UNDERSTANDING LEGAL CONCEPTS THAT INFLUENCE SOCIAL WELFARE POLICY AND PRACTICE

RUDOLPH ALEXANDER, JR.
Ohio State University

THOMSON
BROOKS/COLE

Australia • Canada • Mexico • Singapore • Spain
United Kingdom • United States

THOMSON

BROOKS/COLE

Executive Editor: *Lisa Gebo*
Assistant Editor: *Alma Dea Michelena*
Editorial Assistant: *Sheila Walsh*
Marketing Manager: *Caroline Concilla*
Marketing Assistant: *Mary Ho*
Advertising Project Manager: *Samantha Cabaluna*
Project Manager, Editorial Production: *Stephanie Zunich*

Print/Media Buyer: *Vena Dyer*
Permissions Editor: *Sue Ewing*
Production Service: *Scott Rohr, Buuji, Inc.*
Text Designer: *Jeanne Calabrese*
Copy Editor: *Adrienne Armstrong*
Cover Designer: *Denise Davidson*
Compositor: *Buuji, Inc.*
Cover and Text Printer: *Transcontinental Printing*

For more information about our products, contact us at:
Thomson Learning Academic Resource Center
1-800-423-0563

For permission to use material from this text, contact us by:
Phone: 1-800-730-2214 **Fax:** 1-800-730-2215
Web: http://www.thomsonrights.com

Library of Congress Control Number: 2002104359

ISBN 0-534-59661-4

Brooks/Cole—Thomson Learning
511 Forest Lodge Road
Pacific Grove, CA 93950
USA

Asia
Thomson Learning
5 Shenton Way #01-01
UIC Building
Singapore 068808

Australia
Nelson Thomson Learning
102 Dodds Street
South Melbourne, Victoria 3205
Australia

Canada
Nelson Thomson Learning
1120 Birchmount Road
Toronto, Ontario M1K 5G4
Canada

Europe/Middle East/Africa
Thomson Learning
High Holborn House
50/51 Bedford Row
London WC1R 4LR
United Kingdom

Latin America
Thomson Learning
Seneca, 53
Colonia Polanco
11560 Mexico D.F.
Mexico

Spain
Paraninfo Thomson Learning
Calle/Magallanes, 25
28015 Madrid, Spain

CONTENTS

Chapter 3

Child Protection and the Law   43

Chapter 4

Legal Aspects of Adoption Policy and Practices   65

PREFACE

As an undergraduate criminal justice student in Texas, I became intrigued with a federal court ruling that declared that prisoners have a constitutional right to mental health treatment. Having studied the U.S. Constitution in government classes, I did not remember seeing any such right explicitly stated and wondered how a federal court came up with such a right that changed criminal justice policy in Texas. Later, as a graduate student in social work, I noticed that social work professors tended to focus exclusively on social welfare policy established by two branches of government—the legislative and executive branches—and neglected the third branch of government—the judicial branch. Without a doubt, the right to mental health treatment in a prison setting represents social welfare policy that was not procured by lobbying the Texas legislature to pass a bill and the signing of it by the governor.

When I was given an opportunity to teach a social welfare course as a doctoral student, none of the social welfare books then on the market significantly discussed the role of the law in social welfare policy. Some books did not mention it at all, choosing to focus just on social welfare policy established by

Congress, state legislatures, and presidential executive order. Given another opportunity to teach social welfare as faculty, I wanted to go beyond the social welfare texts and include judicial influence on social welfare policy. However, I had to supplement social welfare texts with articles on the law and social work, which were mostly articles that I had written. This book evolved from these experiences.

After studying this book, students should know basic constitutional and legal principles and how the law shapes social welfare policies and social work practices. For instance, students will learn that "liberty," as stated in the Fourteenth Amendment to the U.S. Constitution, is a very broad concept and applies in a number of areas of concern to social welfare and social work, such as the forced medication of prisoners, the denial of the right of mothers on public assistance and mothers with substance abuse problems to have more children, the termination of parental rights, and the dismissal of problematic students from a college social work program. Instead of just being told that the law has a major influence on social welfare policy, students reading this book will learn, for example, why states cannot enact a law preventing newly arrived state residents from applying for public assistance for a certain period of time. In addition, students will learn how the courts derived a right to mental health treatment for prisoners from the Eighth Amendment, as well as other basic legal concepts that influence social welfare policy.

To show and demonstrate many of these legal concepts, summarized legal cases are presented and referenced using the American Psychological Association (APA) format.

I would like to thank the following reviewers for their assistance in preparing this text: Stephanie Brzuzy, Arizona State University; Kevin Corcoran, Ph.D., J.D., Professor, Portland University; Joyce Everett, Smith College; Esther Langston, University of Nevada, Las Vegas; Katherine Shank, Legal Assistance Foundation of Metropolitan Chicago; Rachelle Zukerman, University of California, Los Angeles.

Rudolph Alexander, Jr.

INTRODUCTION: RATIONALE, FOUNDATION AND EXPLANATION OF CONSTITUTIONAL LAW, AND ORGANIZATION

Speaking to social workers in 1939, Judge L. Ulman of Maryland opined that "there is scarcely a subject of legislative action which may not be subjected to judicial review and control; and this is emphatically true in the field of legislation for social welfare. Every legislative proposal for the amelioration of social hardship is likely to involve an invasion of somebody's rights of property. Every proposal for national action may trench upon the reserved sovereignty of the states. Every comprehensive plan you make, if you want to have it enacted into law, must first be made to fit into the complex pattern of both state and federal constitutions" (Ulman, 1939, p. 743).

Particularly, Judge Ulman observed that social workers had an interest in a number of social welfare areas, such as child labor, mothers' pension, old-age insurance, sickness insurance, unemployment insurance, work conditions, and price regulation. However, the law affected the passage of social workers' plans for ameliorating these social welfare areas. Described as the most significant legislation during Judge Ulman's time, Workman Compensation, when it replaced the common law application of the master and servant law regarding injuries, was held to be unconstitutional by three of four courts (Ulman, 1939). The courts' action regarding Workman Compensation shows the influence of the law on social welfare policy.

Judge Ulman's assessment regarding the importance of the law in social welfare is even more correct today because now the courts are concerned not only with property rights, which they have always sought to protect and preserve, but also with individuals' rights. In the second half of the 20th century, individuals acquired more rights from the courts, Congress, and state legislatures in the areas of privacy and liberty (Stein, 1998). For example, the states can no longer easily give lobotomies involuntarily or easily force sterilization of powerless groups.

Early on, lobotomy was hailed as a revolutionary method of intervening with some groups (Braslow, 1999), earning one of the developers of the procedure the Nobel Prize in 1949 (Clayton, 1987). In the first 20 years after the procedure was developed in 1936, estimates are that between 40,000 and 50,000 lobotomies were performed in the United States (Clayton, 1987). However, a number of studies of this procedure's effectiveness showed negative results (Barahal, 1958; Freeman, 1957). One case study reported the alleged effectiveness of a lobotomy on a sex psychopath (that is, a homosexual who masturbated), while acknowledging that the individual had a significant change in personality (Banay & Davidoff, 1942). Currently, mental health professionals will agree that homosexuality and masturbation do not require treatment. According to Breggin (1972), a primary motivation for performing this surgical procedure was to modify the behavior of socially aberrant people and these people tended to be the poor and other marginalized groups.

Michigan was one of 39 states to adopt laws permitting authorities to sterilize the mentally ill, mentally retarded, and prison inmates to prevent the spread of unfit people (Bates, 1999). For instance, in 1925 the Supreme Court of Michigan upheld the legality of a Michigan statute that authorized the sterilization of mentally defective people, such as those labeled as idiots, imbeciles, and feeble-minded [sic] (*Smith v. Wayne Probate Judge*, 1925). The *Smith* decision cleared the way for the vasectomy of a 16-year-old boy who was deemed to be feeble-minded (*Smith v. Wayne Probate Judge*, 1925).

Later, the Michigan legislature repealed its sterilization statute and replaced it with a revised statute that still permitted sterilization. The Supreme Court of Michigan upheld the new statute, while lamenting the "unfortunate history of forced eugenic sterilization" and noted that "our legislature halted the routine involuntary sterilizations of the past" (*In re Lora Faye Wirsing*, 1998, p. 54).

In 2001, the Virginia legislature passed a resolution expressing its profound regret for forcing 7,450 white Virginians to be sterilized. Passed in 1924 and repealed in 1979, the statute authorized the sterilization of citizens who were thought to be contaminating the white race with mental illness, mental retardation, epilepsy, criminal behavior, alcoholism, and immorality ("Virginia offers regret for sterilizations," 2001). Hence, individuals' rights are more recognized by the courts, and this recognition affects social welfare policy.

RATIONALE FOR TEXT

A number of excellent books exist to teach students about social welfare policy. Most books, however, do not discuss the impact of constitutional law on social welfare policy and practice. Although a few books refer to the law, the overwhelming majority of texts choose instead to emphasize social welfare policy determined by two branches of government—the legislative and executive (see, for example, DiNitto, 2000; Jansson, 1993; Johnson, 1995; Karger & Stoesz, 1998; Miley, O'Melia, & Dubois, 1995; Prigmore & Atherton, 1979). This emphasis is surprising given that, as Segal and Brzuzy (1998) accurately observed, "the impact of the courts on social welfare policy can be significant" (p. 223). Segal and Brzuzy said nothing beyond this statement; however, they did observe elsewhere in their book that the federal judiciary made abortions legal. Briefly mentioning the law, Jansson (1997) wrote that, "court decisions play important roles in American social policy. By overruling, upholding, and interpreting statutes of legislatures, courts establish policies that significantly influence the American response to social needs" (p. 16).

Providing evidence for Jansson's assessment, Prigmore and Atherton (1979), almost 20 years earlier, related how U.S. District Court Judge Frank M. Johnson modified state policies regarding developmentally impaired institutionalized residents and prisoners in Alabama, despite strong opposition from the governor, the state legislature, and citizens. Similarly, Judge Wayne Justice in Texas had a similar effect in shaping social policy regarding treatment in both juvenile and adult correctional institutions (*Morales v. Turman,* 1972; *Ruiz v. Estelle,* 1982), despite strong criticisms and ostracism from fellow Texans. McInnis-Dittrich (1994) wrote an excellent book that described the integration of social welfare policy and social work practice. Near the end of the book, McInnis-Dittrich mentioned the law and briefly discussed three cases, including *Roe v. Wade.* The few books that mention *Roe v. Wade* tell students that this decision gave women the right to terminate a pregnancy. However, students are not told that exceptions or limitations exist in this decision, how the U.S. Supreme Court arrived at this decision, what basic legal concepts are operating in this decision, or what are the full policy implications.

From almost all social welfare textbooks, students learn about the history and impact of the Elizabethan Poor Law Act of 1601 on colonial society and learn about President Roosevelt's New Deal legislation in the 1930s. Of course, the focus in social welfare textbooks on the history of social welfare is important. The Council on Social Work Education (2000) requires that undergraduate and master's students are taught about the history, mission, and philosophy of social work, which would include topics such as the Elizabethan Poor Law Act of 1601 and the analysis of history on current social welfare policy. Moreover, the Council on Social Work Education requires that content be presented on the political and organizational processes used to influence policy, the process of policy formulation, and the framework for analyzing social policies in light of social justice (Council on Social Work Education, 2000).

The latter portions of the accreditation standards would include legal influences. Thus, although students indeed need to know the history of the Elizabethan Poor Law Act of 1601, they should likely know, for instance, that certain provisions of the Elizabethan Poor Law Act of 1601, such as the overseer's authority to apprentice children, were challenged in court. They should likely know also that many aspects of the New Deal were held to be unconstitutional by the courts, causing Congress to alter these statutes.

Showing how the law can influence policy in a more contemporary vein, courts repeatedly struck down protective devices advocated by mental health professionals involving children believed to have been sexually abused and who testified behind screens in court. The almost unanimous view of mental health professionals was that children who have been sexually abused could not testify in open court. But the U.S. Supreme Court found this conclusion to be legally indefensible (*Coy v. Iowa,* 1988), resulting in a change of practice more consistent with the U.S. Constitution (*Maryland v. Craig,* 1990). Moreover, a number of convictions involving interviewing techniques employed by social workers in child sexual abuse cases were found to be problematic by the courts, resulting in the release of prisoners (MacFarquhar, 1995). These actions regarding child sexual abuse suggest rather strongly that the courts play a powerful role in shaping social welfare policy and social work practice.

Although the rationale is given for this book and what it is designed to do, it is necessary also to state clearly what this book is not designed to do and why. As stated, the aim of this book is to acquaint social work students with the basic constitutional and statutory laws that impact principal areas of social welfare policy and social work practice. This book's purpose is not to provide a comprehensive textbook on the law, social welfare policy, or social work practice. Thus, this book was not written to replace existing books on social welfare policy or social work practice. Its primary aim is to fill a gap that exists in many social welfare books that do not address specifically why and how the law shapes and influences social welfare policy and social work practice.

In achieving the objective of discussing the influence of the law on social welfare policy, a number of areas found in most social welfare and social work practice books are purposely omitted. For instance, although the Elizabethan Poor Law Act of 1601 was mentioned earlier, the act itself will not be discussed in this book. Other concepts related to social welfare and social work practice also are not discussed, such as client self-determination, social work values, and ethics. The reason for not discussing these concepts is that they are not connected to the law. For instance, ethical practice might dictate that a social worker refer a client who is objectionable to another social worker. But failing to refer such a client does not constitute a constitutional or legal issue.

Of course, some unethical situations concern the law, such as a counseling professional having sexual relationships with clients. This type of unethical behavior is discussed in this book as malpractice. Concepts such as ethics, the Elizabethan Poor Law Act of 1601, self-determination, and the history of social welfare are ably addressed in other books. However, if client self-determination was argued as a constitutional right as a basis for assisted suicide and there are court challenges, then it falls within the parameters of this book.

Also, fairly recent developments in health care, such as living wills and advance directives, are not addressed. Medical social work, in general, is beyond the scope of this book. However, if an individual claims that he or she was discriminated against or denied equal protection of the law by the state or an employer because of diabetes, for example, this area is discussed, especially if the courts provide policy guidelines.

This book's aim is to discuss mostly how constitutional law influences social welfare policy and social work practice. It does not discuss the history of social welfare, social work practice with gay, lesbian, and bisexual people, social work practice with women or minorities, or culturally sensitive social work practice. A number of excellent social welfare and social work practice textbooks cover these areas, and this book was not developed to replace them. Typically, books on social welfare emphasize policies determined by the legislative and executive branches of government, and this book emphasizes principally social welfare policies and practices determined by the judiciary branch of government.

However, this book includes some congressional and state statutes to illustrate basic legal concepts. Another reason for using federal and state statutes is that sometimes a violation triggers consideration of the Fourteenth Amendment of the Constitution (Stein, 1998). By way of a specific example, if a state statute promises every child in the state a quality education but fails to do so in one rural county because of expense, a lawsuit may be filed that includes claims of a violation of the Fourteenth Amendment. On occasion, a court will conclude that state officials violated their state statute and concomitantly violated the Fourteenth Amendment (*Board of Regents of State Colleges v. Roth,* 1972). In a Wisconsin child protection case, an argument was advanced that the Wisconsin child protection statute provided a severely injured child an entitlement, protected by the Fourteenth Amendment. However, the attorney raised the entitlement argument for the first time in the U.S. Supreme Court, which was a violation of court procedure in that it had to be argued in the initial filing of the case. For this reason, the Court refused to entertain this argument (*DeShaney v. Winnebago County Department of Social Services,* 1989), but it did entertain an entitlement argument in an earlier case in which the **plaintiff** (that is, the person or entity filing a civil lawsuit) prevailed (*Board of Regents of State Colleges v. Roth,* 1972).

Because of the focus of this book, which differs from most books that discuss social welfare policy, and the nature of law itself, readers should be aware of a number of aspects that might seem initially questionable and disconcerting. First, this book utilizes a number of legal cases. Some of these cases involve child protection workers, adoption workers, mental health workers, and social work professionals.

In our approach to understanding cases touching upon social welfare, a case has two important components. First, the statement of the problem or what is it that the plaintiff claims is a problem is important and necessary. Second, the court's application of a legal test or standard to the problem, combined with the court's decision and rationale, is important. From the court's decision, implications may be drawn. Thus, we have endeavored to acquaint readers with the problem and the application of the legal standard in all cases. Accordingly, readers should be looking for these two basic components in reading cases.

In addition, sometimes, the ultimate outcome of a legal conflict is not known. A case may be appealed and returned to a lower court. If the case is settled after it is remanded from a higher court, the public is not likely to know what ultimately occurred. Often, there are legally binding agreements not to discuss publicly the settlement of the case. For instance, an appellate court could rule that a lower court erroneously dismissed a social worker's case and the social worker had indeed made out a **prima facie case** (that is, on its face or being akin to face validity in research) of discrimination. Thus, it is not necessary to know whether the social worker settled before trial for $10,000, $50,000, or $100,000. Even if the social worker plaintiff, for lack of evidence or for insufficient evidence, ultimately loses the case, a case still can give insight into the law and social welfare policy or social work practice.

For example, in a case discussed in Chapter 8, the North Carolina Board for Social Work mandated a social worker to tell her clients that she was under investigation for unethical behaviors. She contended that the person responsible for reporting her injured her reputation, reduced her earnings from her private practice, and violated her rights. A U.S. District Court, in ruling against the social worker, articulated a four-prong test for determining whether the social worker's rights were violated in this case. This four-prong test is the most important information in the case because it tells social workers what needs to be established in order to prevail in such a case. In this particular case, the social worker was able to meet only three of the four criteria. In this case, and others, this book is concerned with the pronouncement of the legal standard and its application, not whether the social worker won.

Cases from the criminal justice arena support the perspective that losing cases can establish social welfare policy. Although criminal justice is not embraced heartily by the vast number of social workers, a significant number of social workers are employed in corrections (Alexander & Brown, 2000). Two prison cases from Texas and Virginia illustrate the problem of focusing on winning cases. Prisoners acquired a constitutional right to mental health treatment based on court rulings in the 1970s. In one case, a Texas prisoner outright lost the case, and in the Virginia case, the prisoner's arguments were not accepted but a hearing was ordered on a different issue. Both cases provided specific guidelines for the states on how to avoid a violation of the cruel and unusual punishment clause of the Eighth Amendment of the U.S. Constitution. Focusing on cases in which prisoners prevailed would overlook critical cases that had social welfare policy implications. Likewise, focusing on cases in which social workers prevailed could lead to overlooking important cases that have social welfare policy implications. Sometimes, much can be learned when a plaintiff has lost a case, and the two prison cases illustrate the influence of the law on social welfare policy in corrections.

This book emphasizes decisions mostly from the federal judiciary, such as the U.S. Supreme Court and Federal Court of Appeals. However, some congressional statutes and state statutes are discussed too because these statutes may have a national effect upon a review by the U.S. Supreme Court. From time to time, the book will indicate that two or three U.S. District Court, state supreme court, or state statutes illustrate a particular point about a case that has social welfare implications. Readers should not take the naming of two cases or statutes as a statement that only two cases or only two states have such a policy. In all probability, other states may have similar statutes or similar case law, but then again, they may not. It is beyond this book's purpose to inform readers of which of the 50 states have the same statute or similar case laws. States have different constitutions, and differences are going to exist in how state courts rule. Listing how each state has ruled on a social welfare issue based on its constitution would be extremely cumbersome. The purpose of this book is to present how the law influences social welfare policy. Thus, this could, at times, be illustrated by two or three cases. If those cases do not represent the state in which the reader resides, the reader would need to conduct research on his or her state.

FOUNDATION AND EXPLANATION
OF CONSTITUTIONAL LAW

The United States consists of three branches of government (executive, legislative, and judiciary). It was not always that way. Following the Revolutionary War with the British, the liberated 13 states established the Articles of Confederation in 1781. As the first American Constitution, the Articles of Confederation was essentially formal recognition of the Continental Congress. It endorsed a Congress but provided for no executive or judicial branch of government. The Congress that was created had only limited powers, such as the power to declare war, establish treaties, regulate weights and measures, manage affairs with Native Americans, establish an army and navy, and run the post office. The states retained considerable autonomy, and the Continental Congress had little authority over the states. More important, Congress had no power to raise taxes. Each state voluntarily donated money to Congress, regulated commerce within its state, and printed its own money (McKay, 2000).

After living under the Articles of Confederation for a few years, many leaders recognized weaknesses and the ineffectiveness of the government. There needed to be a strong person providing leadership for the 13 original states. Revenue needed to be raised to provide for the common defense of all the states. One national currency needed to be established. In addition, a legal system needed to be established to decide disputes between and among states (McClenaghan, 1988).

Dissatisfaction was evident among those who were not well off financially and were in considerable debt, caused by the war and the period that followed. In Massachusetts, very harsh laws existed that crippled debtors. Daniel Shays led a revolt of more than 1,000 people, protesting the harsh debtor law. Although this protest was addressed, the fact that so many people were upset was frightening to political leaders who thought that an ideal society existed in the embryonic United States. These factors caused keen observers to seek to establish a new Constitution and a new government (MacGregor, Peltason, Cronin, & Magleby, 1998; O'Connor & Sabato, 1993).

Although numerous people believed a new Constitution needed to be established, they, and others, were skeptical and fearful. When the convention was called to create this new Constitution and government, some dissenters refused to come. As Patrick Henry said, "I smelt a rat" (Watson, 1985, p. 41). Supporters recognized that they needed a strong central government, but they were concerned about vesting too much power in one place.

Drawing on the writings of national and international political philosophers, key supporters of the Constitution, such as James Madison, proposed the concept of separation of powers, which they took from the French political philosopher, Charles Montesquieu (Watson, 1985). Tyranny, which the Americans had loathed under British rule, was associated with the concentration of power in one area. Liberty, on the other hand, was associated with the dispersion of power. Accordingly, power should be dispersed and separated.

Aligned with separation of powers were checks and balances. Each branch of government checks and balances the other two. Each branch has some effect on the other two branches. Each branch, also, is dependent on the other two, which forces cooperation for each branch's mutual benefit, especially for the legislative and executive branches of government. As Watson wrote:

> The two principles—separation of processes and checks and balances—complement each other to achieve the desired effect in the political system. The first provides that no branch can usurp an activity that is the primary responsibility of another; the second allows the three arms of the government to counteract one another's influence. The end result is a decentralization of political power (Watson, 1985, p. 50).

With these principles, there were still people who were apprehensive about having a strong federal government, even with the checks and balances of the other two branches. The Constitution when it was debated and proposed was a series of compromises (for example, each state would have two senators but each state would have representatives based on its population). One final compromise to get the necessary support for the new Constitution was the inclusion of a Bill of Rights, which was the first ten amendments, which was believed to be needed to check this new federal government and provide rights to citizens that neither Congress nor the president could infringe.

HOW THE FEDERAL COURTS WORK

The underlying theme of this book is that the law plays a significant role in determining social welfare policy and practice. Although Congress or a state legislature may pass a law, it is the courts that determine whether the law is constitutional or unconstitutional. A state court can rule only on the constitutionality of its state's statutes. However, a federal court can rule on the constitutionality of a state statute and a congressional statute. Federal judges are appointed for life—a deliberate strategy to insulate them from political pressures and to give them the freedom to make unpopular decisions. Accordingly, most decisions involving the constitutionality of a statute or recognition of individuals' rights come from the federal judicial system. Moreover, the federal Constitution supersedes state constitutions. For these reasons, this book emphasizes the federal judiciary.

The main federal judiciary consists of the U.S. Supreme Court, 13 courts of appeals, and numerous district courts in each state and the District of Columbia. (There are other federal courts, such as tax and maritime courts, but these are not relevant here.) For instance, Georgia is divided into three districts—the Northern District, the Middle District, and the Southern District. Each district has several judges. A district court decision is binding on those citizens in that district. As an illustration, a U.S. District Court judge might rule that a city ordinance banning nude dancing in a bar is unconstitutional. This decision becomes binding on establishments in that district. If the case is appealed, it is appealed to the Eleventh Circuit Court of Appeals, which consists of Georgia, Alabama, and Florida. A court of appeals ruling upholding that decision then becomes binding on those states within the Eleventh Circuit.

Conceivably, a decision in one circuit may be different from a ruling in another circuit, such as the Seventh Circuit, which consists of Wisconsin, Illinois, and Indiana. An appeal may be taken to the U.S. Supreme Court, and the U.S. Supreme Court may or may not hear the case. It may decline, which leaves the court of appeals decision binding on those states in that circuit. While some individuals promise to take their case "all the way to the U.S. Supreme Court," the odds are that the U.S. Supreme Court will not hear the case. For instance, in the beginning of the 1997–1998 term, the U.S. Supreme Court rejected 1,500 cases and decided to rule on only 58 cases by the time its term ended in June ("Court finds 1,500 ways to say no," 1997). Figure 1.1 shows an overview of the federal judiciary.

In cases going back a number of years, the U.S. Supreme Court sought to indicate that it is equal to the other two branches of government. Congress has the power to amend the Constitution, which is how it can check the judiciary. The classic case in which the U.S. Supreme Court asserted itself is *Marbury*

FIGURE 1.1 | AN OVERVIEW OF THE FEDERAL JUDICIARY

The United States Supreme Court

First Circuit Court of Appeals	Second Circuit Court of Appeals	Third Circuit Court of Appeals	Fourth Circuit Court of Appeals	Fifth Circuit Court of Appeals	Sixth Circuit Court of Appeals	Seventh Circuit Court of Appeals	Eighth Circuit Court of Appeals	Ninth Circuit Court of Appeals	Tenth Circuit Court of Appeals	Eleventh Circuit Court of Appeals	D.C. Circuit Court of Appeals	Federal Circuit Court of Appeals
Maine Massachusetts New Hampshire Puerto Rico Rhode Island	Connecticut New York Vermont	Delaware New Jersey Pennsylvania	Maryland North Carolina South Carolina Virginia West Virginia	Louisiana Mississippi Texas	Kentucky Michigan Ohio Tennessee	Illinois Indiana Wisconsin	Arkansas Iowa Minnesota Missouri Nebraska North Dakota South Dakota	Alaska Arizona California Guam Hawaii Idaho Montana Nevada Northern Mariana Islands Oregon Washington	Colorado Kansas New Mexico Oklahoma Utah Wyoming	Alabama Florida Georgia	District of Columbia	Federal
U.S. District Courts	U.S. District Courts	U.S. District Courts	U.S. District Courts	U.S. District Courts	U.S. District Courts	U.S. District Courts	U.S. District Courts	U.S. District Courts	U.S. District Courts	U.S. District Courts	U.S. District Courts	U.S. District Courts

v. Madison (1803). Almost all political science textbooks discuss this case. Political scientists have maintained that *Marbury v. Madison* established the U.S. Supreme Court's power to conduct judicial review.

More recently, the U.S. Supreme Court ruled in 1997 that Congress exceeded its authority when it passed the Religious Freedom Restoration Act in 1993 and that this act was unconstitutional (*City of Doerne v. Flores*, 1997). Congress had enacted this federal statute in response to a previous U.S. Supreme Court decision in which the justices permitted a lower legal standard in deciding a religious case. Congress sought to reverse this decision and reinstitute the highest legal standard. However, the U.S. Supreme Court held the Religious Freedom Restoration Act was beyond Congress' power and indicated in its decision that the Court determines which legal standard is appropriate for deciding legal disputes (*City of Boerne v. Flores*, 1997).

Another check that Congress has upon the U.S. Supreme Court is that it determines the jurisdiction of the Court and can decide what types of cases the U.S. Supreme Court can hear. For instance, Congress can decide to limit or stop the U.S. Supreme Court from hearing abortion cases. It will never do it, but Congress has this power. Article III, Section 2, of the U.S. Constitution states the following:

> In all cases affecting ambassadors, other public ministers and consuls, and those in which a state shall be party, the Supreme Court shall have original jurisdiction. In all the other cases before mentioned, the Supreme Court shall have appellate jurisdiction, both as to law and fact, *with such exceptions, and under such regulations as the Congress shall make.*

Abortion is a very contentious subject in this country, and people disagree about whether *Roe* is legal or good policy. If Congress could overrule the U.S. Supreme Court, it would have tried to overturn *Roe v. Wade*. All Congress, and some states, have done in the abortion area is to nibble around the edges, with various states trying to decrease abortions or make them more difficult to obtain. Congress can do only two things about *Roe* to overturn it. It can pass a constitutional amendment, which the states must ratify. If the states were to ratify it by the required number, the U.S. Supreme Court, when a case involving abortions comes before it, must base its ruling on this new amendment.

The other thing that Congress can do to reverse *Roe v. Wade* is to change the jurisdiction of the U.S. Supreme Court by saying that it can no longer consider any cases involving abortions and, for instance, all abortion cases are to be left to individual states. In fact, this is what Justice Anthony Scalia has stated numerous times. These are Congress' two options about *Roe v. Wade.* It simply cannot overturn *Roe* by having a majority of Congress vote against it.

ORGANIZATION OF TEXT

The selection of chapter topics for this book was guided by two criteria—areas where social workers are most likely to practice and areas where significant litigation exists that impacts social workers. Statistics from the National Association of Social Workers (NASW) show that the primary areas of practice identified by members are mental health, children, medical clinics, and family (Gibelman & Schervish, 1993). Another survey of social workers showed that most BSWs (46%) and most MSWs (28%) are employed in social service agencies (Teare & Sheafor, 1995). These statistics dictate the topics included in this book.

Although a number of social workers are employed in the health care field, few legal disputes have the potential for affecting or informing social welfare policy or social workers. For instance, although a lot of litigation involves hospitals and physicians for medical malpractice, these cases have little effect on social welfare policy. A physician who operates on the wrong patient or a nurse who has given the wrong medication has little to do with social welfare policy. Hospital discharge planning, which concerns social workers, seldom is the basis for litigation affecting social welfare.

Hence, chapters are devoted to child protection, adoption, mental health, and public assistance. Moreover, this book discusses two issues that social workers may experience personally: malpractice and, broadly speaking, discrimination. For instance, social workers are sometimes sued for malpractice in adoption cases, child protection cases, and mental health practice. These malpractice issues are covered in one chapter. In addition, social work students, professional social workers, and social work professors sometimes feel that they were denied justice themselves. Professional social workers have sued their employers for being denied promotions or for dismissals or for sexual harassment.

Other social welfare textbooks have referred to these areas from the viewpoint of the legislative arena. For instance, DiNitto

(2000) included near the end of her book a chapter called "Challenging Social Welfare: Racism and Sexism." DiNitto's chapter included discussions of gender inequities, equal rights for women, sexual harassment, abortion rights, violence against women, separate but equal, discrimination, and affirmative action. In discussing sexual harassment, DiNitto used the U.S. Supreme Court's definition.

Understanding Legal Concepts That Influence Social Welfare Policy and Practice does much of the same, except that it focuses on social workers involved in litigation. But using social workers does not imply or convey that these legal issues are unique to social workers. The definition of sexual harassment used in corporate America is the same definition used if a social worker claims sexual harassment in a social service agency. The reason for discussing social workers is that social work students might be more interested in reading about cases involving their profession and areas in which they might practice after graduation.

Subsequent to the introductory chapter are eight chapters. Chapter 2 discusses the foundational basis for the law, why legal disputes occur, and critical legal principles that affect cases. Chapter 3 discusses child protection and services, Chapter 4 describes adoption, Chapter 5 discusses public assistance, Chapter 6 concerns mental health, Chapter 7 discusses malpractice, and Chapter 8 covers social workers. At the end of Chapters 3 through 8, the text discusses the implications for social welfare policy and practice. Finally, Chapter 9 summarizes essential points.

CONCLUSION

This chapter described the importance of the law on social welfare policy beginning with observations by a Maryland judge in the late 1930s. Because of the expansion of individuals' rights in the 1960s, the law has had a much greater impact than what the Maryland judge initially noted. The primary purpose of this book, in contrast, is to emphasize the effect of the third branch of government, the judiciary, upon social welfare policy and practice. Next, this chapter explained the rationale for this book, noting that a number of excellent social welfare books have been written but these books tend to focus upon social welfare policy as established by the legislative and executive branches of government. A discussion of the foundation for constitutional law was provided. The selection of chapter topics was determined by two criteria— areas in which social workers are most likely to practice and areas where significant litigation occurs. Last, this chapter outlined the organization of the remaining chapters.

Key Terms and Concepts

Plaintiff
Prima Facie Case

BASIC AND KEY LEGAL CONCEPTS AND PRINCIPLES

A number of concepts and principles affect the outcome of cases. Sometimes, the concepts are explicitly stated or just implied in court rulings. Students should know these concepts and principles in order to understand a court ruling that shapes and influences social welfare policy. Among the concepts and principles defined and explained in this chapter are substantive and procedural law, sources of law, government power and responsibility, conflict between government and individuals, constitutional amendment sections (that is liberty, property, due process, equal protection), right to privacy, legal tests, standards of review, and immunity.

SUBSTANTIVE AND PROCEDURAL LAW

Federal and state constitutions provide both substantive and procedural law (*Spencer Kellogg & Sons Inc. v. Lobban*, 1958). **Substantive law** is "the entire body of law that establishes and defines those rights and duties that the legal system exists to protect and enforce" (Clapp, 2000,

p. 417). On the other hand, **procedural law** involves the methods used in investigating, presenting, managing, and deciding legal cases. Moreover, it is "the body of law that determines which of these methods will be allowed and [the body of law that] governs how they will be used" (Clapp, 2000, p. 343). For instance, the U.S. Constitution provides substantive rights and procedural rights. The Fifth Amendment of the U.S. Constitution recognizes individuals' substantive rights of life, liberty, and property. The Fourteenth Amendment, in theory, protects these rights by declaring that they cannot be taken away without due process. Moreover, a challenged congressional statute may be attacked based on the Fifth Amendment because it applies to the federal government, whereas a challenged state statute may be attacked based on the Fourteenth Amendment because it was specifically adopted to restrain states. However, a challenged state statute may be attacked for substantive violation based on the Fifth Amendment and procedural violation on the Fourteenth Amendment.

SOURCES OF LAW

The law, as a determinant of social policy, flows from three main sources—federal and state constitutions, court decisions, and legislative statutes (Ulman, 1939). Related to court decisions is the common law, a phrase that often appears in legal decisions. The **common law,** materialized in the 11th century in England, consists of rules established by judges to decide cases (Stein, 1998). In part, the U.S. Constitution refers to the promotion of the general welfare of citizens, which many people have said provides the roots for federal social welfare policies (Skidmore, Thackeray, & Farley, 1997). This phrase has been the basis for a number of congressional statutes, such as the Social Security Act of 1935, the Adoption Assistance and Child Welfare Act of 1980, and the Americans with Disabilities Act of 1990 (Jansson, 1993). Court decisions are law, and sometimes the courts will give specific guidelines for states to follow. Another source of law is policies and rules of agencies or institutions, which can become rights protected by the Fourteenth Amendment of the U.S. Constitution (Stein, 1998).

An example of Congress and the state legislatures influencing social welfare policy and practice is with people who suffer from HIV and AIDS, a relatively new disease. Because of the stigma associated with this disease, legislation was enacted protecting the confidentiality of testing and health status. For instance, Pennsylvania passed a statute regarding the confidentiality of records related to HIV. This law provides that no person who obtains confidential HIV-related information in the course of providing health or social services may disclose or be compelled to disclose such information except to 12 listed people or departments (for example, funeral director, health care provider, employees of residential programs) (Pennsylvania Statute 35 § 7607). Georgia passed a statute defining AIDS confidential information, which covers a diagnosis of AIDS, being treated for AIDS, receiving counseling regarding AIDS, and being at risk for AIDS (Official Code of Georgia Annotated, § 31-22-9.1). Texas passed a statute protecting the confidentiality of HIV information regarding prisoners even after their release from confinement (Texas Government Code § 501.054). California, concerned about the disclosure of HIV information to insurance companies, provided civil penalties for those who violated the statute (California Insurance Code § 799.10).

Federal case law also has influenced social welfare policy and social work practice with respect to HIV. The U.S. Supreme Court decided a case involving the refusal of a dentist to fill, in his office, the cavity of a patient who was affected with HIV. The dentist's policy was to do those procedures in the hospital at no additional charge; however, the hospital would bill for use of its facilities. Believing that this policy was discriminatory, the patient filed a lawsuit against the dentist, and several parties joined as plaintiffs. In a divided opinion, the U.S. Supreme Court ruled that HIV was a disability as defined by the Americans with Disabilities Act of 1990 and the Rehabilitation Act of 1973, which were both congressional acts (*Bragdon v. Abbott*, 1998).

WHY CONFLICTS OCCUR BETWEEN GOVERNMENT AND INDIVIDUALS

Government Powers and Responsibilities

Like social work, which has a set of core values, society also has a set of values and principles that it seeks to maintain. Society, or government, possesses power to maintain and further its values and core principles. One of the powers that government has always had is the power to protect itself. This concept is referred to as *police power*. Fisher (1999) defines **police power** as "the power of government to protect the health, safety, welfare, and morals of its citizens" (p. 1243). All criminal laws flow from states' and the federal government's police power to enact laws criminally punishing certain conduct, such as murder, sexual assault, armed robbery, and lesser crimes, such as drug use. These laws are passed to protect citizens' health, safety, and welfare. At one time, the commission of suicide was a criminal offense, and the person committing suicide went to his or her grave as an unconvicted felon. These laws were repealed, but some conduct surrounding suicides is illegal. Currently, states possess laws forbidding the aiding or abetting of suicide (Szasz, 2001). An unsuccessful suicide may mean commitment of an individual to a mental health facility, under the state's police power.

Another historical concept important to government functioning because it serves some of the functions of police power is *parens patriae.* In its early form, **parens patriae** referred to the principle of the king being the ultimate guardian of certain dependent groups, such as children and individuals with severe mental impairment. This meant that as a last resort, the king would become the guardian of these groups if the families failed to provide adequate care. When early settlers came from England to America, they brought these concepts, along with the common law, with them and implemented them in their newly created states. Instead of the king being the ultimate guardian of dependent groups, the state became the ultimate guardian, and its agents, or social workers, could take action under *parens patriae* to protect vulnerable populations. Thus, interventions, such as caring for children or individuals suffering from severe mental illness, may be grounded in either police power or *parens patriae.*

Connected to *parens patriae* is the principle of the **best interest of the child,** a concept frequently heard in contemporary cases involving children in divorce and questionable parenting cases. Because the best interest of the child is a frequently heard concept in contemporary society, this concept is discussed in some detail. The best interest of the child concept emerged during the Chancery Court in the Middle Ages in England. Then, it meant that the Chancery Courts were to protect the oldest male child's right to inherit his father's property; however, these courts were also involved in protecting the welfare of children during this period under the King's *parens patriae* authority (Siegal & Senna, 2000).

In colonial America, and extending into the early 20th century, Chancery Courts were developed to deal with issues involving children, and their primary focus was on the best interest of the child, as in a custody dispute case decided in the Chancery Court of Alabama (*Sparkman v. Sparkman*, 1927). Earlier, in 1897, a Connecticut court endorsed an explanation from a previous court of the best interest of the child. This Connecticut case involved a father recently released from prison whose wife had died and whose son was being cared for by a legal guardian. According to the court,

> the right of the father or mother to the custody of their [*sic*] minor children is not an absolute right to be accorded to them [*sic*] under all circumstances, for it may be denied to either of them if it appears to the court that the parent, otherwise entitled to the right, is unfit for the trust. And in contests between parents and third persons as to the custody by such parents, the opinion is now almost universal that neither of the parties has any right that may be allowed to militate against the welfare of the infant. The paramount consideration is, what is really demanded by its best interests? . . . And the rule is ordinarily the same in contentions between parents for the possession of children. The court is not bound to award the custody to either contesting party in such controversies, but may, subject to the welfare and best interests of the child, award it to a third party. In contentions of this kind the child has the right to the protection of the court against misfortunes of its parents, or the influences of such gross and immoral practices as will seriously endanger its life, health, morals or personal safety. But what measure of wickedness or profligacy on the part of the minor child, must necessarily depend upon the facts and circumstances of each particular case (*Kelsey v. Green*, 1897, pp. 681–682).

The Connecticut court further stated that a child is not the father's property, and a father's right is not absolute or unqualified. A father may relinquish or forfeit his right by contract, by bad conduct, or by misfortune rendering him incapable of giving care or support. Further, the court said that a child is a human being who has rights and cannot be treated like a piece of property. Although the father has legal custody of his child, this right diminishes if the child's welfare is put in peril by the father's imprisonment or misfortune, such as becoming mentally ill. A father cannot break ties formed between his child and a third party when the child and his guardian have formed attachments that, if broken, would lead to the detriment of the child (*Kelsey v. Green*, 1897).

The Minnesota Supreme Court Foster Care and Adoption Task Force, consisting of more than 50 attorneys, child-care advocates, and justices from the Minnesota Supreme Court, recommended that the Minnesota legislature amend its family code to define the best interest of the child. It stated that the best interest of the child in cases involving children in need of protective services and termination of parental rights should include the consideration and evaluation of all relevant factors. These factors are, but are not limited to, the following:

1. The child's current functioning and behaviors;
2. The medical, education, and developmental needs of the child;
3. The child's history and past experience;
4. The child's religious and cultural needs;
5. The child's connection with a community, school, or church;
6. The child's interests and talents;
7. The child's relationship to current caretakers, parents, siblings, and relatives; and the reasonable preference of the child, if the court deems the child to be of sufficient age to express a preference (Hunter, 1997).

California has a provision in its family code entitled "Freedom from Parental Custody and Control" that outlines how the best interest of the child is preserved. A professional shall write a report with a recommendation in a proceeding involving the best interest of the child and parental termination. The report shall include (a) a statement that the person making the report explained to the child the nature of the proceeding to end parental custody and control; (b) a statement of the child's feelings and thoughts concerning the pending proceeding; (c) a statement of the child's attitude toward the child's parent or parents and particularly whether or not the child would prefer living with his or her parent or parents; and (d) a statement that the child was informed of the child's right to attend the hearing on the petition and the child's feelings concerning attending the hearing. In the event that the child, because of his or her age, is unable to understand and appreciate the queries and explanations, then the professional shall document that fact (California Family Code § 7851).

Individual Rights

Individuals have a number of rights, such as the rights established by states regarding HIV testing and HIV status, that are conferred by state legislatures. Moreover, Congress has conferred individuals certain rights regarding taxes and confidentiality of genetic information. Individuals also have constitutional rights, which are more clearly detailed in a subsequent area of this chapter. Suffice to say here, most individuals know they have certain freedoms and rights, such as free speech and freedom of association.

CLASHES BETWEEN GOVERNMENT AND INDIVIDUALS

Although Americans possess many freedoms that are the envy of people in other countries, few rights of Americans are absolute. As stated earlier, the government has rights and interests that it seeks to protect and affirm. As a general rule, people have control over their bodies, but restrictions under a state's police power may be put in place. For instance, juveniles are not permitted to smoke cigarettes, and no person is permitted to use cocaine or LSD, although many of them believe that they have the right to damage their bodies if they so choose. In almost all states, prostitutes do not have the right to sell sexual favors. Governments view many of these behaviors as harmful to society's moral well-being.

Even in the area of abortions, a state's police power is inextricably present. All the abortion decisions are replete with references to the state's police power, and all acknowledge that a state's police power is a strong interest. Though in *Roe v. Wade* the right to abortions was upheld, a reading of this decision reveals that the U.S. Supreme Court permitted abortion during the first three months of pregnancy when the fetus was viewed as nonviable. Writing for the majority, Justice Blackmun employed a trimester approach to describe the extent to which the state could regulate abortions.

During the first trimester of a pregnancy, a woman and her doctor were free to abort a fetus without any governmental interference. During the second trimester, the state could regulate abortions only to protect the mother's health. After six months, or during the last trimester, the fetus was considered to be viable. Then, the state could regulate or ban abortions, provided the mother's life or health was not in peril (Redlich, Schwartz, & Attanasio, 1995). During the last trimester, when the fetus became viable, the state's police power was recognized and restrictions could be placed upon women (*Roe v. Wade*, 1973). Other U.S. Supreme Court decisions, while still permitting abortions, did away with the trimester principle and recognize the state's interest in protecting a fetus a few days after conception or at conception (*Planned Parenthood of Southeastern Pennsylvania v. Casey*, 1992). In effect, the state's police power increased; however, this fact is seldom mentioned in the abortion debates.

Hence, clashes occur involving governments' exercise of their police power in pursuit of their principles and values and individuals' rights. In the past, the government exercised considerable power when dealing with individuals. In many areas, it prevailed over the individual. Probably the greatest advances in individuals' rights occurred during the 1960s (Berstein, 1999; Clark, 1995; Kennedy, 2000; Yamamoto, Serrano, Fenton, Gifford, Forman, Hoshijo, & Kim, 2001).

These advances are illustrated by a number of events in the 1960s. In 1961, the U.S. Supreme Court applied the Fourth Amendment's right of individuals to be free from unreasonable searches and seizures to states (*Mapp v. Ohio*, 1961). A year later, the U.S. Supreme Court applied the Eighth Amendment to states and forbade them from criminalizing a status (that is, an addiction) (*Robinson v. California*, 1962). The following year, the U.S. Supreme Court held that citizens facing felonies must be given an attorney if they cannot afford one (*Gideon v. Wainwright*, 1963). Political scientists have hailed *Gideon* as an example of the importance society had placed on liberty (O'Connor & Sabato, 1993; Watson, 1985). The same has been said about *Miranda v. Arizona* (1966) and its impact on individual freedom. In *Griswold v. Connecticut* (1965), the U.S. Supreme Court gave greater recognition to the right of privacy and individual freedom and forbade states from criminalizing conceptive practices.

Still, the government possesses considerable power over individuals. Most likely, the most important rights that individuals have are the right to life, liberty, and property—rights that are discussed in more detail later in this chapter—yet government may take away each of these rights under certain circumstances. Individuals may be put to death, put in prison, and put out of their homes permanently. Furthermore, children may be taken away from biological parents and reared by the state or put in the homes of strangers. Also, property may be taken away under **eminent domain,** which entails government power to take private property for public use.

Besides the power to take life, liberty, and property, society and the individual may simply disagree regarding what is or is not harmful to a child and when the child's best interest is being threatened. For instance, parents are permitted to decide what is in their child's best interest, such that parents can take their children to an R-rated movie, where violence and sex are shown, or take their children to sport bars, where both alcohol and food are consumed. Further, a growing practice by some parents is to permit their children to see a sibling being born. Society does not prohibit parents from having their children experience the miracle of birth.

However, another parent can logically conclude that if a child can see his or her sibling being born, then the child can see how a sibling is actually conceived. But the government will have something to say about parents who permit their children to watch them having sexual intercourse and attempting to conceive a baby. Society calls this behavior child abuse and may take the child out of the home and criminally prosecute the parents. There likely, then, is a conflict between society's values and parents' values.

Another example of how society and the individual can disagree involves the taking of nude pictures of children. Most people will see nothing wrong with taking nude pictures of babies or very young children, but at some point taking pictures becomes criminal. Hailed as a caring and sensitive person, a 48-year-old bus driver in Oberlin, Ohio, was charged with illegal use of a minor in nudity-oriented material or performance and pandering sexually oriented material involving a minor for taking nude pictures of her 8-year-old daughter. Both charges carried a maximum sentence of 16 years in prison. Since the time that the child was 3 years old, the mother had taken pictures of her daughter rinsing off with the shower sprayer after taking a bath. According to the mother, it was part of her daughter's bathing ritual and the daughter would act silly, prompting the mother to take her picture. However, this time the developer of the pictures called the police. The mother was charged and suspended from her job as a bus driver (Marshall & Wasson, 2000).

In a similar incident, a 65-year-old school social worker was suspended from her job and charged with crimes for taking pictures of her two granddaughters, who were 4 and 6. Specifically, she was charged with endangering the welfare of a child. The grandmother/social worker considered herself to be a portrait photographer and did not see anything wrong with taking nude pictures of her granddaughters (Marshall & Wasson, 2000). Undoubtedly, society has become hypersensitive to child pornography, causing law enforcement to influence what parents do with their children.

Incidents of this nature can often influence the law, and in turn, how the law can influence social welfare policy. The law, emerging from a criminal case and a civil case, may define what is in the best interest of a child and what parents' rights are. The law, through judges, may determine at what age parents should stop taking pictures of a nude child. Experts in child development may help judges establish the dividing age between no crime and a crime or practices not in the best interests of the child and practices within the best interests of the child.

CONSTITUTIONAL PRINCIPLES

The supreme law of a state is its own constitution. The U.S. Constitution is the supreme law of the United States. No state can legally pass a law or statute that violates its constitution or the U.S. Constitution. If a law violates the constitution, the only constitutional remedy is to amend the constitution, which is politically difficult to do. When courts rule on an issue related to social welfare, courts establish minimum standards to meet constitutionality. States or Congress are free to exceed these minimum standards, but they cannot go below the minimum standards.

Broadly written for the most part, a constitution is subjected to interpretations by courts, interpretations that may change as time passes. A constitution is viewed as a living document, adjusting and adapting as society progresses and matures. Hence, what was constitutional several decades ago, such as segregation and separate but equal, is no longer constitutional today. The U.S. Constitution has not changed with respect to the first few amendments, but the justices on the U.S. Supreme Court have changed, and this change explains why separate but equal was first constitutional and later unconstitutional.

One amendment of the U.S. Constitution probably has more applicability to social welfare policy and practice than any other amendment. This is Section 1 of the Fourteenth Amendment. Principally adopted in 1868 as a protection for newly freed people of African descent (Barron, Dienes, McCormack, & Redish, 1992), the Fourteenth Amendment states the following:

> All persons born or naturalized in the United States, and subject to the jurisdiction thereof, are citizens of the United States and of the State wherein they reside. *No state shall make or enforce any law which shall abridge the privileges or immunities of citizens of*

the United States; nor shall any State deprive any person of *life, liberty,* or *property,* without *due process of law;* nor deny to any person within its jurisdiction the *equal protection of the laws.*

As the Fourteenth Amendment was interpreted through the years, it evolved to apply to all citizens as well as businesses and corporations. In terms of those sections of interest to social welfare and social work practice, five italicized portions bear elaboration.

No State Shall Make or Enforce Any Law Which Shall Abridge the Privileges or Immunities of Citizens of the United States

Early in the law, the first ten amendments, which make up the Bill of Rights, were held to be limitations only upon the federal government. Thus, the Fifth Amendment, which provides a privilege against self-incrimination, was interpreted as applying only to the federal government, not the states. According to *Black's Law Dictionary* (1990), a **privilege** is "a particular and peculiar benefit or advantage enjoyed by a person, company, or class, beyond the common advantages of other citizens" (p. 1197). A person who is accused of a crime has the privilege of not being forced to incriminate himself or herself. **Immunity** refers to "freedom or exemption from penalty, burden, or duty" (*Black's Law Dictionary,* 1990, p. 751). Simply, states could not abridge the privileges or immunities of people. However, initially it was not clear how these concepts applied to groups of people. The first case to determine what these prohibitions meant involved a case in Louisiana involving cattle butchers (*Butchers' Union Slaughter-House and Live Stock Landing Company v. Crescent City Live-Stock Landing and Slaughter-House Company,* 1884).

Liberty

Liberty was said to include those rights in the First Amendment, such as freedom of religion, free speech, the right to assembly, and the right to petition the government. These prohibitions were initially directed at Congress; the courts subsequently held that these limitations also applied to the states. In addition, the U.S. Constitution states that individuals have the right to pursue happiness. Thus, liberty was broadened further. Happiness means the right to lawfully pursue those activities that make one happy. This means the freedom to marry whomever one chooses (that is, an adult of the opposite sex, not related by blood; also, a teenager's legal guardian may give consent for the teenager to marry) and the right to have children or not have children. It also means that one has the right to his or her ideas. One also has the right to terminate his or her life under certain conditions. Much of this broadening of liberty, however, did not come until the late 20th century.

Given these parameters, a social worker can see when the states or the federal government may impinge upon liberty. From time to time, a judge, angry with a mother who is addicted to crack cocaine, may order her not to have more children as a condition of probation. A question is then raised whether such a condition violates a woman's liberty. Liberty may mean that even if one is mentally ill, one has the right to be free. Liberty may mean that the government may not force upon a person medications that interfere with his or her ideas. Even in prison, a prisoner may have a limited right to be free within the confines of an institution. A severely disabled person has liberty interests that protect him or her from being physically restrained in an institution. If a behavior modification program would prevent restraints and self-injury of an institutionalized person, liberty requires that state officials so provide, and failing to do so would violate such a person's liberty right (*Youngberg v. Romeo,* 1982). Last, a licensed social worker, reported to a social work licensing board for alleged misconduct, may have his or her liberty interests violated.

Property

To most laypeople, property may mean a house, land, car, or personal possessions. However, the courts have given a broader definition of what property is, as it is referred to in the Fourteenth Amendment. When a person is said to have property interests, this concept refers to almost any tangible commodity that facilitates a person's pursuit of economic and social benefits. For instance, a social worker's job is property that may not be taken without due process. Unemployment benefits, food stamps, and welfare payments are benefits that may not be taken without due process. A conferred college degree, which can be rescinded by a university, is property that may not be taken without due process. A social work license is property that is protected by property interests. Tenure for a university professor is property. Rehabilitation may be property that cannot be denied without due process. Essentially, an institution that promises to provide rehabilitation or treatment and does not may impinge upon a person's property interests.

Additionally, the wording of a state statute or institutional policy may create both liberty and property interests protected by the Fourteenth Amendment. For instance, a state statute that states that a person committed to a mental institution *shall* be provided treatment creates a mandate to do just that for a person so committed. Similarly, a statute that says that a deserving family of a victim of a crime *shall* be given 80% of the cost of a funeral means the family is entitled to this benefit if the family qualifies. *Shall* and *will* create property interests. To relieve a state's obligations, a statute may substitute the word *may* for *shall*. Instead of a statute saying that it *shall* provide rehabilitative programs, it says that it *may* provide rehabilitative programs in a correctional institution. Changing this one word affects the Fourteenth Amendment protection.

Liberty interests, too, are created based on the wording of an institutional policy. If an institutional policy says that restraints will be placed on residents only when they are harmful to themselves or the staff, this policy obligates an institution not to put on restraints for other reasons, such as for punishment. In effect, the wording of such a policy promises freedom or liberty unless harm to self or others is present. Prisoners acquire liberty interests in a similar manner. A parole policy that promises to release a prisoner if that prisoner meets certain release criteria, such as having committed a certain type of felony, having no institutional misconduct, and having served a specified portion of his or her sentence, and then does not parole the prisoner violates the prisoner's liberty interests. In a social work program, a written policy that spells out academic misconduct and the penalty for it cannot be capriciously changed.

Due Process

Both the Fifth and Fourteenth Amendments to the U.S. Constitution contain due process clauses, and both have been used to vindicate numerous classes or categories of rights (Redlich et al., 1995). The Fifth Amendment and its expression that life, liberty, and property shall not be taken unless by due process of law is referred to as substantive due process. It protects citizens from arbitrary decisions. **Substantive due process** restricts the government by requiring the government to be reasonable in the rules or norms it seeks to establish. Stated differently, it refers to what government can do. For example, the state cannot make a law criminalizing being a drug addict or mentally ill (*Robinson v. California*, 1962). Also, legislatures cannot pass a statute making jaywalking a capital offense. Such a law would be unreasonable. On the other hand, the Fourteenth Amendment and its provision that the state cannot deprive a person of life, liberty, or property without due process refers to **procedural due process.** In other words, it refers to the way in which the state may act. If a person is mentally ill and needs commitment, certain steps must be followed. The person simply could not be picked up and taken directly to a mental institution.

Equal Protection

The enactment of public policy by states and Congress invariably creates legal categories. Judgments are made about who is entitled to receive what service or who is to receive what types of treatment. These judgments thus favor or disfavor one group over another group (Ducat & Chase, 1988). For instance, a number of states have enacted policies that compensate victims of crimes. However, if the victim of a crime happens also to be an offender, he or she may be unable to collect victim compensation because some states exclude offenders from collecting victim compensation for five years after the date of their offenses. Accordingly, a person who committed an offense on January 1, 1990, and served two years in prison for theft is not entitled to compensation if he or she is the victim of a violent crime on January 1, 1993. Other examples of the favoring of one group over another occur when veterans are given additional points when seeking civil service jobs or universities charge nonresident students more tuition than students who reside in a state. In effect, legal categories always discriminate. The equal protection clause does not forbid states or Congress from discriminating against some groups, but equal protection requires the court to determine the extent to which government can create legal categories for some people and not others. Unconstitutional classifications are said to discriminate invidiously, but permissible classification does not.

Equal protection challenges often occur whenever economic and social discrimination has occurred, such as distinction based on race, indigency, sex, illegitimacy, alienage, and age. Many of the challenges based on these factors center on whether these classifications affect "suspect classification" or "quasi-suspect classification." **Suspect classification** entails a law's classification of certain people, consisting of groupings by race, ethnicity, national origin, and alienage (Clapp, 2000). **Quasi-suspect classification** entails a law's classification of other people consisting of organization by sex and illegitimacy (Clapp, 2000). Laws involving suspect classification receive the courts' highest scrutiny, and laws involving quasi-suspect classification receive a lesser scrutiny. These different levels of scrutiny are discussed later in the chapter.

Right to Privacy

Another important right that is often discussed is the **right to privacy.** There is no explicit right to privacy in the U.S. Constitution; however, going back to 1891, the U.S. Supreme Court has recognized a right to privacy or zones of privacy. The roots of privacy are found in the First, Fourth, Fifth, Ninth, and Fourteenth Amendments to the U.S. Constitution. These rights are said to have penumbras surrounding them that constitute privacy (*Roe v. Wade*, 1973). In its purest definition, a **penumbra** is a dimly lighted area around an object, such as the moon. Thus, the rights guaranteed by the Constitution have an aura around them that gives the rights life. For instance, the Fourth Amendment says that people should be secure in their homes against governmental intrusion and that in order to enter a home, law enforcement must procure a warrant, supported by probable cause. Thus, this amendment has an aura of privacy surrounding it, which is also true of the First Amendment, which guarantees freedom of association. As long as an organization is lawful, the government has no business prying into membership. If governmental prying were permitted, individuals might be hesitant to join, interfering with the First Amendment right. Thus, a right to privacy exists here too in order to provide true meaning to the right to association.

Currently, the U.S. Supreme Court recognizes that individuals have a constitutional right to avoid the disclosure of personal information by government. The limited areas in which individuals have protection against the disclosure of personal information involve information about reproduction, contraception, abortion, and marriage. Even if information is considered private, disclosure of such information might not violate the Constitution, provided the government can show that its need to disclose outweighs the individual's right in keeping the information private.

For instance, as a general rule, one's medical records are confidential. However, government has always viewed contagious diseases as different from noncontagious diseases, permitting quarantine and forced treatment of those with a contagious disease that affects the public health (*Robinson v. California,* 1962). In some states, a person with a contagious disease, such as tuberculosis, *may* have his or her name and medical problem disclosed to the public via the news media to facilitate containment and treatment. As an illustration, a Louisiana woman with a contagious disease left a treatment facility without that facility's approval. She was identified in the newspapers as a "severe public health threat" and upon going to a federal office, she was recognized and returned to the hospital (Dvorak, 1998). The Louisiana statute states that "in order to prevent the occurrence or spread of communicable diseases, the rules and regulations of the Sanitary Code shall provide for an immunization program and provide for and require the reporting, investigation, and application and implementation of appropriate control measures to expressly include isolation and/or quarantine proceedings and measures, for all communicable diseases of public health significance" (Louisiana Revised Statute 40:4, 2000, p. 1).

In California, a Laotian immigrant who had infectious tuberculosis and who lied and hid from health workers was jailed in a case described as a clash between personal freedom and public safety (Ritter, 1999). An examination of California statute seems to support this type of action and perhaps more. The statute states that "upon being informed by a health officer of any contagious, infectious, or communicable disease the department *may take measures as are necessary to ascertain the nature of the disease and prevent its spread* [italics added]. To that end, the department may, if it considers it proper, take possession or control of the body of any living person, or the corpse of any deceased person" (California Health & Safety Code § 120140, p. 1).

An Alabama statute permits the disclosure of a student with a contagious disease to the Superintendent of Education, permits the disclosure of a person's contagious disease to the prehospital transport personnel, and permits disclosure to a third party where there is a foreseeable, real, and probable risk of transmission. Although the statute states that those receiving the information must keep the information confidential, the statute indicates that those receiving the information "*shall take only those actions nec-*

essary to protect the health of the infected person and others [italics added] where there is a foreseeable, real, or probable risk of transmission of the disease" (Code of Alabama § 22-11A-38).

Of course, no state has a statute that lists individuals' names and diseases as it lists individuals who have gotten married. Further, the news media is not mentioned in either the Louisiana statute, the California statute, or the Alabama statute. But an official can justify the release of someone's name in order to protect the public. This is especially the case when an individual refuses treatment for a contagious disease and purposely infects others or does not care about infecting others. Such a person does not have the right to keep his or her medical condition confidential under those circumstances. It illustrates the classic example of individual rights versus public welfare and which interest shall prevail.

Reflecting the above principle of individual rights versus the public welfare, the Department of Health and Human Services clarified the standards for privacy of individually identifiable health information. These standards, contained in a document consisting of 706 pages, went into effect on February 26, 2001. This document has a section entitled "Uses and Disclosures for Public Health Activities," which permits the disclosure of protected health information without individual authorization. A public health authority, without authorization from an infected person, is authorized to receive information in his or her duties, including public health surveillance, public health investigations, and public health interventions. In addition, information could be given to foreign governments who are collaborating with the United States to limit the spread of an infectious disease (Department of Health and Human Services, 2001). The right to privacy is not absolute.

Information involving births, such as infants who are born addicted to drugs, may also be given to governments. Also, some information involving personal matters may be disclosed to the public without identifying information. Statistics on the number or rate of a community's health information may be disclosed, such as the number of people inflicted with syphilis, gonorrhea, or HIV/AIDS and the number of teenagers giving birth or women having abortions.

In order to encourage individuals to seek drug treatment or participate in research studies, Congress has provided a right to privacy barring government from access to certain information. Individuals in federally funded drug treatment programs have a right to privacy to prevent such information from being given to government officials. In addition, individuals who are research participants have a right to the protection of information given to a researcher. Thus, in a qualitative study, a research participant may disclose that he or she robbed a store, and a prosecutor could not subpoena this information.

Although it is impossible here to discuss for all 50 states, a sample of states reveals the importance of privacy. A number of states recognize individuals' right to privacy in their state constitutions or by state statute. For instance, the New York Constitution contains a section on rights, privileges, and franchise secured, and it discusses the parent-child privilege, referring to the rights of privacy in parent-child relationships (New York Constitution Article I § 1). Similarly, the Kansas Constitution discusses the powers retained by the people and specifically refers to the right to privacy (Kansas Constitution Bill of Rights § 20). The Rhode Island Constitution discusses the right to privacy (Rhode Island Constitution 1, § 6). However, privacy has its limits.

LEGAL TESTS TO DETERMINE THE CONSTITUTIONALITY OF A STATUTE OR POLICY

Social workers apply tests to determine whether clients are entitled to certain benefits. Social workers also apply theories to problems and form conclusions. Similarly, courts apply tests to legal conflicts and apply legal theories to make decisions. Because the government has enumerated values and power and pursuit of them leads to conflicts with individuals, courts generally apply one of three legal tests, depending upon the individual's rights alleged to have been violated. These three tests are *strict scrutiny, intermediate scrutiny,* and *rational basis.* For fundamental rights, strict scrutiny is employed.

Rights can be grouped into fundamental and nonfundamental rights, which determines the type of tests the courts will employ. **Fundamental rights** are those rights explicitly stated in the U.S. Constitution, such as freedom of speech and freedom of association. In addition, fundamental rights are those rights that the U.S. Supreme Court considers to be basic to the concept of liberty, which must be protected from governmental intrusion, absent a **compelling state interest** (a compelling interest is a very strong reason put forth by government). The areas the U.S. Supreme

Court considers to be fundamental are voting, running for office, access to the courts, freedom to travel, freedom of association, and choice in marriage and procreation (Clapp, 2000).

Nonfundamental rights are those rights that are not fundamental, such as receipt of welfare benefits or a promotion. For nonfundamental rights, either intermediate scrutiny or a rational basis test is used. In addition, the setting in which the alleged violation occurred—such as a home, school, or prison—is a factor in which test will be used.

For instance, a person's home is considered sacrosanct, and people have more freedom and privacy there than other places. A high school or prison is an environment in which administrators must have authority to oversee the environment. Hence, to search one's home, law enforcement needs a search warrant. But a student's locker or a prisoner's cell can be searched without a warrant. Courts recognize that these settings differ and thus would use different standards to decide cases arising from each.

Strict scrutiny involves a court examining the extent to which the governmental body passing the legislation shows that the legislation in question promotes a compelling interest and is the least intrusive and extreme (Gifis, 1996). Moreover, the law can be neither too broad nor too narrow. Strict scrutiny is the highest or strictest test in the law; and when it is used to test whether the government has demonstrated a compelling state interest, the government often loses (Gentile, 1996). For instance, a few years ago, New York, like numerous states and the federal government, passed a law to prevent offenders from profiting from their crimes by selling their stories to publishers or the movie industry. The law penalized the publishing industry and thus infringed upon its First Amendment rights. (Remember, a corporation has many of the rights that individuals have.) In a unanimous decision, one in which strict scrutiny was used, the U.S. Supreme Court held this law to be unconstitutional (*Simon & Schuster v. New York State Crime Victims Board*, 1991).

The compelling state interest put forth by the State of New York was the compensation of victims and the prevention of criminals from profiting from their criminal acts. The problem was that the law affected thousands and thousands of books, including those that mentioned a crime only in passing. If a person mentioned any crime in a book, the New York law applied, and this was true whether the person was convicted or not. Accordingly, an author who discussed growing up on a farm and wrote that he or she stole some apples would be subject to the New York law. Furthermore, an activist who wrote that he or she demonstrated against police brutality or unfair labor practices and was arrested and fined $10 would be subjected to the New York law. U.S. Supreme Court Justice Clarence Thomas took no part in deciding this case. However, if Justice Thomas wrote a book and just mentioned in one sentence that he smoked marijuana as a college student, which he admitted in his confirmation hearing to have done, he could not receive payment for a book that he wrote about himself. Thus, this law did not survive strict scrutiny, and states needed to come up with a new law that did not broadly burden free speech.

Intermediate scrutiny is utilized for content-neutral restrictions and involves a court determining whether governmental action is substantially related to an important governmental objective. The government may legally treat some groups unequally and still comport with the equal protection clause of the Fourteenth Amendment. For instance, government may recognize women's unique relationship with their children and reject complaints by fathers that they were treated discriminatorily (*Planned Parenthood of Central Missouri et al. v. Danforth*, 1976). Using intermediate scrutiny, the Court upheld a Georgia law that fathers, but not mothers, of out-of-wedlock children could not inherit from their children unless they had legitimated the children (*Parham v. Hughes*, 1979).

The **rational basis test** is used to determine whether a challenged law bears a reasonable relationship to the accomplishment of some legitimate governmental objective. This test is employed when a general constitutional objection is raised to a law's reasonableness and not when a specific constitutional right is alleged to have been violated (Gifis, 1996). For instance, the U.S. Supreme Court upheld differences in standards for commitment of individuals with mental retardation and individuals with mental illness, noting that there was a rational basis that served a legitimate governmental purpose for differentiating the two groups (*Heller v. Doe*, 1993). Further, a high school student who objects to drug testing or having his or her locker searched is going to have his or her legal challenge determined by the rational basis test.

Related to the rational basis test is the **reasonableness test,** which is used only in correctional institutions. The U.S. Supreme Court has held that strict scrutiny is incompatible with the prison environment regardless of whether the right is fundamental. Thus, the Court decreed that the reasonableness test is to be used in any prison case when prisoners allege that an institutional policy infringes upon their rights (*Turner v. Safley*, 1987).

The Court stated in *Turner* that prisoners have rights that must be protected. However, the Court also stated that administering a prison is a difficult task, and federal judges do not have the expertise to decide what is valid or invalid policy. Therefore, considerable deference should be given to prison administrators. So, a prison policy that conflicts with prisoners' rights is presumed to be valid provided the policy is "reasonably related to legitimate penological interest" (*Turner v. Safley*, 1987, p. 2261). Legitimate penological interests are security and order, deterrence, incapacitation, reformation, and rehabilitation. Whether a prison policy is legitimate is determined by one or more of a four-part test. In deciding whether a prison policy has violated prisoners' rights, the courts must determine:

1. Whether there is a valid, rational connection between the prison regulation and the legitimate government interest put forward to justify it;
2. Whether there are alternative means of exercising the rights that remain open to prison inmates;
3. The impact accommodation of the asserted constitutional right will have on guards and other inmates, and on the allocation of prison resources generally; and
4. The absence of ready alternatives is evidence of the reasonableness of a prison regulation (*Turner v. Safley*, 1987, p. 2261).

The reasonableness test is important in correctional treatment because it has been subsequently used to decide whether the state can involuntarily treat with psychotropic drugs a prisoner who suffers from mental illness (*Washington v. Harper*, 1990). The U.S. Supreme Court also implied that *Washington v. Harper* was instructive in whether the state could treat an insane death-row prisoner involuntarily to restore his or her sanity so that the prisoner can be executed and remanded a Louisiana case (*Perry v. Louisiana*, 1990). However, upon further review, the Supreme Court of Louisiana ruled that forcing medication involuntarily to make a condemned person competent to be executed violated the Louisiana Constitution (*State v. Perry*, 1992).

In another case remanded by the U.S. Supreme Court, the Supreme Court of Nevada instructed the trial court to cease the medication of a Nevada man and required the state to justify forced medication by one of two reasons. First, the state had to show that forced medication was medically appropriate and essential, considering less intrusive means, to ensure Riggins' safety or the safety of others. Or second, the administration of antipsychotic medication was medically appropriate to ensure Riggins' competence to stand trial, and competence could not be maintained by less intrusive means (*Riggins v. Nevada,* 1993). *Riggins* involved the forced medication of a person at trial, and *Perry* involved the forced medication of a person to make the person competent to be executed. Other states have struggled with the issue of forced medication of death-row prisoners to make them competent to be executed, and some states, with uncertainty over their constitutions, allow prisoners to refuse to take medications voluntarily.

LEGAL STANDARDS TO DECIDE CIVIL AND CRIMINAL PROCEEDINGS

The aforementioned four legal tests are used to determine the constitutionality of a congressional or state legislative statute or policy. Three other legal tests are used to determine issues in a legal proceeding and whether the decision-making process comports with due process. These three tests are: *a Preponderance of the Evidence, Clear and Convincing Evidence,* and *Beyond a Reasonable Doubt.*

Individual states may define these three standards a little differently, but Clapp (2000) has provided some definitions. A **preponderance of the evidence** is the lowest standard of proof and has been defined as "the degree of persuasion necessary to find for plaintiff in most civil cases. It requires just enough evidence to persuade a jury that a fact is more likely to be true than not true. If the evidence is equally balanced, then the party with the burden of persuasion loses" (Clapp, 2000, pp. 337–338). **Clear and convincing evidence** is an intermediate standard. It requires that a fact finder (that is, a judge or jury) be persuaded that the fact to be proved is highly probable" (Clapp, 2000, p. 85). **Beyond a reasonable doubt** is the highest standard. It refers to "the degree of certainty necessary to convict a defendant of a crime. It does not mean beyond all possible doubt but beyond any doubt based upon reason and common sense" (Clapp, 2000, p. 52). The first two are employed in civil proceedings, and the last is employed in criminal proceedings. A qualifier is in order here. In many states, juvenile delinquency proceedings are civil, not criminal, but the U.S. Supreme Court has held that due process requires that adjudication of juveniles requires proof beyond a reasonable doubt (*In re Winship*, 1970).

Discussing the three tests in a case, former Chief Justice Warren Burger acknowledged that little is known about how lay juries apply these standards and that society may never know given the secrecy surrounding jury verdicts. The standards, according to Justice Burger, are used to reflect societal values in making decisions. Some legal disputes involve only money, but other legal disputes involve individuals' liberty and maybe their lives. Thus, to comport with the seriousness of the legal dispute and reduce the probability that an erroneous decision would be made, the least stringent test is used in money disputes and the most stringent when people's lives or liberty are at stake (*Addington v. Texas*, 1979).

In areas dealing with mental health policy, such as civil commitment to a mental health facility, the U.S. Supreme Court has held that due process requires the use of clear and convincing evidence before an individual may be civilly committed to a mental institution. The Court rejected the argument that the U.S. Constitution required that the standard needed to be proof beyond a reasonable doubt. A state may use a variation of clear and convincing evidence, such as one state that used clear, unequivocal, and convincing evidence. The main issue is that the standard must be more than a preponderance of the evidence (*Addington v. Texas*, 1979).

Illustrating this point, the U.S. Supreme Court upheld two Kentucky statutes involving the civil commitment of people with mental retardation and people with mental illness. A class of people who suffered from mental retardation contended that their rights to equal protection of the law were violated because the Kentucky statute required civil commitment of them by clear and convincing evidence, but for people with mental illness the standard was beyond a reasonable doubt. Another difference in the statutes was that parents or guardians could be parties to the action involving civil commitment of people with mental retardation, but they could not be parties in civil proceedings for people with mental illness.

The U.S. Supreme Court held that because the classification difference did not involve fundamental rights and did not proceed under suspect reasonings, the Kentucky statutes are constitutional in that the legislature had a rational basis for producing the different civil commitment statutes. According to the Kentucky legislature, diagnosing mental retardation is easier, and parents and guardians may have had a long history with the person and could offer valuable information. On the other hand, diagnosing mental illness is more difficult and it may be more sudden in its occurrence (*Heller v. Doe,* 1993).

ABSOLUTE AND QUALIFIED IMMUNITY

A last legal principle that needs explanation is absolute and qualified immunity. In order for state employees to perform their jobs, they must be provided with legal protection from some lawsuits. For instance, society would be seriously harmed if a prosecutor were permitted to be sued for erroneously trying an innocent person. Simply, this prosecutor would be hesitant to bring a case. The same would be true of a judge who made an erroneous ruling and was permitted to be sued by a losing party. Legislators would be hesitant to pass laws in some areas if they were allowed to be sued. Thus, early on, society recognized that some state officials need to be protected from lawsuits. This protection that is given to them is immunity, which may be either absolute or qualified (Alexander, 1995).

Absolute immunity is quite simple to understand. Essentially, it means that the person who has it cannot be sued in his or her official capacity. This type of immunity is afforded to members of the judiciary, legislatures, and executive branches (Burke, 1985). President Clinton could be sued for sexual harassment, which purportedly occurred when he was governor of Arkansas, because this behavior was not related to his official capacity. However, if he had pardoned a prisoner and this person sexually assaulted an individual, then Governor Clinton could not have been sued for negligently releasing a dangerous person because his action occurred in his official capacity.

Qualified immunity is protection given to some state officials provided that this person did not violate clearly established rights that a reasonable person should know or that the law was not fully developed at the time of the alleged injury. This type of immunity is available to state correctional officers, state mental health professionals, police officers, and social workers employed as child protection workers. For instance, correctional professionals know that prisoners have the right to get married. As long as security is not compromised, a prisoner who wants to get married cannot be denied this right. A warden can permit opposite-sex people to marry and deny this right to same-sex people. If a gay or lesbian prisoner sued the warden for discrimination by permitting opposite-sex people to marry but not same-sex people, the warden likely would move for dismissal of the lawsuit based on qualified immunity. This warden would likely argue, and a court would be likely to agree, that the law sanctioning same-sex marriage is not clearly established. Even if the warden's state legislature just granted gays and lesbians the right to marry, the warden still could argue that this law is not clearly established. The state supreme court or the U.S. Supreme Court could subsequently rule the law unconstitutional.

With respect to social workers, a number of courts have ruled that they enjoy absolute immunity when they initiate abuse and neglect investigations. In effect, these social workers are like prosecutors when they go to a judge, inform the judge that a child has been abused, and request removal of the child from the home. For instance, the Ninth Circuit Court of Appeals stated that:

> although child service workers do not initiate criminal proceedings, their responsibility for bringing dependency proceedings, and their responsibility to exercise independent judgment in determining when to bring such proceedings, is not very different from the responsibility of a criminal prosecutor. The social worker must make a quick decision based on perhaps incomplete information as to whether to commence investigations and initiate proceedings against parents who may have abused their children. The social worker's independence, like that of a prosecutor, would be compromised were the social worker constantly in fear that a mistake could result in a time-consuming and financially devastating civil suit. We therefore hold that social workers are entitled to absolute immunity in performing quasi-prosecutorial functions connected with the initiation and pursuit of child dependency proceedings (*Meyers v. Contra Costa County Department of Social Services*, 1987, p. 1157).

Notwithstanding, all social workers do not have absolute or qualified immunity. Some social workers have no immunity. For instance, social workers in private, clinical practice do not have immunity. If a client tells a clinician about spousal abuse and the clinician conveys this information to others, this clinician cannot claim immunity from a defamation lawsuit. However, a social worker employed in a state mental health agency may have quasi-immunity for some duties involving clients. As an illustration, some federal statutes apply to prisoners, but the extent to which a particular statute does is not known until the U.S. Supreme Court has ruled on the statute. For instance, the Americans with Disabilities Act (ADA) was not written for prisoners, and prisoners were not mentioned in its early legislative history. However, the U.S. Supreme Court has ruled that the act does apply to prisoners

(*Pennsylvania Department of Corrections et al. v. Yeskey,* 1998).
Prior to the U.S. Supreme Court ruling, lower federal courts may
have ruled differently. Thus, a social worker employed in a prison
who violated a prisoner's right under the ADA would be entitled to
claim quasi-immunity for acts prior to the U.S. Supreme Court's
ruling because the law was not clearly established in this area.
After the U.S. Supreme Court ruled and the law became established, a social worker employed in a correctional setting could not
claim quasi-immunity for violating a prisoner's right under the
ADA.

CONCLUSION

This discussion began with an explanation of substantive and
procedural law. It then explained the sources of law and why conflict invariably occurs between governments and individuals, noting that governments have police power and *parens patriae*
responsibilities. Then, it gave an overview of the federal judiciary.
Showing the social welfare implications, the chapter explained key
aspects of the federal Constitution, the right to privacy, and
selected portions of state constitutions and state statutes. The
chapter also discussed the legal tests used to decide the constitutionality of a statute or law and the tests used in civil proceedings,
such as civil commitment of a person with serious mental illness.
Finally, the chapter discussed what absolute and qualified immunities are and how they may affect a case.

Key Terms and Concepts

Substantive Law
Procedural Law
Common Law
Police Power
Parens Patriae
Best Interest of the
    Child
Eminent Domain
Privilege
Immunity
Substantive Due
    Process
Procedural Due
    Process

Suspect
    Classification
Quasi-Suspect
    Classification
Right to Privacy
Penumbra
Fundamental
    Rights
Compelling State
    Interest
Nonfundamental
    Rights
Strict Scrutiny
    Test

Intermediate
    Scrutiny
Rational Basis Test
Reasonableness
    Test
Preponderance of
    the Evidence
Clear and Convinc-
    ing Evidence
Beyond a Reason-
    able Doubt
Absolute Immunity
Qualified Immunity

CHILD PROTECTION
AND THE LAW

Child protection involves a number of areas that implicate social welfare policy and practice. These areas consist of abuse and neglect investigations, the removal of children from their homes because of abuse, and parental termination (Courtney, 1998). In addition, some children, for their own protection, such as children who are unsupervised or neglected, may be in need of protection under *parens patriae* (*In re Lukas B. et al. v. Rungsun*, 2000; *In the Matter of Department of Social Services v. Bonnie Mitchell*, 2000). For instance, a 14-year-old girl weighing 300 pounds was removed from her parents and put in foster care because the parents were allowing the girl to eat too much. The girl was put in foster care, resulting in her weight coming down, but when returned to her parents, her weight went up again, resulting in another removal from the home (Mayhood, 2000).

Children may also need to be protected from parents who do not maintain a clean home (*A. J. et al. v. L. O.*, 1997; *Fred Phillips and Yolanda Lopez v. Texas Department of Protective and Regulatory Services*, 2000; *In the Interest of*

M. C., 2000; "Mother of Four Charged with Endangerment," 1997; "10 Children Taken Out of Brooklyn Apartment," 1997). Occasionally, social workers take some children from their homes because the houses in which the children lived were filthy. These parents were discarding trash in the house and human feces were smeared throughout the house, which was a significant health hazard.

Although this chapter discusses parental separation, this discussion, consistent with the chapter's title, should be understood as involving child protection. All states have statutes for dealing with child protection issues, but the federal Constitution also is implicated in some cases. This chapter begins with the legal standard for separating a child and parent, the legal standard for termination of parental rights, cases in which parental terminations have been upheld, cases in which parental terminations have been reversed, fetuses as children needing protection, protection of children from violence, and the implications for social welfare policy and practice.

LEGAL STANDARD FOR SEPARATION OF PARENT AND CHILD

The law protects both the right of parents to their children and the right of children to their parents. A social worker, acting as an agent of the state, can interpose between a parent and child by taking a child temporarily out of the home and placing the child in foster care. Such a decision must be made for sound reasons. *Parens patriae* gives social workers the authority to act in the best interests of the child. When a child's welfare is being threatened by virtue of abuse or neglect, a social worker is empowered to act by temporarily removing the child. A plethora of decisions have supported this policy, as long as the parent is afforded due process and the removal decision is justified.

In *White by White v. Chambliss* (1997), a child who was killed by foster parents sued (through her mother as next of kin) numerous social workers in South Carolina. Among the many grounds for the lawsuit was that the social workers had violated the mother and child's liberty interest by separating them though an emergency removal. As a result, their rights to substantive due process were violated, according to the lawsuit.

The Fourth Circuit Court of Appeals stressed that few rights are more fundamental in our society than those of parents to retain custody of their children and to rear them as they see fit. However, this right is not absolute, and "the parent's right to custody is subject to the child's best interest in his [or her] personal health and safety and the state's interest as parens patriae in protecting that interest" (*Jordan ex rel. Jordan v. Jackson,* 1994, p. 346). The South Carolina law states that when a social worker has probable cause to believe that a child's life or physical safety is periled by abuse or neglect, the social worker is authorized to remove the child from the home (South Carolina Code § 20-7-610). Examining the South Carolina law, the Fourth Circuit Court of Appeals ruled as constitutional South Carolina law governing emergency removal of children (*Jordan ex rel. Jordan v. Jackson,* 1994).

In this case, the social worker was called to the emergency room of a hospital where another child of the mother was treated for a fractured arm. The mother's story that the child had fallen out of the crib was inconsistent with the nature of the fracture, according to the treating physician and a consulting physician. The social worker, in addition, went to the child's home to see the crib, and its structure and height suggested that the mother's story was improbable and that physical abuse had occurred. The Fourth Circuit Court had previously ruled that an emergency removal of children is constitutional when there is some evidence of child abuse, which there was in this case (*White by White v. Chambliss,* 1997).

LEGAL STANDARD FOR PARENTAL RIGHTS TERMINATION

States vary in determining when to terminate parents' rights to their children. A specific parent's behavior may result in the termination of custody of a child, but in another state, the same behavior might result in this parent keeping a child. Of course, the best interest of the child is subjective, and judges may rule differently. Since the passage of the Adoption and Safe Families Act of 1997, states have been encouraged to terminate parental rights speedily so that abused and neglected children could be quickly adopted (Genty, 1998). Notwithstanding, the U.S. Supreme Court has uniformly established the legal standard that needs to be used in terminating parental rights.

This landmark case occurred in New York. New York law provided that parents' right to their children could be terminated by a fair preponderance of the evidence. In this case, the Santoskys had two children. First, one was taken away because of neglect for several months. Later, the Ulster County Department of Social Services took away the other child because of neglect. During this process, the Santoskys had a third child and when he was three days old, he, too, was taken away. In all cases, the contention was that the children were in danger by virtue of neglect.

Believing that it was in the best interests of the children, the Ulster County Department of Social Services sought under New York law to terminate the Santoskys' parental rights to the three children. While court proceedings were occurring, officials learned that the Santoskys had had two more children, but these children were not removed from the Santoskys. With respect to the three oldest children, the Santoskys' parental rights were terminated, which the New York appellate court upheld (*Santosky et al. v. Kramer et al.*, 1982).

However, the U.S. Supreme Court ruled that the legal standard New York used was insufficient and violated the Santoskys' due process rights under the Fourteenth Amendment. As the Court reasoned, parents have a fundamental liberty interest in the care, custody, and management of their children, which is protected by the Fourteenth Amendment. Failing to be model parents or temporarily losing custody of their children to the state does not erase this right. When the state moves to permanently terminate, weakened families' bonds, the parents are entitled to fundamentally fair proceedings, and a lower legal standard violates this fundamental fairness. The fair preponderance of the evidence is inadequate and violates parents' due process rights because it can permit more errors adverse to parents. Thus, states must use at least the standard of clear and convincing evidence to satisfy due process before parental termination may occur (*Santosky et al. v. Kramer et al.*, 1982).

Later, the Court held that a parent facing termination of her parental rights must be afforded an opportunity to appeal the case, provided the parent wanted to appeal, even if the parent could not pay the filing fee. This ruling came about because of a Mississippi case in which a mother's parental rights were terminated and custody awarded to the biological father and his new wife. In addition, the court ordered that children's birth certificates list the adopting stepmother. To appeal a case in Mississippi, a party must pay filing fees and record preparation fees. The filing fee was $100, which the mother paid, but the record preparation fees were $1,900 for the trial transcript, $438 for other documents, $4.36 for binders, and $10 for mailing. The mother could not pay the $2,352.36, and as a result, the Supreme Court of Mississippi denied her the right to appeal (*M. L. B. v. S. L. J.*, 1996).

However, the U.S. Supreme Court ruled that denying the mother the right to appellate review based on an inability to pay appeal costs violates the mother's due process rights of the Fourteenth Amendment. The Court stressed that the severance of a parent's right to his or her child constitutes very severe state action and concerns a fundamental right. In the parental cases that the Supreme Court of Mississippi had handled since *Santosky*, almost half of them were reversed because the Mississippi trial courts had not used the clear and convincing standard (*M. L. B. v. S. L. J.*, 1996). With the standard of clear and convincing evidence in place, parental termination cases have been upheld and reversed.

Cases in Which Parental Terminations Were Upheld

In a Georgia case, a mother's parental rights to her four children were terminated; however, she appealed the termination of only two of them, twin boys. On appeal, she contended only that the trial court erred in finding by clear and convincing evidence that the twins' deprivation, a component of the Georgia statute, was likely to continue. The Georgia statute delineates a two-step procedure to be employed in parental termination of rights cases. First, there must be a finding of parental misconduct or inability, which requires clear and convincing evidence that (a) the child is deprived; (b) the lack of proper parental care or control is the cause of the deprivation; (c) the cause of the deprivation is likely to continue; and (d) the continued deprivation is likely to cause serious physical, mental, emotional, or moral harm to the child.

If these four factors are satisfied, the trial court must then determine whether termination of parental rights is in the best interests of the child, considering the child's physical, mental, emotional, and moral condition and needs, including the need for a secure and stable home (*In the Interest of D. B. et al.*, 2000).

In ruling on a parental termination case on appeal, the Court of Appeals of Georgia decided the case in a light most favorable to the **appellee** (that is, the party responding in the appellate court), or the trial court. This means that court of appeals must determine whether any rational **trier of fact** (that is, a judge or jury who decides the facts of a case) could have found by clear and convincing evidence that the biological parental rights had been lost. Thus, examining the evidence in the record showed that the mother left the twins, when they were about a year old, and the other two children with their alcoholic father. Supposedly, she left the city to look for work. When the mother left, there was no food, electricity, or heat in the home. The father contacted the police, saying that he did not know when the mother was returning and that he was unable to care for the children. At that point, the Department of Family and Children Services took custody of all four children (*In the Interest of D. B. et al.*, 2000).

The Department of Family and Children Services tried to work with the mother, and the mother promised to keep the department informed of her address and situation. However, the mother missed 10 scheduled appointments with social workers, and three certified letters were returned to the department. During the time the department had her children, the mother missed 19 of 55 scheduled bimonthly visits with her children, and she also had lived in about 18 different places. The mother was required to attend substance abuse counseling, but she failed to complete the program. She called the foster mother only once and never sent the children birthday cards or wrote them letters (*In the Interest of D. B. et al.*, 2000).

Hence, the Department of Family and Children Services moved to have the mother's parental rights terminated. At the time of the hearing, the mother admitted that she could not at the present time care for her children. She indicated that she had hoped to be in a better situation in about four months. She stated that she intended to care for her children by relying upon the children's Social Security benefits and other government aid. The trial court noted that the mother had never lived independently and had no vocational skills. For 18 months, the Department of Family and Children Services had offered help and assistance, but the mother's behavior had not changed appreciably. At the termination hearing, the mother could only state a vague promise to have a suitable home for the children in the future (*In the Interest of D. B. et al.*, 2000).

Thus, the trial judge found all four factors of the Georgia statute to exist and concluded that the children's best interests had to rest on more than the mother's positive promises. Reviewing the evidence and the law, the Court of Appeals of Georgia ruled that any rational trier of fact would have found by clear and convincing evidence that the mother's parental rights should be terminated (*In the Interest of D. B. et al.*, 2000).

In another Georgia case, a mother was convicted of attacking her 14-year-old daughter with a hammer and a screwdriver. She pled guilty to simple assault. Two years later, she was convicted of cruelty to her two youngest children for injuring them with an electrical cord during a beating, a conviction which resulted in the mother being put on probation. The youngest children were put in foster care. To get the children back, the mother agreed to a reunification plan that consisted of her improving her parenting skills by attending parenting and anger management classes and receiving evaluation of and treatment for her chronic alcohol and drug abuse. Two years after the plan was developed, the Department of Family and Children Services petitioned to have the mother's parental rights terminated on the grounds that the mother failed to maintain a meaningful parental role and failed to comply with the court-ordered reunification plan. After hearing the evidence, the family court judge granted the petition to terminate parental rights (*In the Interest of L. S. D. et al.*, 2000).

The mother appealed, contending that the evidence did not suffice to sustain a finding that her parental misconduct was likely to continue or would not likely be remedied. She reported that she had completed substance abuse and parenting classes. However, the department contended that the mother had not completed these programs until she received notice that her parental rights were to be terminated. Prior to receiving this notice, the mother had not attended counseling despite agreeing to do so. Also, the mother did not visit her children until she received notice that a hearing was planned to have her parental rights terminated. Thus, the court noted that the mother's plan to change came too late and was unconvincing. Furthermore, the mother was still on probation for cruelty to her children, and her probation required that she not have unsupervised contact with the children. This probation condition precluded her from getting the children back anyway (*In the Interest of L. S. D. et al.*, 2000).

In a case that had a tinge of antigay bias, a Mississippi judge in Pike County Chancery Court awarded custody of two children to their grandparents. In this case, the father and mother divorced due to long-standing problems involving the father's substance abuse problem and both parents' unfaithfulness. After the separation and divorce, the mother moved into a trailer with a female friend, and they began a lesbian relationship. One day, the father picked up the children for a visit and took them to their paternal grandparents. The grandparents kept the children and subsequently pressed charges against the mother for being unfit and immoral.

At an evidentiary hearing, the mother admitted that she and her partner smoked marijuana when the children were nearby. The mother, who was subsequently unemployed, also admitted that she did not get up in the morning until about 11 a.m. and often the children would play outside unsupervised. Reportedly, the children were hungry at times and ill dressed during cold weather. Finding both biological parents unfit, the judge, with the Mississippi Supreme Court concurring, ruled that the children's best interest required that the children be placed in the custody of their grandparents. The mother argued that the judge was biased against her because of her lesbian relationship, which was illustrated by the portion of the ruling that described her as leading an immoral life. Nevertheless, the Supreme Court of Mississippi held that there was more than enough evidence to find that the mother was unfit (*White v. Thompson et al.,* 1990).

Cases in Which Parental Terminations Were Reversed

In a reversal of a family court judge's decision to terminate parental rights, the Court of Appeals of Minnesota remanded the case for a new hearing. In this case, a mother and her child were living with a man in a home fraught with violence. Both adults had substance abuse problems, and both were threatening each other and threatening each other with weapons. The man was reported to have threatened the mother and child with a knife, and on another occasion, the mother had shot at the man with the bullet hitting a wall. The mother sought and received a protective order, and her live-in partner was ordered out of the home. At some point, the mother's 11-year-old child was put in foster care, and parental termination was ordered, but stayed.

As part of the assistance to the mother, the Hennepin County Department of Children and Family Services formulated a reunification plan for the mother. Part of the plan required that she not have consensual contact with her former live-in boyfriend. Despite agreeing to this provision, the mother began seeing the boyfriend again and permitted him to move back in, despite having a protective order against him. When the Hennepin County Department of Children and Family Services learned of the mother's behavior, it sought to have the stay lifted, which was granted. The mother contended that this decision was illegal because the judge did not make a specific finding that the issue of the former boyfriend was the basis for the judge's decision. Although the judge noted that the mother's renewed involvement was a problem, the judge failed to show by clear and convincing evidence that the mother violated aspects of the Minnesota statute governing parental termination. For this reason, the Court of Appeals remanded the case and ordered a new hearing (*In the Matter of the Welfare of P. R. I.*, 2000).

A father in California who had his parental rights to his two sons terminated appealed the termination decision. His contention was that he was not given proper notice of the termination hearing. The California Code requires that whenever a juvenile court schedules a hearing regarding a minor, the court assures the following: The father, presumed and alleged, the mother of the minor, the child if 10 years of age or older, and any counsel of record shall be notified of the time and place of the proceeding. Moreover, the notice shall advise them of their right to counsel, the nature of the proceeding, and that at the proceeding the court shall select and implement a plan of adoption, legal guardianship, or long-term foster care. Service of notice shall be completed at least 45 days before the date of the hearing, except in cases where notice is by publication, in which the number of days is 30. If the termination of parental rights is sought, this intention shall be included in the notice and served within the time period specified This notice may also be provided by separate notice to all people entitled to receive notice by first class mail at least 15 days before the scheduled hearing (California Welfare & Institution Code § 366.26, p. 1).

The record showed that the case was set for a hearing on March 18, 1999. Attorneys were appointed for the children at this March 18, 1999, hearing and the father was present. The case was continued to April 20, 1999, but the father was not present. The case was continued until May 20, 1999, and again the father was not present. Then, the case was continued because the children's birth certificates were not available. On May 24, 1999, a fourth hearing was held, and at this hearing the father's parental rights were terminated. Neither the father nor his attorney was present at this last hearing. The department agreed that the father did not have proper notice, and the termination order was vacated and remanded (*In re Rashad H. et al. v. Steven H.*, 2000).

FETUSES AS CHILDREN NEEDING PROTECTION

The issue of pregnant women using drugs and incurring interference from the state is often discussed as a women's issue that violates women's right to privacy. However, this book discusses it from the perspective of child protection because this appears to be where society is headed. The issue here is the extent to which the state may force and coerce a pregnant woman who is using drugs to get treatment, ensuring the health of her fetus and future fetuses. Also, coercing a mother to get treatment for a drug problem could help the mother ultimately in parenting. Because some states have recognized fetuses as people meriting state protection, this section discusses fetuses as children in need of protection.

The foundation for coercing mothers into treatment appears to have its roots in two South Carolina cases. The South Carolina Supreme Court ruled that a fetus was a person with respect to South Carolina criminal statute (*State v. Horne*, 1984). Moreover, the South Carolina Supreme Court upheld the conviction of a woman who was convicted of criminal child neglect for taking cocaine while she was pregnant with a viable fetus (*Whitner v. State*, 1997). More significant, this case was appealed to the U.S. Supreme Court, but certiorari was denied (*Whitner v. State*, 1998). (**Certiorari** is a written order by the U.S. Supreme Court to a lower court to send certified records of a proceeding in the court below. The Court will grant certiorari, which means it will hear the case, or deny certiorari, which means it will not hear a case.) The refusal of the U.S. Supreme Court to hear the Whitner case is consistent with this author's assertion that while abortion decisions were upheld, the U.S. Supreme Court had strengthened the recognition that the state possesses significant police power in protecting viable and nonviable fetuses.

South Carolina officials, concerned with the number of children born with cocaine in their systems, undertook a policy that has been highly criticized. A collaboration of people and institutions in Charleston, South Carolina—the Medical University of South Carolina, the Solicitor General (that is, the district attorney), the Chief of Police, the City of Charleston, and various social services agencies—implemented a policy of coerced drug treatment for pregnant women whose urine tested positive for cocaine. Women who tested positive were referred to the prosecutor's office, and the prosecutor could charge the women with delivery of cocaine to the children. The women were told that they had to complete substance abuse counseling if they wanted the charge dropped. The clientele of the hospital was poor women, and most of the women referred to the prosecutor's office were African American.

Assisted by the Center for Reproductive Law and Policy, the women sued the parties involved in the creation of the policy, contending that the policy violated their rights under the Fourth Amendment to be free of warrantless searches; the Civil Rights Act of 1904 that protects minorities against policies that have a racially disparate impact; their right to privacy; and South Carolina law against abuse of process (*Ferguson et al. v. City of Charleston*, 1999). While the Fourth Circuit Court of Appeals upheld this policy, the U.S. Supreme Court reversed the decision of the Fourth Circuit Court of Appeals, holding that the policy was illegal.

Drawing a distinction between the women in Charleston and previous cases in which the Court sanctioned drug testing, the Court ruled that the Charleston policy was unconstitutional because law enforcement was heavily involved. Previously, the U.S. Supreme Court sanctioned drug testing of students, railroad conductors, and some federal officials involved in sensitive areas. The Court recognized that some situations involved "special needs," and these were constitutional under the Fourth Amendment. **Special needs** is "a balancing test used by the U.S. Supreme Court to determine whether certain searches (such as administrative, civil-based, or public-safety searches) impose unreasonably on individual rights" (Garner, 1999, p. 1404).

In law enforcement, the task is frequently to conduct investigations and gather evidence of a crime. However, a transportation department may have a need to ensure that a train conductor is not under the influence. None of the previous cases where special needs were sanctioned by the Court involved law enforcement officials, and there was no intention to turn over the results of drug testing for arrest and prosecution. In the Charleston case, law enforcement was involved initially, information was being shared with law enforcement from case conferences, and the hospital staff helped to coordinate arrests of the women (*Ferguson et al. v. City of Charleston et al.*, 2001).

Justice Kennedy wrote a concurring opinion and stated:

> In my view, it is necessary and prudent to be explicit in explaining the limitations of today's decision. The beginning point ought to be to acknowledge the legitimacy of the State's interest in fetal life and one of the grave risks to the life and health of the fetus, and later the child, caused by cocaine ingestion. . . . There can be no doubt that South Carolina can impose punishment upon

an expectant mother who has so little regard for her own unborn that she risks causing him or her lifelong damage and suffering. The State, by taking special measures to give rehabilitation and training to expectant mothers with this tragic addiction or weakness, acts well within its powers and its civic obligations. . . . The holding of the Court, furthermore, does not call into question the validity of mandatory reporting laws such as child abuse laws which require teachers to report evidence of child abuse to the proper authorities, even if arrest and prosecution is likely to result. . . . We must accept the premise that the medical profession can adopt acceptable criteria for testing expectant mothers for cocaine use in order to provide prompt and effective counseling to the mother and to take proper medical steps to protect the child. If prosecuting authorities then adopt legitimate procedures to discover this information and prosecution follows, that ought not to invalidate the testing. One of the ironies of the case, then, may be that the program now under review, which gives the cocaine user a second and third chance, might be replaced by some more rigorous system. We must, however, take the case as it comes to us; and the use of handcuffs, arrests, prosecutions, and police assistance in designing and implementing the testing and rehabilitation policy cannot be sustained under our previous cases concerning mandatory testing (*Ferguson et al. v. City of Charleston et al.*, 2001, pp. 1294–1295).

PROTECTION OF CHILDREN FROM VIOLENCE

The issue of protecting children from violence needs to be put into a broader context in order to understand the law and policy in this area. In *DeShaney v. Winnebago County Department of Social Services*, 1989), the U.S. Supreme Court reiterated a basic principle that encompassed children, public assistance programs, and society in general. This important principle is that the due process clause of the Fourteenth Amendment provides no duty upon states or the federal government to provide basic needs. Simply put, government is under no legal duty to provide citizens food, housing, clothing, financial help, education, medical care, or protection from violence. People do not have a right to housing or affordable housing. Hungry people do not have a right to food. A person who is robbed or sexually assaulted in the home or on the streets cannot blame the government for failing to protect him or her from criminals. (However, a person who is robbed or assaulted in a hotel may have a case against the hotel for a lack of security, but such a claim is likely based on state tort law.)

The U.S. Supreme Court has established that no individual, including children, has an affirmative right to protection from violence that was administered by a private person. This ruling occurred in a Wisconsin case in which social workers failed to take a child from the child's father, and the father subsequently seriously and permanently injured the child (*DeShaney v. Winnebago County Department of Social Services*, 1989). However, the Court indicated that the situation would be different if a child was injured in a state-operated foster home (*DeShaney v. Winnebago County Department of Social Services*, 1989). The next section of this chapter explains when and how government bears responsibility to protect children from violence.

PROTECTION OF CHILDREN FROM CASEWORKERS' DECISIONS

The cases discussed in this section could be discussed as the basis for professional malpractice. However, they are discussed here because these cases also indicate rather clearly the degree to which children must be protected. Two theories have been proffered as exceptions to the standard in *DeShaney* by the Tenth Circuit Court of Appeals, the largest circuit in the country. One is the special relationship theory, and the other is danger creation theory.

A **special relationship** in federal law exists when government restrains an individual's freedom so as to cut the individual off from basic needs (that is, food, clothing, shelter, and sometimes safety) and causing an individual to be dependent on the government for those needs (*Armijo v. Wagon Mound Public Schools et al.*, 1998). The classic examples of a special relationship are prisoners, detainees, institutionalized people with mental illness, and children in foster care or detention. These groups are dependent upon the government for their basic needs, such as food, shelter, clothing, and medical care. A special relationship does not exist between a child and a public school teacher or a correctional officer and the state. A correctional officer who is assaulted cannot claim a special relationship between him or her and a state or federal prison system.

Danger creation theory provides that if a government's affirmative conduct places a person in danger, then the government may be liable for the harm inflicted on that person by a third party (Garner, 1999). It consists of several components, according to the

Tenth Circuit Court of Appeals (*Armijo v. Wagon Mound Public Schools et al.,* 1998). First, the plaintiff must demonstrate that he or she was a member of a limited and specifically definable group. Second, the defendant's conduct put the plaintiff at substantial risk for serious, immediate, and proximate harm. Third, the risk was obvious or known. Fourth, the defendant acted recklessly in conscious disregard of that risk. Fifth, the conduct, viewed in total, is conscience shocking. Sixth, the defendant created the danger or increased the plaintiff's vulnerability to danger in some way (*Armijo v. Wagon Mound Public Schools et al.,* 1998).

Yvonne L. v. New Mexico Department of Human Services (1992) illustrates the special relationship theory. In this case, the New Mexico Human Services Department placed two children in Child Haven, a not-for-profit facility. While at this facility, Yvonne contended that she was raped and sodomized by another girl, while Demond, the other child placed with Yvonne, watched. Both children sued, contending that the social workers for the Department of Human Services violated their rights by placing them at Child Haven. Specifically, the children argued that if the social workers had monitored Child Haven properly, the social workers would have known about the general operations at Child Haven and the type of children who were placed there. Though a district court granted summary judgment for the defendants, the Tenth Circuit Court of Appeals reversed this decision.

The children in *Yvonne L.* argued that they had a special relationship with the New Mexico Department of Human Services because they were removed from the community and placed at Child Haven. (In fact, the children had to be moved because they were being cared for by their grandmother who died, but legally this would not matter.) This removal required that social workers use professional judgment in making placements. Particularly, they contended that social workers departed from Section 671 of the Social Security Act, which required that social workers ensure that Child Haven was following national standards. Among the standards were admission and classification policy, safety, and civil rights protection. Reportedly, Child Haven failed to screen and isolate children with serious psychological problems and children with delinquent behaviors, failed to have proper supervision of the children in its care, and failed to hire and train competent staff. In short, if the social workers had monitored Child Haven, they would have known that the staffing was a problem and various children were placed there with inadequate supervision. Accordingly, the Tenth Circuit remanded the case, ruling that a special relationship exception existed in the law and that the plaintiffs had raised questions that were for a trial to decide (*Yvonne L. v. New Mexico Department of Human Services*, 1992).

The danger creation theory could be said to exist in *Yvonne L.* But it is a separate theory that might be applicable when social workers have not placed a child with a contracted program, such as Child Haven. In short, danger creation theory exists when the state has created the danger of attack or mistreatment by private individuals or has rendered a person more vulnerable to such conduct. In *DeShaney*, the father seriously injured his son, but the Wisconsin social workers did not place the child with the father. The following cases illustrate an essential difference between *DeShaney*, where the state was considered not responsible, and cases where the state was considered responsible or possibly responsible.

In *Currier v. Doran* (1998), social workers took a 3-year-old child from his mother's custody. They placed the child with the father, who killed the child by scalding the child with boiling water. Unlike in *DeShaney*, the social workers in *Currier* placed the child with the father. Thus, one could argue that the social workers placed the Currier child in danger. Five social work professionals were sued. The judge granted summary judgment for two, rejected summary judgment for two, and one defendant apparently did not ask for summary judgment. But the import of the ruling was that danger creation theory exists, and two individuals might have violated the child's rights (*Currier v. Doran*, 1998).

A series of cases have established that children who have been abused or assaulted by foster parents (who are viewed as agents of the state) have a cause of action against social workers and social work supervisors who have been negligent by placing them in harm. A case from Gillette, Wyoming, illustrates this protective requirement. Appearing on the surface to be upright people, Beth and Homer Griswold, who relocated to Wyoming, were made foster parents there. Dr. Beth Griswold was hired as the staff psychologist for the Northern Wyoming Medical Center. She was also a member of the Weston County Child Protection Team. Dr. Griswold's husband, Homer Griswold, was a dispatcher for the Newcastle Police Department (*T. M. et al. v. Carson et al.*, 2000).

Reportedly, Homer Griswold had a history of abuse in his family; he stated that he had been abused by his father. As an adolescent, Homer was accused of molesting his sisters. In Louisiana, as an adult, Homer and his brother were alleged to have sexually assaulted two nieces. When the Griswolds lived in Newcastle,

Wyoming, they were approved as foster parents by a social worker. Two girls were placed with the Griswolds, and one reported to the social worker that Homer Griswold was having sex with her. A meeting was held that was attended by Beth Griswold, the county attorney, and several social workers from children services. They decided to remove the children. Strangely, Dr. Griswold, Homer's wife, was asked to conduct a psychological evaluation of the girl that her husband was accused of sexually molesting.

The Griswolds subsequently moved to Gillette, Wyoming. They were approved again as foster parents despite Homer's problem in Newcastle, Wyoming, and Homer's loss of two jobs in Wyoming because of inappropriate sexual behavior. Homer was fired from his job as a police dispatcher for sexual harassment, and he was fired from a job as a school worker for inappropriate sexual behaviors. Nonetheless, the Griswolds were approved as foster parents. A 5-year-old girl and a 7-year-old girl were placed with the Griswolds. Both were sexually assaulted by Homer Griswold, resulting in several sentences of life imprisonment for Homer (*Griswold v. The State of Wyoming*, 1999). Through their **guardian ad litem** (a special guardian appointed by the court to represent a ward in that litigation) both girls sued 11 social work professionals in the Department of Family Services in Newcastle and Gillette, Wyoming, contending that the social workers failed to conduct a proper investigation of the Griswolds and caused them to be sexually assaulted (*T. M. et al. v. Carson et al.*, 2000).

The defendants moved for a dismissal of the lawsuit. The plaintiffs countered, in part, with an affidavit from a social work professor at the University of Michigan who wrote that the placement of the two children in Gillette was done without social workers exercising sound professional judgment. Further, the social work professor wrote that no competent social worker who exercised professional judgment after conducting a proper home study would have certified Homer Griswold as a foster parent in either Newcastle or Gillette. The home study was said to be defective in several areas, and no competent social work supervisor, according to the University of Michigan social work professor, would have concurred in what the lower line social worker did. In short, their performance was so lacking as not only to reflect unsound professional judgment but to reflect instead no professional judgment. Based on this affidavit, as well as a review of applicable theories (that is, special relationship and danger creation theories), the defendants' motion for summary judgment was rejected (*T. M. et al. v. Carson et al.*, 2000).

IMPLICATIONS FOR SOCIAL WELFARE POLICY AND PRACTICE

Although states may vary somewhat regarding when a social worker should remove a child, *White by White v. Chambliss* (1997) indicates that "some evidence" is sufficient to temporarily remove a child from home. Intuition and hunches are not evidence. Evidence would be inconsistent or contradictory parental reports, inconsistency between a physical injury and a parent's report, reliable eyewitnesses, and parental admission. Surely, this list is not exhaustive; other types of evidence exist. But professional social work practice requires evidence of this nature.

A professional social worker would not personally want a parent's parental rights to be terminated and would assess, gather, and report the information present in a case. *Santosky* tells a social worker that clear and convincing evidence needs to be provided before a court will terminate parental rights. For instance, a child's injury may have been caused by a parent or by the child falling. If the parent denies injuring the child and the physical circumstances do not contradict the parent, there is no convincing evidence to recommend or begin the process of parental rights termination. Furthermore, a grandparent's report that the parent was believed to be physically abusive although the grandparent did not see the parent abusing the child is not convincing evidence. Recall in Chapter 2 that a social worker took nude pictures of her grandchildren. There are perhaps legitimate differences of opinion in this case. This incident would not be clear abuse. However, hitting a child with a hammer or weapon or repeatedly leaving a child unsupervised constitutes clear and convincing evidence that may require a petition for parental termination, or perhaps just counseling is needed.

The due process clause of the Fourteenth Amendment also requires that social workers adhere to state law in parental termination cases. Because states differ regarding the notice that must be given to parents before terminating their parental rights, due process requires adherence to state laws. California law requires 15 days' notice to parents, but another state could require 10 days, and a third state could provide 7 days. Whatever the number of days specified in the statute, due process requires that social workers comply with the law. Notwithstanding, a state cannot be unreasonable, and due process protects parents. If a state passes a law that parents must be given 3 days' notice, such a provision would likely be ruled unconstitutional because it is unfair and violates due process. Such a limit could be reasonably argued as not enough time to hire an attorney and gather evidence to counter the social workers' claim.

The Mississippi case involving the mother who lost custody of her children after she began a relationship with another woman, indeed, smacks of a biased judicial opinion (*White v. Thompson et al.*, 1990). Reportedly, the judge referred to the mother's immoral lifestyle in the decision to terminate parental rights, and the Supreme Court of Mississippi upheld the decision. Although the decision was biased, it indicates something else regarding the issue of gay and lesbian parents. In the record were reports that the mother admitted that she and her partner smoked marijuana in the children's presence. She admitted that she did not get up in the morning until about 11 a.m., and the children would already be up and outside playing without supervision. In addition, the children were hungry and ill dressed at times. Thus, the evidence indicated a parenting problem regardless of sexual orientation. If the mother was parenting adequately and her sexual orientation was the sole issue, the decision to terminate parental rights likely would have been reversed if pursued in the federal courts.

White says that an irresponsible parent may be heterosexual or homosexual. Even if bias or prejudice is present in a case, a tainted decision may not be reversed if there is clear and convincing evidence that the parent is unfit. Removing the taint likely would have resulted in the same decision to terminate parental rights and place the children with their grandparents. In criminal law, a principle referred to as **harmless error** means that there was an error, but such error did not materially affect the outcome of the case. It would be no different if a white woman was staying with an African American man, and a judge indicated that such interracial relationships were against nature. A decision to terminate parental rights in such a case would not likely be disturbed if there was clear and convincing evidence, for example, that the woman and man were smoking crack cocaine regularly, the children were not fed, the children were not attending school, or the parents were physically abusing the children. An appellate court would likely uphold the decision to terminate parental rights while rebuking or reprimanding the judge for his comment about interracial relationships.

The South Carolina case involving drug testing of pregnant women and using the legal system to force them into treatment has implications for social welfare policy. As stated previously, the U.S. Supreme Court held that this policy violated the U.S.

Constitution, which was a victory for the women in South Carolina. The concurring opinion by Justice Kennedy in *Ferguson* clearly suggests that another approach would be legal as far as he is concerned. Because this decision was 6 to 3, another justice, besides Justice Kennedy, could uphold testing and prosecution of pregnant women who use drugs. In fact, Justice Kennedy's concurring opinion seems to provide suggestions for states in how to create a lawful policy of testing and prosecution.

A reading of both the majority opinion and the concurring opinion instructs hospital officials and social service professionals to take law enforcement out of its initial procedures and policy. This appears to be the key problem. If hospital workers and social service professionals created such a policy by themselves and then discover a violation of the law, such policy might be legal.

For example, no one would question a call to the police by a nurse or hospital social worker if the hospital determined that a 3-year-old child had overdosed on her mother's illegal drugs. Such a situation might be viewed as child neglect and/or abuse. As Justice Kennedy stated, the *Ferguson* decision does not call into question mandatory reporting by teachers when they learn of child abuse, even if an arrest and prosecution occur involving the parent. Just as teachers learn of child abuse, so can hospital social workers learn of child abuse, requiring them to report. Further, South Carolina law recognizes that a fetus is protected under its law, and the U.S. Supreme Court has so far not rejected this stance, although the Court had an opportunity to hear and reverse a case involving a fetus, but the Court refused to hear the case.

A lawful policy *might* be as follows. A hospital creates a policy of testing for pregnant women, and one of these tests is for drugs. Its rationale for testing is that good medical care involves testing for various problems and conditions, and often the patient does not consent to each test that a doctor orders. A number of tests may be ordered, such as a test of the urine for infection, a test of the blood for liver functioning, or a test for blood sugar levels. Then, a test for drugs may also be ordered in order to provide the best care for women and their fetuses. When a child is born, additional tests are conducted to determine if the child is healthy or has some problems that need to be treated. If upon learning that the child has illegal drugs in its system, a call is made to the police. Upon arriving to investigate an alleged crime, law enforcement discovers evidence of a crime. As Justice Kennedy wrote, if prosecuting authorities adopt legitimate procedures to discover information regarding a child being born with drugs in its system and prosecution follows, this ought not to invalidate the testing. Even the attorney for the women, Ms. Priscilla Smith of the Center for Reproductive Law and Policy, conceded that the Court gave "a message to state legislatures to go ahead and criminalize behavior during pregnancy" (Goodman, 2001, p. E7).

Children have a right to be protected from violence caused or facilitated by state actors under the special relationship theory or the danger creation theory. However, children have no legal right to be protected from violence committed by their parents when social workers are unaware of a problem or have made sound, justifiable decisions. For instance, a parent who has slapped a child in anger and who has no previous history of abuse may be viewed by social workers as amenable to counseling. If the social worker arranges for counseling and later the parent kills the child, no fault is attributed to the social worker. One can second-guess and feel badly, but a tragic result such as this incident is not foreseeable. However, if the social worker has a special relationship with a child or puts the child in danger, the social worker may be culpable.

The special relationship and danger creation theories are linked to protecting children from violence and provide guidelines for social workers. Professional practice requires knowing as much as possible about a noncustodial parent or a residential treatment program. If a social worker is contemplating removing a child from a parent and placing the child with another parent, sound social work practice is required. Such practice would mean conducting a background check, taking a social history, and perhaps interviewing neighbors to learn if they had seen problems. Failing to perform activities of this type is not professional social work practice. This is what occurred in the Wyoming case, where essentially nothing was done.

CONCLUSION

This chapter discussed the range of activities covering children protection, including abuse and neglect investigations, removing children from their homes, and parental termination. Children have been taken from parents for permitting a child to eat too much, which endangered the health of the child. Also, children have been removed from their homes because the homes have been filthy and unsanitary, which posed a danger to the children's health. The legal standard for removing children from their homes was discussed, revealing that social workers needed only some evidence of abuse or neglect. The chapter explained that in terminating parental rights, the legal standard is clear and convincing evidence. Situations in which parental terminations were affirmed and reversed by courts were described.

The extent to which children were owed protection from violence was discussed. Generally, children are not owed protection from violence committed by private individuals. Thus, the state has no legal responsibility to protect a child from a violent parent. However, if the social worker places a child with a parent or places a child in foster care, the social worker may be legally responsible. Either the special relationship theory or the danger creation theory govern these situations.

Key Terms and Concepts

Appellee

Trier of Fact

Certiorari

Special Needs

Special Relationship Theory

Danger Creation Theory

Guardian Ad Litem

Harmless Error

LEGAL ASPECTS OF ADOPTION POLICY AND PRACTICES

The law, consisting of federal statutes and case law, has had some effect on adoption policy and practices. Congress passed the Adoption Assistance and Child Welfare Act of 1980 and amended this act by passing the Adoption and Safe Families Act of 1997. Also, Congress passed the Indian Child Welfare Act in 1978 to protect Native American children from being adopted by white parents. Similarly, Congress passed a statute regulating interracial adoption involving mostly the adoption of African American children by white parents, but later repealed this act, forbidding consideration of race in making adoption decisions. Also, litigation has occurred over adoption practices.

Various adoption issues have emerged involving social welfare policy (Barth, 1996; Reitz, 1999), and some of these issues have legal implications (*Derzack v. County of Allegheny, Pennsylvania County of Allegheny Children and Youth Services et al.*, 1996). For instance, discrimination has existed when gays and lesbians have sought to adopt children (Crawford, 1999; Huppke, 2000). In Indiana, a gay white male was permitted to adopt three African American brothers, but child welfare and the community balked at him adopting the boys' sister (Huppke, 2000). This Indiana adoption was not litigated, but it reflects a type of discrimination actionable in the courts.

All states have laws regarding adoption and the factors that adoption workers should assess. A key aspect of the process is the information that is given to parents regarding the health and background of the child. Some parents have contended that adoption workers misled them regarding the health and behavioral problems of children the parents adopted. These malpractice issues are discussed in Chapter 7. This chapter discusses the principal federal statutes governing adoption, including the Indian Child Welfare Act. In addition, this chapter discusses a state statute from Texas regarding adoptions, adoption issues relating to subsidies, adoption by gays and lesbians, transracial adoption, and access to adoption records.

FEDERAL STATUTES GOVERNING ADOPTION

Adoption guidelines are often discussed in statutes that address foster placement as well. Title 42 regarding the state plan for foster care and adoption assistance specifies the extent to which reasonable efforts should be made; however, *reasonable efforts* is a broad term (Blome, 1996). In determining reasonable efforts, the child's health and safety shall be the paramount concern. Reasonable efforts shall be made to preserve and reunify families prior to the placement of a child in foster care to prevent or eliminate the need for removing the child from the home. If reasonable efforts are inconsistent with a child's permanency plan, necessary steps should be taken to finalize permanent placement of the child. Reasonable efforts shall not be required when a court has determined that the parent has subjected the child to aggravated circumstances, such as abandonment, torture, chronic abuse, or sexual abuse. In addition, reasonable efforts are not required when the parent has been convicted of murder, voluntary manslaughter, aiding or conspiring a murder or manslaughter, or a felony assault involving a child (Title 42 USCS § 671).

Title 42 regarding the state plan for foster care and adoption assistance provides that after January 1, 1997, neither the state nor any entity receiving federal funds may (a) deny to any person the opportunity to become an adoptive or foster parent on the basis of race, color, or national origin of the adoptive parent, foster parent, or child or (b) delay or deny the placement of a child for adoption or into foster care on the basis of race, color, or national origin of the adoptive parent, foster parent, or child. However, preference may be given to the adult relative over a non-related caregiver when determining a placement for a child, provided that the relative caregiver meets all relevant state child protection standards (Title 42 USCS § 671).

NATIVE AMERICAN ADOPTION

As stated earlier, in the Indian Child Welfare Act of 1978, Congress exempted from the requirement that race not be a factor in adoption decisions the case of the adoption of Native American children. Native Americans, unlike Latinos, Asian Americans, or African Americans, occupy a unique position because they were an independent nation within the embryonic United States. Native Americans negotiated treaties with the United States, though the United States broke many of the treaties that it signed. Many Native American issues that arise on Native American reservations are, because of past treaties, addressed either by Native American institutions or the federal government. Illustrating this point, a Native American who was living on a reservation in Michigan was tried for child sexual abuse in the federal courts (*United States of America v. Scott William Moses,* 1998). Further, the State of Oklahoma has no jurisdiction over social welfare issues that occur on Native American reservations in Oklahoma. However, the federal government, in agreement with Native American people, may designate some social welfare issues to be covered by state law and policy.

Exemplifying the special nature of Native Americans, Congress found that Article 1, Section 8, Clause 3, of the U.S. Constitution gave Congress the power to regulate commerce with Indian tribes and that Congress had plenary power over Indian affairs. Moreover, Congress found

> "(a) that Congress, through statutes, treaties, and the general course of dealing with Indian tribes, has assumed the responsibility for the protection and preservation of Indian tribes and their resources; (b) that there is no resource that is more vital to the continued existence and integrity of Indian tribes than their children and that the United States has a direct interest, as trustee, in protecting Indian children who are members of or are eligible for membership in an Indian tribe; (c) that an alarmingly high percentage of Indian families are broken up by the removal, often unwarranted, of their children from them by nontribal

public and private agencies and that an alarmingly high percentage of such children are placed in non-Indian foster and adoptive homes and institutions [that is, these removals were mostly carried out by white social workers seeking to Americanize Native Americans]; and (d) that the States, exercising their recognized jurisdiction over Indian child custody proceedings through administrative and judicial bodies, have often failed to recognize the essential tribal relations of Indian people and the cultural and social standards prevailing in Indian communities and families" (Title 25 USCS § 1901).

As a result, Congress declared that the policy of the United States is to protect the best interests of Indian children and to promote the stability and security of Indian tribes and families. This policy would be pursued by the establishment of minimum federal standards for the removal of Indian children from their families. The placement of such children would be in foster or adoptive homes that would reflect the unique values of Indian culture. Finally, assistance would be provided to Indian tribes in the operation of child and family service programs (Title 25 USCS § 1902). To further this policy, Congress declared that any adoptive placement made under state law would be with (a) a member of the child's extended family; (b) other members of the Indian child's tribe; or (c) other Indian families, unless evidence exists that such placement would not be in the child's best interest (Title 25 USCS § 1915).

The U.S. Supreme Court was asked to interpret a provision of the Indian Child Welfare Act in *Mississippi Band of Choctaw Indians v. Holyfield et al.* (1989). The case centered on whether a Native American's mother was domiciled. According to Garner (1999), **domicile** is "the place at which a person is physically present and that the person regards as home." It is "a person's true, fixed, principal, and permanent home, to which that person intends to return and remain even though currently residing elsewhere" (p. 501). A white couple attempted to adopt two Native American children. The children's mother was domiciled on a reservation in Neshoba County, Mississippi, but her children were born nearly 200 miles away and not on a reservation. The mother agreed to give the children for adoption to the white couple. However, the Mississippi Band of Choctaw Indians objected, contending that the adoption violated the Indian Child Welfare Act. The act states that Native American children who are domiciled on a reservation are governed by the tribal courts. But the Chancery Court of Harrison County noted that the children were not domiciled on the reservation and approved the adoption, which the Supreme Court of Mississippi upheld.

The U.S. Supreme Court reversed the Mississippi courts, ruling that the Chancery Court had no jurisdiction over Native American adoptions because the children were, in theory, domiciled on the reservation. Interpreting Congress' intent, the Court stated that the purpose of passing the Indian Child Welfare Act was to protect Native American children, whose problems were essentially caused by social workers taking them and instituting adoptions by whites. Further, in the federal common law, being domiciled is determined by the mother's status. If the mother is domiciled on a reservation, then her children are too, regardless of where the children were born. Moreover, the Court declared that Congress never intended to leave it to individual states and their different definitions of *domicile.* Instead, Congress wanted Native American children to be covered by one, national definition, although the Indian Child Welfare Act did not specifically state the definition of being domiciled (*Mississippi Band of Choctaw Indians v. Holyfield et al.,* 1989).

ONE STATE STATUTE GOVERNING ADOPTION

Every state has adoption statutes providing legal requirements for adoption workers to follow. It is beyond the scope of this book to delineate all 50 state statutes; however, one state, Texas, is discussed because it is a large state with a large number of children available for adoption. Further, Texas Administrative Code lists specific areas that adoption workers must assess. A discussion in Chapter 7 indicates that some adoption workers were accused of not making a professional assessment in a malpractice case. Although the malpractice case is not from Texas, students will have a rough idea of what a comprehensive assessment guide entails. Another reason for examining one state is to examine whether an adoption statute, which details what information is collected from and about prospective parents, indicates what parents should be told about a child's medical and social history. The lack of accurate information given by adoption workers to prospective parents also has been the source of malpractice claims.

Texas promulgated specific guidelines for conducting a foster or adoptive home study and provided specific rights to individuals involved in the process. For instance, the home study must be completed within four months after submission of paperwork by prospective parents or the last pre-service training. A social worker conducting such a home study must submit it to a supervisor, who has 30 days to approve or disapprove the parents as foster parents or adoptive parents (Texas Administrative Code § 700.1504). Foster parents, foster parent recruits, and applicants have a right to an administrative review of a decision not to approve an application to be foster parents or to close a foster home (Texas Administrative Code § 700.1505). Furthermore, adoptive recruits and applicants are entitled to an administrative review of the decision not to approve their adoptive home for placement of a child (Texas Administrative Code § 700.1505).

When inquiries are made regarding foster care or adoption possibilities, staff are required to respond in writing within 10 business days regarding the process for becoming foster or adoptive parents (Texas Administrative Code § 700.1502). The following specific areas are assessed.

1. *Age:* All applicants must be at least 21 years of age. Age is evaluated in terms of the life expectancy of the applicant. The applicant's life expectancy must be long enough for the applicant to be able to raise the child to adulthood. Applicants nearing retirement age usually are only considered and approved for adolescent children.
2. *Marriage:* If married, both spouses must apply, and if separated and not divorced, the divorce must be finalized before an applicant is approved as an adoptive parent.
3. *Length of Marriage:* Couples must be married at least two years before the Texas Department of Regulatory Services approves an adoption application. However, if the couple cohabited for two years, an exception is made. The social worker must assess the impact of the marriage on the stability of the couple's relationship.
4. *Single Parents:* Single parents are evaluated in terms of their ability to nurture and provide for a child without the assistance of a spouse.
5. *Disabilities:* Disabilities are evaluated in relation to the applicant's adjustment to the disability and the effect of the disability upon a child.
6. *Residence:* Adoptive home studies are started only if the applicant will live in the community long enough for a social worker to complete a study and make a placement.

7. *Adoption by Foster Families:* Foster families are evaluated using the same criteria applied to any other adoptive applicant.

8. *Family's Ability to Help the Child:* Applicants are evaluated based on their ability to help the child develop a sense of identity consistent with the child's racial, cultural, and ethnic background and learn to cope with difficulties that may arise from racial, cultural, or ethnic differences, both within and outside the adoptive family. An adopting parent must help the child develop a plan for managing racial, cultural, and ethnic issues as the child reaches developmental milestones.

9. *Finances:* No specific income level is required, but an applicant must have enough income and manage it well enough to care for the child.

10. *Health:* The applicant's physical and mental health must be sufficient to assume parenting responsibilities and to protect the child from loss occurring as the result of a parent's death or incapacitation.

11. *Religion:* There are no specific religious requirements. Applicants are evaluated based on their willingness to respect and encourage a child's religious affiliation and must have a health plan that will be used if the parent's religion bars certain medical procedures.

12. *Discipline:* Physical discipline may not be used prior to consummation of the adoption.

13. *Criminal History:* Criminal background checks must be conducted on all prospective adoptive or foster parents and all members in the household who are 14 years old or older.

14. *Fertility:* Fertility may be assessed if a couple is ambivalent regarding their ability to conceive and how this might affect their adoption of a child.

15. *Citizenship and Immigration:* Only U.S. citizens, permanent residents, and other qualified aliens can be approved as foster or adoptive parents (Texas Administrative Code 700.1502).

LEGAL CASES CONCERNING ADOPTION ISSUES

Adoption Subsidy

Overturned by a local judge, the repeated denials by Franklin County, Ohio, Children Services of a subsidy to a mother who adopted an African American girl suggested an issue of gender discrimination. A single mother, who was employed as a patient care assistant at a hospital, adopted a girl through a private agency. The mother was told that she was eligible for adoption assistance, but assistance was rejected for 11 years by two government agencies. State officials contended that the mother was not entitled to assistance because the baby she adopted was a healthy girl, and assistance was primarily for boys, older children, and children with health problems, all of whom were more difficult to place.

However, the Ohio Administrative Law indicated that all minorities were eligible for assistance. Interpreting the law literally, a local judge overturned the denial of assistance to the mother and ordered assistance retroactively for all the years the mother was eligible. Despite the adverse ruling, the state has appealed the decision to the Franklin County Court of Appeals (Nirode, 2000b), which is likely to uphold the local judge. Even if the Franklin County Court of Appeals reverses, other courts, either the Ohio Supreme Court or the federal courts, are likely to uphold the awarding of the adoption assistance.

The Ohio Attorney General's Office is handling the appeal, but someone in that office should have strongly recommended that Franklin County Children Services give the mother the adoption assistance. The agency's position has two primary weaknesses. First, the Ohio Administrative Law says that minorities are eligible for adoption assistance. Thus, state officials cannot change the law based on their personal or professional opinion. If the law says all minorities are eligible and the girl is African American, then it is clear that the child is eligible. The assistance is property protected by the Fourteenth Amendment and cannot capriciously be taken away. Second, the decision to deny the assistance is clearly gender discrimination and thus also violates the Fourteenth Amendment.

Although African American males may be harder to place for adoption, assistance cannot be denied to African American girls who are healthy. The federal courts have been especially vigilant in protecting females' right to equal protection, either in entering formerly all-male schools or in the awarding of equal amounts of athletic scholarships. A subsidy is intended to offset some of the expenses when adopting a child. It is to help pay for food, clothing, and perhaps recreational activities. Thus, it is quite indefensible to say that African American boys up for adoption are entitled to food, clothing, and recreational activities, but African American girls are not. This is a clear losing case for Franklin

County Children Services, which it has fought, through its denials, for 11 years and a case that the Ohio Attorney General's Office chose to appeal. However, the state agencies and the attorney general decided to drop the case, and the mother was given the assistance.

Gay and Lesbian Adoption

A couple of cases at the federal level have far-reaching implications for gay and lesbian adoptions. The first case involved a referendum that purported to ban the giving of special rights to gays, lesbians, and bisexual Cincinnatians. The case arose when the Cincinnati City Council enacted two ordinances that strove to end discriminatory practices in the city. A group named "Equal Rights Not Special Rights" opposed the ordinances and instituted a ballot initiative. The purpose of the ballot initiative was to ban special class status based on sexual orientation, conduct, or relationships. A majority of the citizens in Cincinnati approved the ordinances. Affected and concerned gay, lesbian, and bisexual people filed a lawsuit to block implementation of the referendum. The U.S. District Court held that the referendum violated the rights of gays, lesbians, and bisexual citizens, and thus was unconstitutional (*Equality Foundation of Greater Cincinnati et al. v. The City of Cincinnati,* 1994).

An important facet of the ruling is that the trial judge made 23 findings of facts based on expert witnesses. Among those findings were:

1. Sexual orientation is a characteristic that exists separately and independently from sexual conduct or behavior.
2. Sexual orientation is a deeply rooted, complex combination of factors including a predisposition toward affiliation, affection, or bonding with members of the opposite and/or the same gender.
3. Sexual orientation bears no relation to an individual's ability to perform in, contribute to, or participate in society.
4. Homosexuals have suffered a history of pervasive, irrational, and invidious discrimination in government and private employment, in political organization, and in all facets of society in general, based on their sexual orientation.
5. Pervasive private and institutional discrimination against gays, lesbians, and bisexuals often has a profound negative psychological impact on gays, lesbians, and bisexuals.

6. There is no meaningful difference between children raised by gays and lesbians and those raised by heterosexuals. Similarly, children raised by gay and lesbian parents are no more likely to be gay or lesbian than those children raised by heterosexuals (*Equality Foundation of Greater Cincinnati et al. v. The City of Cincinnati*, 1994, pp. 426–427).

The last finding described here means that in the city of Cincinnati the policy surrounding adoption of children cannot be made based on any perceived adverse affect on children or that such an adoption might not be in the best interest of the child. (*Equality Foundation of Greater Cincinnati* was appealed to the Sixth Circuit Court of Appeals and remanded by the U.S. Supreme Court back to the Sixth Circuit based on the Supreme Court's ruling in *Romer v. Evans et al.* (1996), which is discussed below. Upon a second review by the Sixth Circuit Court of Appeals, which the U.S. Supreme Court refused to hear, the Sixth Circuit held that the Cincinnati ordinance was different from *Romer v. Evans et al.* (1996). Simply, it held that the Cincinnati ordinance did not disempower gays and lesbians (*Equality Foundation of Greater Cincinnati v. City of Cincinnati*, 1997). Despite this ultimate ruling, the initial findings adopted by the district court were not rejected.

Although the case in Cincinnati involved just one city in Ohio, another case from the U.S. Supreme Court has national implications. In this case, the U.S. Supreme Court upheld the rejection of an amendment to the Colorado Constitution that adversely affected gays and lesbians. This case has implications for adoption and other social welfare policies and practices for the following reasons.

As background to the Colorado case, a number of municipalities and institutions passed ordinances and policies forbidding discrimination based on sexual orientation in health and welfare services, as well as in housing, employment, education, public accommodations, and other activities. Alarmed that gays and lesbians were receiving perceived special rights, Colorado citizens passed a constitutional amendment forbidding the executive, legislative, and judicial branches of Colorado governments from recognizing gays and lesbians' rights to redress discriminatory practices. A lower Colorado court enjoined the enforcement of the amendment, and the Colorado Supreme Court held that, under a strict scrutiny test, the amendment violated the Fourteenth Amendment's equal protection clause of the U.S. Constitution. Upon further appeal to the U.S. Supreme Court, this Court also held that the amendment violated the equal protection clause of the Fourteenth Amendment (*Romer v. Evans et al.*, 1996).

The effect of this case on social welfare policies and practices is that it recognizes that gays and lesbians cannot be denied the opportunity to foster parent and adopt children. In the introduction to this chapter, a reference was made to a gay white male's adoption of three African American brothers, but not the brothers' sister. Clearly, this type of discrimination violates the Fourteenth Amendment. A determination that a gay or lesbian parent is unsuitable or unfit must be made on other disqualifying factors, such as having a serious criminal record, drug and alcohol abuse, or a disposition incompatible with caring for children. But a gay or lesbian person cannot be denied the opportunity to foster parent or adopt children based just on his or her sexual orientation (Crawford, 1999).

Transracial Adoption

Transracial adoption involves parents of one race adopting a child of another race. This racial dyad can consist of a variety of combinations, such as Korean parents adopting a child of Japanese ancestry, or white parents adopting a child of Chinese or Vietnamese ancestry (Higginbotham, 1998; Lewin, 1998). Certainly, the most controversial combination, and the one that involves the law more than others, involves white parents adopting African American children (Boyer, 1999; Strausberg, 1999; Teicher, 1999).

In the 1900s, the percentage of white parents adopting African American children began to increase. However, in the late 1960s, these adoptions took a steep decline because of the strong opposition voiced by the National Association of Black Social Workers (NABSW) (Curtis & Alexander, 1996). Later, some white parents began to sue when after caring for African American foster children, their adoption requests were rejected in favor of African American prospective parents (Curtis, 1996).

Congress then got involved and passed the Multiethnic Placement Act. The primary sponsor for this legislation was former Senator Howard Metzenbaum of Ohio, who believed that a rigid policy of same-race adoption violated the civil rights laws and was not in the best interest of African American children who tended to stay in foster care longer than white children. The Multiethnic Placement Act of 1994 forbade the sole use of race in making placement decisions; however, race could be one of several factors in making placement decisions. Later, Congress repealed the Multiethnic Placement Act and passed the Adoption and Safe

Families Act of 1997. This new act forbids any use of race in making placement decisions. The Adoption and Safe Families Act provides that:

> A person or government that is involved in adoption or foster care placements may not (a) deny to any individual the opportunity to become an adoptive or foster parent, on the basis of race, color, or national origin of the individual, or of the child, involved; or (b) delay or deny the placement of a child for adoption or into foster care, on the basis of race, color, or national origin of the adoptive or foster parent, or the child, involved (Title 42 USCS § 996b).

This statute further provides that noncompliance with the act was a violation of Title VI of the Civil Rights Act of 1964, but the statute did not apply to the Indian Child Welfare Act of 1978 (Title 42 USCS § 1996b). One might think then that the issue of transracial adoption involving white parents adopting African American children was legally settled.

However, several reports have emerged that some social workers are still using race in making adoption decisions and are discriminating against white prospective adoptive parents. For instance, a social worker alleged that he was fired from his job in the Hamilton County Department of Human Services, located in Cincinnati, Ohio, because he insisted that the agency follow the law and not discriminate against white parents who wanted to adopt African American children (Michaud, 1999a). The social worker, who was identified in the lawsuit as John Doe, stated that the agency was using race despite congressional law that forbids the consideration of it (Michaud, 1999a), and the white family that was alleged to have been discriminated against joined the lawsuit (Michaud, 1999b).

Although the agency denied that racial bias was a factor in making adoption decisions (Michaud, 1999c), one of the county officials who was sued countersued, arguing that race should be a factor in making adoption decisions regardless of congressional law (Kaufman, 2000). Barbara Manuel, an African American and Assistant Director of the Hamilton County Department of Human Services, countersued, contending that the social worker who filed the initial lawsuit was racist and greedy and had violated her (Manuel's) rights. Moreover, she asked that the court permit greater freedom in placing African American children with African American families when it is in the best interest of the child.

According to Manuel, she was following Ohio law in making adoption decisions, and the federal law was vague. Age and disability are clearly acceptable factors to use in making adoption decisions, and race is an acceptable factor as well. Manuel maintains that African American infants are different from Caucasian infants in several important physiological ways. At a minimum, Caucasian parents must be sensitive to racial characteristics particular to an African American in such areas as hair care, skin care, and subtle changes in skin tone color or hair texture that are caused by illnesses. Placing an African American child with parents who are unaware of or unwilling to understand these issues negatively affects the child (Kaufman, 2000).

Although Manuel expresses the concern of a number of African American social workers, she is not likely to prevail in her lawsuit. The current climate in the legal system is not to understand or accept the racial differences in children that would justify same-race adoption. The view now is that society is color-blind. However, other African American professionals contend instead that this policy of banning race as a factor in adoptions so that white parents can adopt African American children is racist (Kupenda, Thrash, Riley Collins, Dukes, Lewis, & Dixon, 1998).

Notwithstanding the furor over the adoption of African American children by whites, some African American professionals have underscored a very important point. For instance, Kupenda et al. (1998) state that Congress and the courts are interested only in one-way transracial adoption: White parents adopting African American infants and children. They document instances where social workers and judges have strongly resisted African Americans adopting white children. One judge ordered the immediate removal of a child from a foster home after learning that the child was a little white girl and the parents were African American. In addition, African American parents have reported receiving resistance when trying to adopt white infants. In short, if a white baby is available for adoption and two sets of parents, one white and one African American, are seeking to adopt, the adoption system is going to place the white infant with a white family (Kupenda et al., 1998). When one sees a transracial story in the news media, one invariably sees a white parent with a minority child. One never sees an African American parent lamenting problems with child welfare over a white child, and Congress and the courts are unconcerned with this racism. However, this practice is just as illegal, though it is not debated and discussed.

The extent to which racism is practiced in adoption, according to Kupenda et al.'s insight, will be quickly known. For instance, a very high proportion of adoptive parents want infants, and it does not matter whether the adoptive parents are white, Latino, African

American, or Asian American. If race is no longer used as a criterion for adoption, as the Adoption and Safe Families Act requires, then white infants, if everything is fair and nonracial, will be placed with African American, Latino, and Asian American adoptive parents. If white adoptive parents receive all the white infants or an extremely high percentage of them, then it is clear that same-race adoption is being practiced.

ACCESS TO ADOPTION RECORDS

Several decades ago, females could have babies, give them up for adoption, and move on with their lives. Often, these females did not know who adopted their children, and the adopting parents were given only general information. Agencies acted as liaisons, limiting information on each side. Agency and court records were often sealed with promises of confidentiality to the birth mothers and adopting parents. Only upon exigent circumstances and supported by a court order could adoptees gain access to their adoption records. However, some biological mothers, feeling guilty about giving up their children years earlier and wondering what the children were doing, have searched for their children. For example, a Minnesota mother learned that a son she had given up years previously had died mysteriously, and she sought to prove that the adopted mother had murdered him. Following a reopened investigation, Minnesota authorities proved that the adopted child's death in 1965 was a homicide and convicted the adopted mother in 1987 (Duchschere & O'Connor, 1995).

Some children have searched for their biological mothers, hoping to learn why they were given up for adoption and seeking to address some psychological issues. In one instance, a teenager who never met her biological mother or father stated that she wanted to meet her biological mother because she wanted to know if she looks like her mother (Woods, 2000). In short, a variety of reasons exist why parents and children might want access to adoption records.

Perhaps balancing biological mothers' interests and children's interests in seeking answers and satisfying questions, some states have passed statutes permitting open adoptions (Yngvesson, 1997) and allowing adult adoptees access to their adoption records. In Columbus, Ohio, the Dave Thomas Center for Adoption Law held a conference at Capital University, which was attended by social workers, lawyers, and youth advocates, to discuss access to adoption records. Some attendees supported access, while others questioned the practice. In many states, adoptees have the burden of demonstrating why records about their biological background should be opened. Joan Hollinger, a law professor at the University of California at Berkeley, argued that the burden should be on biological parents to demonstrate why their children should be denied access to the adoption records. Critics countered that increasing access would lead to a higher number of abortions. However, Alaska and Kansas, states that provide easy access to adoption records, had abortion rates of 14.6 and 18.9, respectively, per 1,000 females compared to a national rate of 22.9 (Nirode, 2000a).

Tennessee's adoption statute underwent changes in 1949, 1982, 1985, and 1996. The latest revision permitted the release of information to adopted children over the age of 21 years. Prior to the change, the only way that an adopted person could get information was through a court order indicating that the release of information was in the best interests of the child or if the birth mother agreed. The new law provided a contact veto through which a birth parent could veto any personal contact although her name would be released to the child she gave up for adoption. A violation of the contact veto subjected the violator to both criminal and civil liabilities. Another feature of the revised law was that it applied prospectively and retrospectively. The latter provision prompted several people to challenge the law. At first, the plaintiffs sued in federal court, contending that the revised law violated their right to privacy. This contention was rejected by a federal district court (*Doe v. Sundquist*, 1996), which was upheld by the Sixth Circuit Court of Appeals (*Doe v. Sundquist*, 1997).

Then, the plaintiffs, consisting of two birth mothers, two adoptive parents, and an adoption agency, sought an injunction in Tennessee state court, arguing that the Tennessee Constitution prohibits retroactive laws. All three sets of plaintiffs argued that they were negatively affected by the change. The birth mothers argued that they were promised confidentiality. The adoptive parents argued that they disclosed personal and sensitive information to an adoption agency, and this information was now a part of the adoption record. The adoption agency argued that it had made promises regarding confidentiality to adopting parents. Accordingly, the Court of Appeals of Tennessee held that the latest change in the Tennessee statute violated the Tennessee Constitution (*Doe et al. v. Sundquist et al.*, 1998). Although the Tennessee state appellate ruling was favorable to the plaintiffs, its ruling did not apply to adoption cases that occurred after July 1,

1996, the date the latest adoption revised statute went into effect.

In Oregon, the voters approved a measure permitting adoptees access to adoptees' original birth certificates. Seven women sought an injunction contending that the law violated their rights under both the federal and state constitutions. The women contended that the law violated or interfered with contracts that they had with adoption agencies, and thus the law violated the state and federal constitutions. They also contended that the Oregon adoption laws existing at the time they gave up their children for adoption promised them confidentiality. The women argued that under the landmark decision granting women the right to abortion, a right of women to privacy was established. However, the Court of Appeals of Oregon rejected all claims of constitutional violations. The court stated that a birth, unlike an abortion, is both a private and public event. The state has an interest in recording the births, as well as deaths, of all people. The state needs to know the identity of children's parents, and a public agency collects this information. Although birth mothers have an interest in privacy, society also has interests. Balancing both sets of interests, Oregon citizens chose to make information available to adoptees (*Jane Does v. The State of Oregon*, 1999).

IMPLICATIONS FOR SOCIAL WELFARE POLICY AND PRACTICE

The Texas adoption factors, and other factors of individual states, indicate what a social worker must consider in making a professional assessment and practicing in the adoption field. Assessing less than what the law required would not constitute a professional assessment. In Chapter 3, references were made regarding Wyoming social workers who were said not to have made a professional assessment in a foster placement. A person with a trail of child sexual abuse was approved as a foster parent. Although this chapter and the Texas law are about adoption, factors similar to those used in adoption apply to foster care. Furthermore, the list of factors can indicate to adoptive parents whether a social worker had conducted a professional adoption assessment and can provide the basis for legally challenging a negative decision if all the listed factors were not assessed.

More important, the Texas Administrative Code does not indicate what information should be given to parents. Just as the

Texas Code states what information should be collected from prospective parents, it could easily state what information should be given to the prospective parents. A fair and protective policy for adoption workers, state or private, would legally require them to be forthright regarding a child's health and background. Full disclosure would prevent future problems, such as parents contending that they had been deceived.

The law seems to have signaled the end to overt discrimination against gays and lesbians adopting children, although the account of a gay male in Indiana illustrates that bias still exists. Reportedly, the gay male was allowed to adopt two brothers, but not the sister. The U.S. Supreme Court ruled that the Colorado statute violated gays and lesbians' right to equal protection of the law. Equal protection would embrace a number of areas, including social welfare concerns. In addition, a federal court made a number of findings in *Equality Foundation of Greater Cincinnati v. City of Cincinnati,* 1997. Prominent among the findings were that sexual orientation bears no relation to an individual's ability to perform, contribute to, or participate in society and there is no meaningful difference between children reared by gays and lesbians and those reared by heterosexuals. These rulings make it very difficult, but not impossible, for discrimination in adoption cases involving gays and lesbians.

The Adoption and Safe Families Act of 1997 indicates that the policy of the country is that race cannot be used in an adoption decision. Most adoption agencies likely will comply with this policy, and the number of African American children adopted by whites likely will increase somewhat. However, there may be situations, such as the Ohio case, where African American social workers attempt to circumvent and challenge this policy. African American social workers who believe that African American children should be adopted by African American parents are likely to alter their practice by not indicating in writing or verbally that their aim is to pursue same-race adoption.

African American professionals are quite correct when they state that Congress and the courts are concerned about transracial adoption only when the child is a minority and the prospective adoptive parents are white. They would not be as passionate in supporting transracial adoption if adoptive parents were African American and the children were white. As some professionals stated, African Americans adopting whites is more natural because African Americans have always cared for white children (Kupenda, Thrash, Riley-Collins, Dukes, Lewis, & Dixon, 1998).

They did so during slavery, and after slavery, African American domestic workers in white homes often served as surrogate parents (Kupenda et al., 1998).

CONCLUSION

This chapter began by discussing Congress' influence on adoption and particularly its attention to transracial adoption, with the passage and repeal of the Multiethnic Placement Act and the passage of the Adoption and Safe Families Act. One state's, Texas', factors used in making an adoption assessment were described. A case from Ohio involving gender discrimination in subsidy payments for African American children was described. This chapter discussed gay and lesbian adoption and two cases that would facilitate adoptions by gay, lesbian, and bisexual people. Transracial adoption was discussed also, noting that some African American professionals are still against transracial adoption. One administrator believes it is not in the best interests of African American children. Other professionals noted that society, the law, and Congress are interested in transracial adoption only when the parents are white and the children are African American or another minority. They stressed that Congress and society are not as passionate about transracial adoption if the adoptive parents are African American and the children are white. Last, the issue of a growing number of states permitting access to adoption records was discussed.

Key Terms and Concepts

Domicile

LEGAL CHALLENGES SHAPING PUBLIC ASSISTANCE

Public assistance consists of all forms of financial programs or benefits available to citizens. Examples of public assistance include aid to families, food stamps, Social Security benefits, and disability payments. In the past, advocates have argued that individuals have a right to welfare payments (Abramovitz & Blau, 1984; Atherton, 1990; Blau, 1989; Idelson, 1996; Kitchen, 1979). When these arguments were made, the reference was to Aid to Families with Dependent Children (AFDC). But this contention is without legal support. Most individuals realized that there was no legal right to welfare when Congress abolished the AFDC program and replaced it with the Temporary Assistance to Needy Families program (TANF)—a much more limited program. Although some recipients of aid sued, all of them lost their cases in the courts because there is no legal right to public assistance (Kim, 2001). Congress could easily have abolished AFDC and replaced it with no program. Litigation to restore the AFDC program would have been fruitless. Despite the discussion about the word *welfare* being in state and federal constitutions, no constitutional or legal right to public assistance exists.

As noted above, Congress in its discretion replaced AFDC with TANF. Congress also conferred discretion upon states in administering TANF. In addition, Congress authorized states, if they so choose, to terminate under TANF recipients who have been convicted of possessing or using illegal drugs. Congress and society have the right not only to terminate but also to limit all public assistance. People denied public assistance have legal recourse only when they have been denied due process or equal protection of the law. Due process and equal protection come into effect when states try arbitrarily and capriciously to terminate benefits or penalize citizens from moving from one state to another state. This chapter provides examples of the influence of the law on several forms of public assistance, including the legal standard for terminating benefits, TANF and the right to travel, legal restrictions on receiving food stamps, Social Security disability benefits, drug testing of recipients receiving TANF, and implications for social welfare policy and practice.

LEGAL REQUIREMENTS
FOR TERMINATING BENEFITS

The U.S. Supreme Court heard a case in which it decided whether people who received AFDC could have their benefits terminated without a hearing. The case, *Goldberg v. Kelly et al.* (1970), has implications for states attempting to terminate benefits under TANF. Consolidated from two cases, a group of about 20 people argued that Goldberg, the Commissioner of Social Services in New York, terminated or was about to terminate their benefits without a hearing. Mrs. Altagracia Guzman alleged that her benefits were about to be terminated because she was accused of not helping the Department of Social Services in suing her estranged husband. Another case involved Juan DeJesus, whose benefits were terminated because he refused to accept counseling for a drug problem. Mr. DeJesus denied that he had a drug problem. After the lawsuit was filed, the Department of Social Services enacted some rules regarding the termination of benefits, but a lower federal court held that these new rules were inadequate (*Goldberg v. Kelly et al.*, 1970).

As the U.S. Supreme Court recalled, "from its founding the Nation's basic commitment has been to foster the dignity and well-being of all persons within its borders. We have come to recognize that forces not within the control of the poor contribute to their poverty. . . . Public assistance, then, is not mere charity, but a means to promote the general Welfare, and secure the Blessings of Liberty to ourselves and our Posterity" (pp. 264–265). In essence, the Court defined *welfare* as property under the Fourteenth Amendment. Hence, **due process requirements for terminating benefits** are (a) adequate notice detailing reasons for termination; (b) an opportunity to confront adverse witnesses; (c) an impartial decision maker; and (d) a statement of the reasons for the decision to terminate benefits. Although due process does not provide for a recipient to have a lawyer, the recipient can retain an attorney and have the attorney present to assist him or her (*Goldberg v. Kelly et al.*, 1970).

These standards, established when the United States had AFDC, would also apply to TANF. Though TANF is temporary and has a maximum period for receiving benefits, a decision to terminate benefits earlier would trigger the legal protection pronounced in *Goldberg v. Kelly et al.* (1970). Some states, under the AFDC program, attempted to prevent individuals who were receiving AFDC in other states from moving to their states and receiving the same benefits that current residents receive. The Court held this restriction to be illegal. Despite the U.S. Supreme Court holding state policies regarding AFDC to be illegal, Congress authorized similar policies regarding TANF. The Court also held these restrictive policies regarding TANF to be illegal, as the section below illustrates.

√TANF AND THE RIGHT TO TRAVEL

When Congress passed the Personal Responsibility and Work Opportunity Reconciliation Act of 1996 (PRWORA), PRWORA specifically gave states the authority to pay for 12 months of TANF benefits to new residents based on the amount of benefits the residents were receiving prior to relocating. The underlying motivation for this provision was to discourage poor individuals from moving from one state that paid low benefits to another state that paid significantly higher benefits.

Three new residents to California filed a lawsuit over this new durational residency policy. These women moved to California from other states to escape abusive relationships. One moved from Oklahoma, one from Colorado, and one returned to California after living in Louisiana for seven years. California at the time was providing a TANF benefit of $641 a month for a family of three and $504 a month for a family of two; however, the woman from Louisiana was set to receive $190, the woman from Oklahoma $341, and the woman from Colorado $280. Both the U.S. District Court and the Court of Appeals found this durational residency policy to be unconstitutional (*Saenz v. Roe and Doe et al.*, 1999).

A majority of the U.S. Supreme Court justices concurred with the lower courts. The Court noted that liberty entails the **right to travel** and that the right to travel embraces three different components: (a) the right to enter and leave another state; (b) the right to be treated as a welcome visitor while temporarily present in another state; and (c) for those people who choose to become permanent residents, the right to be treated like other citizens of the state. Thus, any social welfare policy that has as its aim the inhibition of citizens' right to travel violates the equal protection clause of the Fourteenth Amendment of the Constitution, unless the state can demonstrate a compelling governmental interest (*Saenz v. Roe and Doe et al.*, 1999).

An analysis of the decision quickly demonstrates why such laws are unconstitutional. Essentially, these laws constitute discrimination and penalize some people because of where they formerly resided. For example, California had the sixth highest benefit level. Accordingly, five states paid higher benefits than California and 44 paid lower benefits. If Minnesota was one of the states that paid higher benefits and Georgia was one of the states that paid lower benefits, then a person moving from Minnesota would be treated like a lifelong resident of California, whereas a person moving from Georgia would be penalized. Moreover, a resident of Minnesota would be encouraged to move to California, but a resident of Georgia would be discouraged. When a social welfare policy has this effect, it constitutes discrimination.

Though Congress authorized PRWORA and though Congress gave the states the authority to set different benefits for new arrivees, the U.S. Supreme Court rebuked Congress for what it had done. Specifically, the Court declared that Congress cannot give states the power to violate the Fourteenth Amendment. The protection given to citizens by the Fourteenth Amendment citizenship clause limits not only the states but also the national government. Though Congress has power to legislate based on Article 1 of the U.S. Constitution, this power may not be exercised in a fashion that conflicts with other specific provisions of the U.S. Constitution (*Saenz v. Roe and Doe et al.*, 1999).

Emboldened by PRWORA like California was, Pennsylvania passed a statute that families arriving in Pennsylvania from another state shall receive during the first 12 months either the benefits available to similarly situated Pennsylvania residents of 12 months or more or the benefit level the family would have been eligible to receive in their former state had they not moved to Pennsylvania, whichever amount was less. One family, consisting of a husband, wife, and six minor children, moved to Pennsylvania from Puerto Rico. Pennsylvanians with a 12-month residency were eligible for cash benefits of $936, but the Maldonado family was eligible for cash benefits of $304. They sued, contending the statute violated their right to travel and equal protection of the law.

A U.S. District Court enjoined Pennsylvania from carrying out the statute, ruling that the Maldonados had supported their argument that the lower benefits were a penalty but ruling also that there was no rational basis for the two-tiered system. However, the Third Circuit Court of Appeals went further. It stated that the district court had used the wrong test and that rational basis was inappropriate. The appeals court held that strict scrutiny should have been used, and, based on it, the Pennsylvania statute was wholly unconstitutional (*Maldonado et al. v. Houstoun et al.*, 1998).

Saenz v. Roe and Doe et al. (1999) and *Maldonado et al. v. Houstoun et al.* (1998) are consistent with what the Court ruled in 1969 in an AFDC case involving Connecticut, Pennsylvania, and the District of Columbia. In *Shapiro v. Thompson* (1969), a newly arrived resident to a state had to wait a year before being eligible for AFDC. The Court held that:

1. The statutory prohibition of benefits to residents of less than a year creates a classification which denies equal protection of the laws because the interests allegedly served by the classification either may not constitutionally be promoted by government or are not compelling government interests.
2. Because the Constitution guarantees the right of interstate movement, the purpose of deterring the migration of indigents into a State is impermissible and cannot serve to justify the classification created by the one-year waiting period.
3. A state may no more try to fence out those indigents who seek higher welfare payments than it may try to fence out indigents generally.
4. The classification may not be sustained as an attempt to distinguish between new and old residents on the basis of the contribution they have made to the community through payment of taxes because the Equal Protection Clause prohibits

the States from apportioning benefits or services on the basis of the past tax contributions of its citizens.

5. In moving from jurisdiction to jurisdiction appellees were exercising a constitutional right, and any classification which penalizes the exercise of that right, unless shown to be necessary to promote a compelling government interest, is unconstitutional.

6. Appellants do not sue and have no need to use the one-year requirement for administrative and government purposes suggested, and under the standard of compelling state interests, that requirement clearly violates the Equal Protection Clause.

7. Section 402 (b) of the Social Security Act does not render the waiting period requirements constitutional (*Shapiro v. Thompson*, 1969).

LEGAL RESTRICTIONS ON RECEIVING FOOD STAMPS

Following the passage of PRWORA, the Michigan state legislature authorized the Michigan Family Independence Agency to revise its policies that sanctioned some individuals receiving TANF. Among the sanctions was that a family member who failed to cooperate for three consecutive months in establishing paternity of the member's children could be terminated from receiving benefits. One woman receiving TANF had two children, a 3-year-old son, Ethan, and a 5-year-old daughter, TéAsha. Ethan's father acknowledged paternity and was paying child support. However, the mother presented false information about TéAsha's father, causing one man to be tested and cleared of paternity.

The Michigan Family Independence Agency, under its revised policy, sought to terminate both TANF and the food stamps of the mother. Ethan, the 3-year-old suing through his mother, filed a lawsuit, contending that he should not be punished because of his mother's action, especially because the Michigan statute did not authorize the taking of food stamps from everyone in the household. Ethan's lawsuit was established as a class action lawsuit including all similarly situated children in Michigan (*Walton et al. v. Hammons*, 1999).

Holding that the Michigan Family Independence Agency had to revise its food stamp program, the U.S. District Court granted summary judgment in Ethan's favor. The Sixth Circuit Court of

Appeals upheld the district court. Reading the strict language of the Michigan statute, the appeals court ruled that all members of a household could not be deprived of food stamps. Each member of the household, including Ethan, his sister, and his mother, were receiving food stamps (*Walton et al. v. Hammons*, 1999). In effect, Ethan and his sister were being punished unfairly.

Another aspect of PRWORA was to bar people who had been convicted of drug offenses from being eligible for TANF or food stamps. The statute says that an individual convicted on August 22, 1996, or thereafter under federal or state law involving the possession, use, or distribution of a controlled substance shall not be eligible for (a) assistance under any state program funded under Part A of Title IV of the Social Security Act or (b) benefits under the food stamp program or any state program carried out under the Food Stamp Act of 1977. However, the statute provided that states could exempt their citizens from the disqualification of either program.

Indiana chose not to exempt its citizens disqualified from either program based on a drug conviction, and a lawsuit followed (*Turner v. Glickman et al.*, 2000). Henry Turner, an Indiana resident, was receiving food stamps prior to the passage of PRWORA. In 1997, Turner was convicted of felony possession of heroin and cocaine. In 1998 when Turner came up for recertification for food stamps, his conviction was uncovered. Based on this conviction, Turner was permanently barred from receiving food stamps. With the assistance of the Indiana Civil Liberties Union, Turner sued in a class action lawsuit the Secretary of the U.S. Department of Agriculture, Daniel R. Glickman, and the Secretary of the Indiana Family and Social Services Administration, Peter J. Sybinsky (*Turner v. Glickman et al.*, 2000).

Turner argued that the federal disqualification statute violated the due process clause of the Fifth Amendment, the equal protection clause of the Fourteenth Amendment, and the double jeopardy clause of the Fifth Amendment. Turner contended that the statute was unconstitutional because it did not have any rational basis that was connected to a legitimate government interest. Because the law did not involve any fundamental rights, such as the right to travel, and did not involve a suspect classification, the legal test required to decide this argument was the rational basis test. This test is highly deferential to government and presents a very high burden to any plaintiff.

Courts are not mandated to determine whether a statute is fair, wise, or logical. The issue is whether the government can present any rational basis for the statute. In this case, the government offered three. First, the statute sought to deter drug use. Second, the statute sought to reduce fraud in the food stamp program. Third, the statute sought to curb welfare spending. Based on these arguments, the U.S. District Court in Indiana and the Seventh Circuit Court of Appeals rejected Turner's challenge. Turner also alleged that the disqualification constituted a second punishment and thus violated his right to be free from double jeopardy. The courts rejected this argument as well (*Turner v. Glickman et al.*, 2000). According to Turner's attorney, no further appeals are planned (Jackie Bowie, personal communication, April 27, 2000), which establishes law in all the states in the Seventh Circuit.

The City of Chicago challenged the constitutionality of the Welfare Reform Act, especially the provision that related to the eligibility of legal aliens to receive benefits under the food stamp program, or to receive Supplemental Security Income, or other benefits. Initiating the suit for the City of Chicago was its commissioner of Human Services. This commissioner brought suit against the Secretary of Health and Human Services, the Acting Commissioner of Social Security, and the Secretary of Agriculture. The lawsuit raised issues regarding whether the City of Chicago had standing to sue; however, members of the affected group asked to intervene, and the case was decided on the merits (*Alvarez et al. v. Shalala et al.*, 1999).

Congress declared that some aliens would be eligible to receive benefits but others would not. Among some of the groups that were eligible were refugees, asylees, aliens whose deportation was being withheld, certain Cuban and Haitian entrants, and Hmong and Highland Laotians. However, illegal aliens were not eligible and lawful aliens were ineligible. Essentially, Congress differentiated within the class of aliens, and this differentiation seemed to provide the argument that the Welfare Reform Act was unconstitutional. The case was quickly dismissed by the U.S. District Court and affirmed by the Seventh Circuit Court of Appeals, which noted that Congress had a rational basis for its decisions and the statute. Among the reasons were that Congress wanted to encourage self-sufficiency among immigrants, prevent public benefits from serving as an incentive to immigrate, and ease the burden on the public welfare system (*Alvarez et al. v. Shalala et al.*, 1999).

The Seventh Circuit Court of Appeals recounted congressional intent in this area, which was spelled out under the heading

"Statements of National Policy Concerning Welfare and Immigration." It states:

1. Self-sufficiency has been a basic principle of the United States immigration law since this country's earliest immigration statutes.
2. It continues to be the immigration policy of the United States that
   a. aliens within the Nation's borders not depend on public resources to meet their needs, but rather rely on their own capabilities and the resources of their families, their sponsors, and private organizations, and
   b. the availability of public benefits not constitute an incentive of immigration to the United States.
3. Despite the principle of self-sufficiency, aliens have been applying for and receiving public benefits from Federal, State, and local governments at increasing rates.
4. Current eligibility rules for public assistance and unenforceable financial support agreements have proved wholly incapable of assuring that individual aliens not burden the public benefits system.
5. It is a compelling government interest to enact new rules for eligibility and sponsorship agreements in order to assure that aliens be self-reliant in accordance with national immigration policy.
6. It is a compelling government interest to remove the incentive for illegal immigration provided by the availability of public benefits.
7. With respect to the State authority to make determinations concerning the eligibility of qualified aliens for public benefits in this chapter, a state that chooses to follow the federal classification in determining the eligibility of such aliens for public assistance shall be considered to have chosen the least restrictive means available for achieving the compelling government interest of assuring that aliens be self-reliant in accordance with national immigration policy.

The Seventh Circuit Court of Appeals acknowledged that reasonable people might disagree regarding the wisdom of controlling immigration through such a policy. Further, the executive branch noted that another purpose of making legal aliens ineligible is to provide them with an incentive to become citizens. The plaintiffs challenged this position also. However, a decision in favor of the government based on a rational basis test does not mean that

Congress and the executive branch must provide a perfect fit between their objectives and the statute. In sum, under a rational basis test, the Welfare Reform Act was ruled to be constitutional (*Alvarez et al. v. Shalala et al.*, 1999).

Alvarez differs from previous cases that sought to discourage poor people from moving from one state to another state for higher benefits. As shown above, such restrictions were held to be unconstitutional. But aliens do not have the same rights as citizens. First, aliens do not have a constitutional right to travel or immigrate to the United States. Further, because of aliens' status, they cannot claim a denial of equal protection like new residents can claim. If the case involved fundamental rights, strict scrutiny would have been appropriate to determine the constitutionality of the Welfare Reform Act. Perhaps if it had been used, the plaintiffs might have made a stronger case that differentiating was either underinclusive or overinclusive.

SOCIAL SECURITY DISABILITY BENEFITS

Disability benefits are governed by congressional statute, which creates property interests protected by the Fifth Amendment. In order to receive disability benefits from Social Security, a person must meet all five parts of a **disability test** (*Sanchez v. Apfel*, 2000), which are:

1. the person must not be presently employed;
2. the person's impairment must be severe;
3. the impairment must meet or medically equal a listed impairment as defined by the Social Security Administration;
4. the person must not have the residual functional capacity to perform his or her former work;
5. the person must not have the residual functional capacity to perform any other substantial gainful activity (Title 20 C.F.R. § 404.1520). **Substantial gainful activity** is defined as work activity involving significant physical or mental abilities for pay or profit (*Newton v. Apfel*, 2000).

Some courts have approached the issue differently but with the same results. To qualify for disability benefits, an individual must establish that he or she (a) is insured for disability insurance benefits; (b) has not attained retirement age; (c) has filed an application for disability insurance benefits; and (d) is under a disability. To make this determination, an examiner considers several issues:

1. If the claimant is doing substantial gainful activity, he or she is not disabled;
2. If the claimant is not doing substantial gainful activity, his or her impairment must be severe before he or she can be found to be disabled;
3. If the claimant is not doing substantial gainful activity and is suffering from a severe impairment that has lasted or is expected to last for a continuous period of at least 12 months, and his or her impairment meets or equals a listed impairment, the claimant is presumed disabled without further inquiry;
4. If the claimant's impairment does not prevent him or her from doing his or her past relevant work, he or she is not disabled;
5. Even if the claimant's impairment does prevent him or her from doing his or her past relevant work, if other work exists in the national economy that accommodates his or her residual functional capacity and vocational factors (that is, age, education, skills), he or she is not disabled (*Hammond v. Apfel*, 2000).

Once the person satisfies the first four components of the test, the burden of proof shifts to the commissioner regarding the fifth component. To meet this burden, the commissioner may employ the opinion of a vocational expert and pose germane hypothetical questions regarding the extent to which the person seeking benefits has the capacity to perform other substantial gainful employment. Often the District Office of the Social Security Administration makes the actual decision. An adverse decision may be appealed, and a hearing by an Administrative Law Judge may be requested (*Underwood v. Commissioner of Social Security*, 2000).

If a decision is adverse to a claimant, the decision may be appealed. The review standard is whether there is substantial evidence in the record to support the findings that were made. **Substantial evidence** means such relevant evidence that a reasonable mind might accept as adequate to support a conclusion. The substantial evidence standard includes a zone of choices in which the decision maker could go either way. As long as there is substantial evidence to support the decision, the courts would not overturn the decision, despite there being some evidence to support the claimant's position (*Underwood v. Commissioner of Social Security*, 2000).

Applying these standards, the Sixth Circuit Court of Appeals upheld the denial of benefits to an Ohio man who claimed to be disabled because of respiratory problems. The man claimed that smoke, fumes, and dust interfered with his breathing, causing him to be unable to hold a job. A vocational expert was called as a witness, and she testified that there were positions in Ohio that the man could hold with his medical condition. Based on this testimony, the decision to deny benefits was upheld despite the evidence existing that supported and refuted the claimant (*Underwood v. Commissioner of Social Security*, 2000).

But in another case, *Newton v. Apfel* (2000), the Fifth Circuit Court of Appeals reversed the decision of the Administrative Law Judge. In this case, Newton was diagnosed with systemic lupus erythematosus (SLE), a condition that caused swelling in her joints and other ailments. Newton saw a rheumatologist and another physician for treatment. Federal regulations require the assessment of several factors in making a decision of how much weight to assign medical testimony, including the physician's length of treatment of the claimant, the physician's frequency of examination, the nature and extent of the treatment relationship, the support of the physician's opinion afforded by the medical evidence of record, the consistency of the opinion with the record as a whole, and the specialization of the treating physician. The Administrative Law Judge did not give sufficient weight to the medical opinions of Newton's physicians, holding instead that Newton's pain was not severe and her functional limitations were not as great as the physicians reported. Because the Administrative Law Judge appeared not to assess fairly the physicians' reports regarding Newton, the Fifth Circuit Court of Appeals reversed and remanded the case for reconsideration of the physicians' report (*Newton v. Apfel*, 2000).

Disability benefits are not limited to individuals suffering from physical disability; it is also possible to receive such benefits for a mental disability. A psychiatric review form must be completed, and the Administrative Law Judge assesses whether the mental disability prevents the individual from working. One woman, Ms. Ray, who lost her job reportedly because her employer was downsizing, contended that she might have been released from her job because of a disability. She was diagnosed with a mild affective mood disorder. The Administrative Law Judge requested an additional psychiatric evaluation and history (*Ray v. Apfel*, 2000).

A psychiatrist saw the woman on May 10, 1995. She reported that she was laid off in November 1994 and began to feel lousy. She read about depression and visited a mental health center. A professional at the mental health center told the woman that she was depressed and placed her on a waiting list for treatment. The psychiatrist also informed the woman that her depression was mild but had the potential to become major. The specific diagnosis was depressive disorder, not otherwise specified, mild to moderate. With treatment, the prognosis was that the woman would probably receive considerable relief. The woman began treatment a few months later and was diagnosed then as having severe, major depression. The Administrative Law Judge concluded that on the date the mental health treatment began, October 27, 1995, the woman's mental impairment only slightly restricted the activities of daily living and social functioning. Also, her condition seldom affected her concentration, persistence, or pace in work settings, and never resulted in episodes of deterioration or decompensation. Accordingly, the Administrative Law Judge concluded that the woman did not have a severe mental impairment and that a non-severe mental impairment would not significantly limit the woman's mental ability to do basic work activities (*Ray v. Apfel*, 2000).

In 1996, Congress passed the Contract with America Advancement Act, which eliminated disability benefits for people whose disability is materially caused by alcohol or drug addiction. The statute advises that if a person is disabled and has evidence of drug addiction or alcoholism, a determination must be made regarding whether the person's addiction is a contributing factor material to the disability. To make this determination, a fact finder must determine if the person would still be disabled if he or she stopped drinking or using drugs. If the answer is yes, then benefits would be granted; however, if the answer is no, then benefits would be denied (*Mittlestedt v. Apfel*, 2000).

Legal Congruence of Social Security Disability Insurance and the Americans with Disabilities Act

The U.S. Supreme Court was asked to decide whether an application for Social Security Disability Insurance (SSDI) precludes a lawsuit based on the Americans with Disabilities Act (ADA). On the surface, one might appear to be incompatible with the other. For instance, to apply for SSDI, an individual asserts that he or she is totally disabled and incapable of working. But by pressing a claim under ADA, an individual contends that she or he is capable of doing a job with reasonable accommodations. In different parts of the country, Courts of Appeals had ruled contradictorily regarding this issue, convincing the U.S. Supreme Court to decide this issue (*Cleveland v. Policy Management Systems Corporation et al.*, 1999).

In the case that the U.S. Supreme Court decided, Carolyn Cleveland was hired in 1993 by Policy Management Systems to perform background checks on applicants. A year later Cleveland suffered a stroke, which affected her memory, concentration, and language skills. A few weeks after her stroke, Cleveland filed an SSDI application contending that she was disabled and incapable of working. Cleveland's condition improved after three months and she returned to work. When informed that Cleveland had returned to work, the Social Security Administration denied the application. A few days later, Cleveland was fired from her job. Cleveland then asked the Social Security Administration to reconsider her application based on her dismissal. After another rejection and reconsideration in September 1995, the Social Security Administration granted SSDI benefits to Cleveland and made her benefits retroactive to the time of her stroke.

A week before the Social Security Administration's decision, Cleveland had initiated a lawsuit against her former employer, charging that she was fired because of her disability in violation of the ADA (*Cleveland v. Policy Management Systems Corporation et al.*, 1999). When Cleveland filed her lawsuit in U.S. District Court, her employer's lawyers argued that Cleveland had represented to the Social Security Administration that she was totally disabled. Therefore, she could not claim that she was a qualified person with a disability who was discriminated against by her former employer. The U.S. District Court agreed and granted summary judgment to Policy Management Systems, and the Fifth Circuit Court of Appeals concurred. The Court of Appeals indicated that in one setting, Cleveland was declaring "I am too disabled to work," but in another setting, she was saying "I am not too disabled to work." Still, the U.S. Supreme Court reversed the Court of Appeals (*Cleveland v. Policy Management Systems Corporation et al.*, 1999).

The Court noted that both SSDI and ADA have similar goals in mind—assisting individuals with disabilities. SSDI provides monetary benefits to qualified individuals with a disability. The Social Security Act defines **disability** as an inability to engage in any substantially gainful activity because of a physical or mental impairment that could be expected to result in death or to last continuously for at least 12 months. The ADA defines a **qualified individual with a disability** as a disabled person who is capable of doing the essential functions of a job when that job provides reasonable accommodations. The Court noted that the Social Security Administration does not take into account reasonable accommodation when it makes a decision regarding whether to grant benefits, and an applicant does not need to factor in reasonable accommodations when applying for SSDI. In addition, SSDI is awarded to individuals who can work and are working. The contextual environment of SSDI and ADA are different, and an applicant can tailor responses to satisfy each without contradicting himself or herself. Moreover, the law provides individuals with the right to present two or more statements of a claim or defenses alternatively or hypothetically (*Cleveland v. Policy Management Systems Corporation et al.,* 1999).

For instance, a criminal defendant may claim that a criminal statute is unconstitutional because it is vague and did not put him or her on notice of the forbidden conduct, but if he or she committed the crime, it was because of duress or insanity. These two defenses are not incompatible. Thus, Cleveland was not being inconsistent in requesting relief based on two statutes. Though the Court did say that responses geared to SSDI and ADA can be inconsistent and potentially problematic for an applicant, summary judgment was inappropriate in this case and both parties should have been allowed to argue their cases (*Cleveland v. Policy Management Systems Corporation et al.,* 1999).

DRUG TESTING OF RECIPIENTS RECEIVING PUBLIC ASSISTANCE

As part of welfare reform, Congress authorized states to mandate drug testing of recipients of TANF. This policy has been roundly condemned as a violation of women's rights (Hentoff, 2000; Simon, 1999). On the other hand, Congress and some states were sensitive to the effects of women using drugs on their children—the born and unborn (Howard, 1999). For instance, one woman in Atlanta with a drug problem gave birth to four children. Two children were born prematurely and died shortly after birth, and a third child died at age 2. The fourth child was born with permanent disabilities and was thus taken from the mother (Hansen, 2000). In Atlanta during a two-year period, 37 babies died because their mothers used drugs (Hansen, 2000). Supporters of drug testing of women who were on Aid to Dependent Children contend that a significant number of these women were using drugs and, as a result, their children suffered. Instead of spending money for necessities, the benefits money was used to buy drugs and the food stamps were sold or traded to pay for drugs. The end result was that children were not fed and they were neglected (Simon, 1999).

A. Hamid, an anthropologist, conducted a qualitative study in 1992 on the impact of crack cocaine use on the African American community of Harlem. He noted that the use of crack had a different impact on men and women. For women on AFDC, crack cocaine forced them to leave home to get money for the drugs. Prior to the introduction of crack cocaine, many women on AFDC stayed home, watched television, and smoked marijuana or drank beer. Crack created a need for more money than what AFDC provided and thus forced women on the streets to hustle nonstop for money or drugs. According to Hamid (1992), research participants described this behavior as being on "a mission." One of the effects of women on AFDC being on a mission is that children suffer. Money provided by the welfare system for support of children goes to the purchase of crack, and children often are neglected while their mothers are on "the mission."

A number of legal professionals have examined the issue of drug testing of welfare recipients and have determined that such testing is unconstitutional (Carey, 1998; Guthrie, 1991). However, they also indicate, based on current case law, that the likelihood of an appellate court holding drug testing to be illegal is very slim. The courts have sanctioned drug testing of school athletes, railroad workers, and air traffic controllers. These groups have been held to have a limited expectation of privacy and can be tested although there is no probable cause to suspect that members of these groups have used drugs.

Compounding further the issue for welfare recipients, the courts have rejected legal arguments that social workers could not enter welfare recipients' homes to check for violations of welfare policy and regulations. The recipients argued that caseworkers coming into their homes violated their Fourth Amendment right to be free from unreasonable searches. But the courts rejected this argument, holding that a home visit is not a search. Furthermore, the Court stated that even if it were a search, welfare recipients waive their right by accepting welfare benefits (*Wyman v. James*, 1971).

IMPLICATIONS FOR SOCIAL WELFARE POLICY AND PRACTICE

The law has had more effect on social welfare policy with respect to public assistance programs than other benefit programs. Whenever Congress or a state creates a policy providing benefits, it creates property interests that are protected by the

Fifth or Fourteenth Amendment. As the Fourteenth Amendment states, property shall not be taken without due process. Thus, a commissioner of a Public Welfare Agency cannot terminate benefits without a hearing and cannot deny the right of the recipient to contest in a fair forum. The U.S. Constitution also protects public assistance recipients' right to travel without being penalized. A decision to restrict benefits based on a resident's newness to a state violates that person's liberty interests and equal protection.

Whether the government agency is following the statute or applying the statute fairly governs legal issues surrounding disability benefits. When seeking redress in a legal forum regarding whether disability benefits should have been granted or should not have been granted, individuals explicitly argue a violation of the Fifth or Fourteenth Amendment. Significantly deviating from a written policy or statute violates the Fourteenth Amendment. An administrative law judge who unfairly disallows or discredits a claimant's physician injects unfairness into the process, thus violating due process.

A contentious area has been drug testing of recipients of TANF and terminating TANF and food stamp recipients who have been convicted of a drug offense. A case can be made that a policy mandating drug testing is on the surface unfair to recipients. Mostly, these recipients are poor and powerless women. Moreover, there is another side to this issue, which is the effect of denying TANF and food stamps on children in these families.

Although some states have provisions that allow women who have tested positive for drug use to continue receiving TANF or food stamp benefits, a single person who is convicted of drug use is permanently barred from receiving food stamps in other states, such as Indiana. This policy of permanently banning convicted offenders is much more punitive than drug testing TANF recipients. Even if a person successfully completes treatment, he or she will never again be allowed to receive food stamps. (Perhaps a pardon from the governor might make a difference.) This policy is likely to create other social welfare issues. In California, for example, where there is a three-strikes law, some individuals are serving life or 25-years-to-life sentences for stealing sandwiches and pizzas. For some people stealing food was their third strike. A person who is denied food stamps is likely to cost residents of California much more in the price of incarceration for a number of years than giving that person a small amount of food stamps would cost. If Indiana had a similar three-strikes law as in

California, Indiana would pay much more in long-term incarceration than in providing food stamps.

Some social workers likely approve of the changes passed by Congress, and some social workers likely disapprove. Regardless, the current law is what must be followed and implemented through practice. For clients who are nearing the end of their benefits under TANF, social workers must try harder to help them find employment. In addition, they must help clients try to secure other resources in the community, if needed. Such assistance might include food, assistance with rent payments, and assistance with utilities. In effect, a case would not be closed because a client is no longer receiving public assistance. A case would be closed only when the client is firmly established in the community.

CONCLUSION

This chapter began by explaining the legal requirements for terminating benefits, indicating that due process of law must be provided before benefits can be terminated. The standards for terminating benefits under AFDC are applied to TANF. Similarly, public assistance policy designed to discourage residents from moving from one state to another state by paying lower benefits was ruled unconstitutional under AFDC and equally is unconstitutional under TANF. However, termination of benefits under both TANF and the food stamp program is legal for people who have been convicted of drug offenses. The test for establishing disability benefits was presented. An explanation was given for why illegal aliens can be legally denied benefits. Finally, the chapter discussed the forced drug testing of people as a condition for receiving public assistance.

Key Terms and Concepts

Due Process Requirements for Terminating Benefits	Disability Test Substantial Gainful Activity	Disability Qualified Individual with a Disability
Right to Travel Components	Substantial Evidence	

THE LAW'S EFFECT ON MENTAL HEALTH POLICY

The law has had a major impact on mental health policy and practice in this country (Clark, 1999; Madden & Parody, 1997). It has shaped the civil commitment of individuals with mental illness and developmental disability. It has influenced the treatment of institutionalized individuals with mental illness, providing this group with a constitutional right to mental health treatment. The law has provided guidelines for the involuntary treatment of people who refuse to take psychotropic drugs. The law has had a similar effect in correctional institutions, giving prisoners the right to psychiatric treatment and outlining when prisoners may be involuntarily treated with drugs.

This chapter describes the influence of the law on mental health policy, beginning with an important legal principle affecting mental health policy and intervention with people suffering from mental illness. Then, the chapter discusses the standard for civil commitment, the right to mental health treatment in mental institutions, the right to mental health treatment in the least restrictive setting, the right to mental health treatment in correctional institutions, and the right to refuse treatment in mental institutions and correctional institutions. Next, the chapter discusses the right to access mental health records. At the end, this chapter discusses the implications for social welfare policy and practice.

LEGAL PRINCIPLES AFFECTING MENTAL HEALTH POLICY

Several legal concepts are implicated in mental health policy. One is liberty, which was discussed in Chapter 2. Being free in this country is the norm, and restraints of this freedom must be justified and must conform to due process. A person cannot be taken out of his or her home or taken off the street simply for behaving deviantly or criticizing someone such as the president of the United States. In order to curtail a person's liberty interests, the government must have reason and justification. Then, it must afford due process in providing a hearing and an opportunity for a person whose liberty is being threatened to respond to the allegations. Involuntary treatment threatens liberty as well as an individual's First Amendment right to his or her thoughts. Altering a person's thoughts through surgery or drugs interferes with that person's right to think freely.

In the prison environment, prisoners have acquired the right to treatment through the Eighth Amendment to the U.S. Constitution, which forbids states from inflicting cruel and unusual punishment upon citizens. A prisoner who is mentally ill and not receiving treatment is being inflicted with wanton pain that has no penological justification. The administering of pain to prisoners must serve a penological justification, and permitting the suffering of prisoners due to mental illness constitutes cruel and unusual punishment. For the government to avoid this constitutional violation, it must provide treatment.

INTERVENING WITH INDIVIDUALS WITH MENTAL ILLNESS

A consistent legal issue that emerges when discussing individuals with mental illness is the extent to which the government can restrict these individuals' liberty interests, interests that are guaranteed by the Fourteenth Amendment to the U.S. Constitution and by individual state constitutions. People with various stages of mental illness have been institutionalized for decades. A cardinal law emerged in the 20th century that requires that in order for government to restrict an individual's liberty, the individual must be both mentally ill and currently dangerous. Both prongs must be established in order to commit an individual to a mental institution involuntarily. A person who is just mentally ill and not dangerous poses no threat to society. Thus, this person has a right to walk the streets as freely as other citizens. Also, dangerous individuals (that is, sane people who have a propensity to be violent) cannot be confined unless they have been convicted of a crime. Dangerous individuals walk the streets all across America, and they have a right to be free as long as they have not broken any laws. Neither states nor Congress can pass a law prohibiting anyone from being dangerous. Accordingly, in the civil arena, a person who is mentally ill and currently dangerous can be committed to an institution until one of these factors dissipates. At that point, the person is entitled to his or her freedom or to have his or her full liberty interests recovered (*Foucha v. Louisiana*, 1992).

Standard of Proof Needed for Civil Commitment

The issue of liberty interests arose in determining what level of proof is needed to satisfy a decision maker to commit involuntarily an individual to a mental institution. The case involved Frank O'Neal Addington, whose mother initiated an involuntary civil commitment process for him in Texas. There was no question that Addington was assessed to be both mentally ill and dangerous, as determined by a civil jury. The issue was the standard of proof that the jury was instructed to use in making its determination. The judge charged the jury to use the standard of clear, unequivocal, and convincing evidence. On appeal, the appellate courts in Texas differed regarding the proper standard. The Texas Court of Civil Appeals ruled that because Addington's substantive rights were threatened, the standard for commitment was proof beyond a reasonable doubt. But the Texas Supreme Court reversed, holding the proper standard was a preponderance of the evidence (*Addington v. Texas*, 1979).

Addington asked the U.S. Supreme Court to hold that his commitment required proof beyond a reasonable doubt, which had been decided in a case involving a juvenile threatened with commitment to a juvenile institution. The Court restated the purpose of the standard of proof. Writing for the majority, Chief Justice Warren Burger stated that "the function of a standard of proof, as that concept is embodied in the Due Process Clause and in the realm of factfinding, is to 'instruct the factfinder concerning the degree of confidence our society thinks he [sic] should have in the correctness of factual conclusions for a particular type of adjudication'" (*Addington v. Texas*, 1979, p. 423).

This standard serves to allocate the risk of error to the parties in a trial, hearing, or litigation and to the degree of importance attached to the ultimate decision. In civil cases, where just money is involved, the standard is a preponderance of the evidence. This is so because society has minimal concern with the outcome of private lawsuits, and the parties share the risk of error about equally. In criminal cases, the standard is beyond a reasonable doubt because the risks are great, and thus the government should shoulder this risk almost entirely. Equally, it serves to denote the importance of the outcome, where lives and freedom are at stake. The intermediate standard, using words such as *clear, cogent,* and *unequivocal,* is used when the interests at stake are more than money but less than being executed or going to prison for the rest of one's life (*Addington v. Texas,* 1979).

Chief Justice Warren Burger stated that it is indisputable that involuntary commitment to a mental hospital based on a finding of mental illness and dangerousness to self or others can produce adverse social consequences. Whether this adverse social consequence is called *stigma* or something else, it is quite apparent and can have a significant, negative impact on the individual. As indicated by the Chief Justice:

> the state has a legitimate interest under its parens patriae powers in providing care to its citizens who are unable because of emotional disorders to care for themselves; the state also has authority under its police power to protect the community from the dangerous tendencies of some who are mentally ill. . . . At one time or another every person exhibits some abnormal behavior which might be perceived by some as symptomatic of mental or emotional disorder, but which is in fact within a range of conduct that is generally acceptable. Obviously, such behavior is not a basis for compelled treatment and surely none for confinement. However, there is the possible risk that a factfinder might decide to commit an individual based solely on a few isolated instances of unusual conduct. Loss of liberty calls for a showing that the individual suffers from something more serious than is demonstrated by idiosyncratic behavior. Increasing the burden of proof is one way to impress the factfinder with the importance of the decision and thereby perhaps to reduce the chances that inappropriate commitments will be ordered. . . . We conclude that the

individual's liberty interest in the outcome of a civil commitment proceeding is of such weight and gravity that due process requires the state to justify confinement by proof more substantial than a mere preponderance of the evidence (*Addington v. Texas*, 1979, pp. 426–427).

Right to Mental Health Treatment in Mental Institutions

The U.S. Supreme Court has not explicitly ruled that under the U.S. Constitution individuals committed to mental institutions have a constitutional right to psychiatric treatment. However, indirectly the Court has strongly suggested that individuals committed to mental institutions based on mental illness have a right to treatment. Again, the Court focused on the concept of a person's liberty interests. In this case, Kenneth Donaldson, an institutionalized patient in a Florida mental institution, sued Dr. J. B. O'Connor, the superintendent, for depriving him of his liberty. Donaldson, who was institutionalized for 15 years mostly under Dr. O'Connor's tenure, contended that he was neither mentally ill nor dangerous. Moreover, Donaldson repeatedly requested that Dr. O'Connor discharge him, but Dr. O'Connor refused. Further, friends and advocates of Donaldson requested that Donaldson be released into their care, but Dr. O'Connor still refused. Donaldson sued for damages under the theory that Dr. O'Connor had maliciously deprived him of his liberty and had not given him any treatment for his supposed mental illness. A jury found for Donaldson and the Fifth Circuit Court of Appeals concurred, contending that Donaldson's right to treatment was violated.

The U.S. Supreme Court chose to view the case more narrowly and refused to rule that individuals have a right to psychiatric treatment. Instead, the Court focused on the liberty issue. Speaking for a unanimous Court, Justice Stewart wrote that

> we have concluded that the difficult issues of constitutional law dealt with by the Court of Appeals are not presented by this case in its present posture. Specifically, there is no reason now to decide whether mentally ill people dangerous to themselves or to others have a right to treatment upon compulsory confinement by the State, or whether the State may compulsorily confine a nondangerous, mentally ill individual for the purpose of treatment. As we view it, this case raises a single, relatively simple, but nonetheless important question concerning every man's [sic] constitutional right to liberty (*O'Connor v. Donaldson*, 1975, p. 573).

The Court posed and answered two questions that spoke to liberty interests. First, it posed whether the state can confine the mentally ill merely to ensure them a living standard superior to that they enjoy in the private community. The answer is no. Second, it posed whether the state can fence in the harmless mentally ill solely to save some citizens from exposure to those whose ways are different. The answer again is no. According to the Court, a finding of mental illness alone cannot justify a state institutionalizing a person against his or her will and keeping the person indefinitely in simple custodial confinement. Simply, a state cannot constitutionally confine without *more* [italics added] a nondangerous person who is capable of surviving safely in freedom by himself or herself or by the assistance of friends (*O'Connor v. Donaldson*, 1975).

In *O'Connor*, the U.S. Supreme Court would not say that individuals have a right to treatment, but it suggested that the "more" involves justification or purpose. The Court referenced *Jackson v. Indiana* (1972), in which it ruled that due process required that the nature of confinement bear a reasonable relationship to its purpose. Some statutes may state that the purpose of compulsory confinement is to protect society, to protect the individual, or to provide treatment. Thus, if the purpose of confinement is treatment, then treatment has to be provided in order to conform to due process. Most state statutes say clearly that individuals with mental illness are institutionalized for treatment; therefore, they have a right to treatment when confined.

Another case that involved liberty and that also has implications for the right to treatment is *Youngberg v. Romeo* (1982). Romeo was severely developmentally disabled with an IQ of between 8 and 10. He could not speak and could not perform basic self-care. Romeo's parents cared for him until the death of his father. Unable to care for him alone, the mother had Romeo institutionalized when he was 26 years old. In the institution, Romeo was violent, injured himself, was injured by other patients, and was frequently put in physical restraints. Despite his severe limitations, Romeo had liberty interests that were protected by the U.S. Constitution. His confinement restricted his liberty, and his being put in physical restraints restricted his liberty even further. Though Romeo's confinement was in his best interests, the nature of his confinement was problematic.

Thus, to preserve his liberty interests, Romeo was entitled to a safe environment and freedom from physical restraints. To facilitate these ends, he was entitled to **habilitation** (that is, the teaching of basic skills). For instance, if he were taught how to behave better, physical restraints would be unnecessary. The Court noted that even prisoners have limited liberty interests, protecting them from unjustified solitary confinement. Therefore, if convicted people have liberty interests, then Romeo, said the Court, had liberty interests protected by the U.S. Constitution (*Youngberg v. Romeo,* 1982).

Similar to *O'Connor, Youngberg* can be interpreted as providing a right to treatment. If Romeo had to be provided with habilitation to preserve his liberty interests, then the same would apply to people with mental illness. If a person were committed to a mental institution due to mental illness and were violent on the unit, requiring restraints or seclusion, then one could argue that such a person was entitled to behavior modification or treatment in order to prevent him or her from being put in restraints or seclusion.

Right to Mental Health Treatment in the Least Restrictive Setting

Two women with diagnoses of developmental disability, schizophrenia, and antisocial personality disorder contended that their liberty interests were violated by their treatment in an institution rather than in the community when treatment professionals concluded that both women could be treated. In addition, they contended that treatment in an institution unnecessarily violated their rights under the Americans with Disabilities Act (Title 42 U.S.C. § 12132). The court refused to decide this issue on constitutional grounds and decided instead to decide it on statutory grounds because Congress passed the Americans with Disabilities Act in 1990 and authorized the Attorney General to promulgate regulations (*Olmstead et al. v. L. C. et al.,* 1999).

The U.S. Supreme Court ruled that the proscription against discrimination, embodied in the Americans with Disabilities Act and the Attorney General's regulations, suggested that treatment of individuals with mental disabilities should be in the community, rather than in an institution. This right, however, is qualified. The right to community treatment depends upon the state's treatment professionals determining that community placement is appropriate, that the client does not oppose a transfer from institutional care, and that the placement can be fiscally accommodated without depriving other individuals with mental disabilities who are under the care of the state (*Olmstead et al. v. L. C. et al.,* 1999).

RIGHT TO MENTAL HEALTH TREATMENT
IN CORRECTIONAL INSTITUTIONS

If one were to examine closely the U.S. Constitution, one would not find an explicit right to mental health treatment in a prison setting, and these words are not mentioned at all in any of the amendments (Alexander, 1989). To understand such a right, one must look to the Eighth Amendment and its prohibition against cruel and unusual punishment (Mayer, 1989). The foundation for prisoners' rights to mental health treatment is *Estelle v. Gamble* (1976). In this case, a Texas prisoner brought a lawsuit contending that he had been subjected to cruel and unusual punishment because he was inadequately treated for a back injury. Although this prisoner lost his lawsuit, the U.S. Supreme Court established when a prisoner could make a valid claim of an Eighth Amendment violation based on medical issues.

Writing for the majority, Justice Marshall stated that "in order to state a cognizable claim, a prisoner must allege acts or omissions sufficiently harmful to evidence deliberate indifference to serious medical needs" (*Estelle v. Gamble*, 1976, p. 106). Simply, a prisoner who has a serious medical problem that is being ignored by prison administrators is being inflicted with cruel and unusual punishment. The pain inflicted by a lack of medical treatment serves no legitimate penological interest. The Eleventh Circuit Court of Appeals, repeating this sentiment with respect to juveniles, held that juveniles have the same right to medical treatment that was established in *Estelle v. Gamble* (1976). Further, a wait of three days to treat an injured juvenile constituted cruel and unusual punishment, for which the superintendent was liable (*H. C. by Hewett v. Jarrard,*1986).

With *Estelle v. Gamble* (1976) clearly establishing a prisoner's right to medical treatment, such a right was quickly extrapolated to psychiatric care. Like Gamble, Bowring, the prisoner involved, did not prevail, but his lawsuit established the parameters for a right to mental health treatment. This prisoner was turned down for parole, in part, because a psychiatric report had indicated that his chance of success on parole was low because of a psychological problem. After getting his rejection for parole, he filed a lawsuit. He contended that because his freedom was being denied because of a psychological problem, the state had a duty to provide mental health treatment to him so that he could make parole. The U.S. District Court rejected the claim without a hearing, but the Fourth Circuit Court of Appeals reversed the district court's decision and ordered a hearing on Bowring's claim (*Bowring v. Godwin,* 1977).

The Fourth Circuit Court of Appeals did not accept that Bowring had a psychological problem but stated that a hearing had to be held to determine the extent to which he had a serious medical problem. This hearing was necessary in light of *Estelle v. Gamble* (1976) because psychiatric treatment was considered to be medical treatment. Just as the U.S. Supreme Court had outlined how a prisoner could make a valid claim of an Eighth Amendment violation because of a medical issue, the Fourth Circuit Court of Appeals outlined how a prisoner could make a valid claim of an Eighth Amendment violation because of a psychiatric problem. The Fourth Circuit Court of Appeals wrote that:

> A prison inmate is entitled to psychological or psychiatric treatment if a physician or mental health care provider, exercising ordinary skill and care at the time of observation, concludes with reasonable medical certainty (1) that the prisoner's symptoms evidence a serious disease or injury; (2) that such disease or injury is curable or may be substantially alleviated; and (3) that the potential for harm to the prisoner by reason of delay or the denial of care would be substantial (*Bowring v. Godwin,* 1977, p. 47).

Logically tied to *Estelle, Bowring* provides that a prisoner with serious psychiatric problems has the right to be free from cruel and unusual punishment. When a prisoner with a serious psychiatric problem is allowed to suffer needlessly and painfully, the Eighth Amendment is violated. *Bowring* does not mean that the prison must provide counseling for minor psychological distress. The psychological problem must be serious, such as a prisoner who is suffering from schizophrenia and is causing harm to himself or herself. A prisoner who is suffering from depression would not have a right to counseling for that depression, unless the depression is quite severe and is significantly affecting the prisoner's functioning in the institution.

RIGHT TO REFUSE MENTAL HEALTH TREATMENT

Though some individuals have litigated their right to receive mental health treatment, other individuals have litigated their right to refuse psychotropic treatment (Brooks, 1998). Mental health professionals have not criticized the development of the right to receive treatment by state statutes or federal case law; however, professionals have strongly criticized the concept that individuals have both the right to treatment and then the right to refuse treatment. Numerous legal observers have debated and discussed these seemingly divergent perspectives (Blackburn, 1990; Cichon, 1992; Plotkin, 1978). Supporters of the right to refuse treatment argue that this right is consistent with the right to refuse treatment in general. Furthermore, they suggest that some treatment decisions are based more on institutional needs than on the patient needs. This is especially true in the correctional system, where medication has sometimes been given to control individuals or been given to prisoners who are not mentally ill. Despite the right to refuse treatment, states may easily override these rights. The sections below elaborate upon the right to refuse treatment in mental institutions and correctional institutions.

State Mental Institutions

Liberty involves the ability to make decisions to either accept or reject treatment. With people who are mentally ill, the belief is that they are incapable of knowing what is best for them, and people with mental illness, unlike other people, may pose problems for staff and other residents. One of the early decisions on the right to refuse treatment involved an individual who challenged Boston State Hospital's use of seclusion rooms and forced medication. A U.S. District Court agreed that the right to privacy includes the right both to accept and to reject treatment. However, the state might override this right to protect residents and staff (*Rogers v. Okin*, 1979). Another decision, *Rennie v. Klein* (1978), provided the same conclusion. Further, the district court concluded that a mental institution must evaluate four factors when a patient refuses to take psychotropic medication. These are (a) the patient's degree of physical threat; (b) the patient's ability to make decisions regarding treatment; (c) whether a less restrictive alternative exists; and (d) the degree of risk from the side effects of the medication (*Rennie v. Klein*, 1978).

Rennie was appealed to the U.S. Supreme Court, but the Court remanded it in light of the ruling in *Youngberg v. Romeo* (1982) (*Rennie v. Klein*, 1982). The Court ruled in *Youngberg* that Romeo's right to habilitation or treatment is not violated unless it substantially departs from accepted professional judgment, practice, or standards. Conversely, a patient could not refuse psychotropic treatment or drugs unless the decision to treat substantially departs from accepted judgment, practice, or standards. Thus, subsequent courts have adopted this approach in ruling against individuals' right to refuse mental health treatment.

A number of states have defined the contours of a citizen's right to refuse psychiatric treatment. For instance, California states that any person who is subject to detention shall have the right to refuse treatment with antipsychotic medication subject to certain provisions (California Welfare & Institution Code § 5325.2). Another section of the California Code provides the criteria for involuntary medication. Specifically, if any person deemed appropriate for antipsychotic medication refuses, the treatment staff shall determine in a hearing whether treatment alternatives to involuntary medications are unlikely to meet the needs of the patient (California Welfare & Institution Code § 5332).

In Texas, the state legislature has provided a mechanism for creating a committee to determine the best interest of people suffering from mental illness, which may include medication issues. According to the statute, the committee shall make a determination, based on clear and convincing evidence, of whether the proposed treatment promotes the client's best interest. According to its determination of the client's best interest, the committee shall consent to or refuse the treatment on the client's behalf. The statute provides immunity from criminal and civil penalties for any person serving on such a committee (Texas Health & Safety Code § 597.049).

Correctional Institutions

Prisoners have a long history of resisting involuntary mental health treatment. At one time, prison administrators transferred sane but troublesome prisoners to mental institutions, which meant that these prisoners could not be paroled and were confined longer (Alexander, 1988). The courts limited these practices as violations of prisoners' rights. The U.S. Supreme Court held that a prisoner facing involuntary treatment in a mental institution is entitled to due process. In this case, due process required a hearing, the right to present witnesses, the right to notice of the need for treatment, and an impartial person to decide if forced treatment was required (*Vitek v. Jones*, 1979).

Additionally, the courts began to scrutinize therapies provided to prisoners. Aversive therapy, legitimately used in psychiatric practice, had become punishment in the prison setting. For instance, because of a violation of an institutional rule, an Iowa prisoner contended that he was given a medication that caused him to vomit. The prisoner contended that this constituted cruel and unusual punishment, but the state countered that this treatment was aversive therapy. However, the Eighth Circuit Court of Appeals agreed with the prisoner and stated that this was cruel and unusual punishment (*Knecht v. Gillman*, 1973). In California, the Ninth Circuit Court of Appeals made a similar ruling regarding another aversive therapy that gave a prisoner the feeling of being suffocated. The California prison authorities called it treatment, but the court held it to be cruel and unusual punishment (*Mackey v. Procunier*, 1973). Neither the Iowa case nor the California case involved prisoners with a recognized diagnosis of mental illness, and the courts properly found these practices unconstitutional.

Of course, some prisoners have universally recognized mental illnesses. The extent to which these prisoners could reject involuntary treatment has not been debated by professionals and advocates as it has been debated regarding free citizens (see Bentley, 1994; Brown, 1984; Poythress & Miller, 1991; Rhoden, 1980; Rosenson, 1994; Shobat, 1985). Alexander (1991) argued that discussions regarding prisoners' right to refuse psychotropic treatment were slighted because of the qualitative difference between the rights of free citizens and prisoners. Simply, prisoners are a neglected group. More importantly, the U.S. Supreme Court has permitted the involuntary treatment of prisoners with psychotropic medication. This issue does not involve the Eighth Amendment like *Knecht v. Gillman* (1973) and *Mackey v. Procunier* (1973). Instead, it involves the reasonableness test.

The U.S. Supreme Court decided a case of a prisoner's right to refuse mental health treatment and used the reasonableness test in ruling against the prisoner. Walter Harper, a prisoner in the state of Washington, was assessed by mental health professionals to be mentally ill. He voluntarily took medication for his illness. After serving a portion of his sentence, he was paroled. As a condition of parole, he was required to get psychiatric treatment in the community. While in the community, Harper experienced a relapse and was subsequently civilly committed to a mental institution. In the mental institution, he assaulted two nurses. Because these assaults were a violation of his parole, he was returned to prison and placed in a psychiatric unit. Harper briefly took psychotropic medication voluntarily, but he stopped. His refusal caused the prison system to invoke its involuntary medication policy, which was developed to accommodate the due process requirements of *Vitek v. Jones* (1979).

Washington State's involuntary medication policy required a panel consisting of a psychiatrist, a psychologist, and the associate superintendent to conduct a hearing. The prisoner had (a) the right to 24 hours' notice of the prison's desire to medicate involuntarily, (b) the right to be present at the hearing, (c) the right to introduce evidence in his or her behalf, (d) the right to cross-examine the prison staff witnesses, (e) the right to assistance by a lay adviser, (f) the right to appeal the decision to the superintendent of the prison, and (g) the right to periodic review subsequent to the initial hearing (*Harper v. the State of Washington,* 1988). These procedures were followed, and a decision was made to medicate Harper forcibly. On appeal, the Supreme Court of Washington held that these procedures violated Harper's rights. The court stated that because forcibly administered medication involved a significant body intrusion with a medication that had serious side effects, the state had to overcome the strict scrutiny legal test before a judge. This requirement is similar to the rights of a free citizen if the state proposes to perform a lobotomy on that person (*Harper v. the State of Washington,* 1988).

However, the U.S. Supreme Court disagreed. The Court stated that the strict scrutiny test was incompatible with deciding issues in a prison environment and would make it more difficult for prison administrators to manage dangerous prisoners. Instead, the reasonableness test should be used, which the Court had articulated in *Turner v. Safley* (1987). Applying the reasonableness test, the Court ruled that prison administrators could override Harper's constitutional right to liberty. The Court reasoned that Harper's mental illness made him dangerous to staff and others. Therefore, Harper's limited right to liberty had to yield to the prison's legitimate interest in maintaining security and order in the institution. Also, the Court held that providing Harper with a judicial hearing would take scarce resources away from the prison and that the cost of accommodating a prisoner's right must be taken into account. In conclusion, the Court stated that the prison psychiatrist knew best how to treat Harper, understood the side effects of the prescribed medication, took an oath to provide medical services only in the patient's medical interest, and, therefore, should not be second-guessed by federal judges (*Washington v. Harper,* 1990). Later, the U.S. Supreme Court suggested that pretrial detainees who are mentally ill could be medicated involuntarily, provided jails followed the procedures in *Washington v. Harper* (1990) (*Riggins v. Nevada*, 1992).

Riggins involved a mentally ill defendant who was involuntarily medicated to make him competent to be tried. At Riggins' trial, Riggins was convicted and given the death penalty. The Court also remanded a death penalty case to Louisiana involving whether the State of Louisiana could forcibly medicate a mentally ill death-row prisoner to make the prisoner sane enough to be executed. In remanding this case, the U.S. Supreme Court instructed the State of Louisiana to use the reasonableness test (*Perry v. Louisiana*, 1990). The U.S. Supreme Court's ruling in these two cases shows that the Court wants the reasonableness test to be used in all prison-related cases involving mental illness. However, the Supreme Court of Louisiana decided that forcing medications upon death-row prisoners to make them sane enough to be executed violated the Louisiana Constitution.

ACCESS TO MENTAL HEALTH RECORDS

Ordinarily, mental health counselors believe that mental health records are confidential and cannot be released without the consent of clients. However, mental health professionals have been perturbed to learn that some criminal defendants who have been charged with sexual assaults have successfully subpoenaed mental health records of victims to aid these defendants in trial. Counselors are rightly concerned that clients would be reluctant to go to mental health professionals or disclose some information in a therapeutic session if they knew that this information could be released to alleged perpetrators.

However, some disclosure of confidential information benefits both sides in sexual assault cases. For instance, some defendants on trial have argued that they have a constitutional right to some access of their alleged victim's mental health records, a position with which the courts have agreed. At the same time, some sexual assault victims have argued that they should have access to records of perpetrators who were in state custody to show in civil cases that these perpetrators had a history of sexual assaults. This section of the chapter elaborates upon each side of the issue.

Defendants have grounded their requests for access to mental health records in the confrontation clause of the Sixth Amendment to the U.S. Constitution. Similar provisions may be found in individual states' constitutions. The **confrontation clause** of the Sixth Amendment provides that a defendant should be given the right to confront evidence against him or her and to be given **compulsory process** (that is, the court's authority to issue a subpoena) for obtaining witnesses in his or her favor. Hence, confrontation entails the right to cross-examine witnesses, which could be aided by use of mental health records. For instance, suppose an accuser who is a child states that a male defendant touched her inappropriately. Suppose further that in counseling the child accused a TV character, the police chief, and her sister's teddy bear of the same behavior. A defendant without access to this information might be convicted, but with this evidence, he might be able to convince a jury that the child victim should not be believed. If convicted, the accused could claim that not being given access to this information in the victim's mental health records deprived him of an effective means of cross-examining the child witness. It is possible that the child might recant on the witness stand when confronted with questions regarding when and how the TV character, the police chief, and the teddy bear touched her. Thus, access to mental health records could affect the fundamental fairness of the judicial process, especially when a defendant is facing a sentence such as life without parole.

In *Pennsylvania v. Ritchie* (1987), the U.S. Supreme Court reviewed a conviction involving a man's sexual abuse of his daughter. In this case, reports were given to Pennsylvania Children and Youth Services of the sexual abuse of a child, which ultimately resulted in a criminal trial of the father. Prior to trial, the defendant requested access to the Pennsylvania Children and Youth Services records involving his daughter so that he might discover the names of favorable witnesses and formulate questions for cross-examination of his daughter. This motion was denied, and the defendant was convicted. The decision was then appealed and the Pennsylvania Superior Court held that the failure to disclose the daughter's statements contained in the Children and Youth Services file violated the confrontation clause of the Sixth Amendment. The State of Pennsylvania appealed to the Pennsylvania Supreme Court, and it went even further in ruling for the defendant. The Pennsylvania Supreme Court held that the failure violated the confrontation clause as well as the compulsory process clause of the Sixth Amendment. In addition, the Pennsylvania Supreme Court held that the defendant's attorney must be given access to the file (*Pennsylvania v. Ritchie*, 1987).

The U.S. Supreme Court seemed to concur with the Pennsylvania Superior Court and rejected the broader interpretation of the Pennsylvania Supreme Court. However, the Court viewed the primary issue as falling within the due process clause of the Fourteenth Amendment. Under due process, a defendant is entitled to any favorable information in the state's possession, but a defendant does not have, under the compulsory process clause, the right to learn the identity of a favorable witness. The compulsory process clause requires the state's assistance in compelling the attendance of favorable witnesses. Acknowledging that the protection of confidential information is strong, the Court ruled, nonetheless, that this interest could not prevent disclosure of information in all circumstances. Agreeing with the limitations expressed by the Pennsylvania Superior Court, the U.S. Supreme Court held that a defendant is entitled to have the trial court review a file *in camera* (in the judge's chambers), with the trial judge determining whether any information is favorable to the defendant. If information is found that is favorable to the defendant, the information is given to the defendant's attorney, but the attorney is not entitled to unfettered access to a confidential file (*Pennsylvania v. Ritchie*, 1987).

Although the records in *Pennsylvania v. Ritchie* involved files maintained by Pennsylvania Children and Youth Services, the import of the ruling, combined with specific state statutes, has been extended to mental health records held by both public and private agencies. For instance, the Supreme Judicial Court of Massachusetts cited *Pennsylvania v. Ritchie* and the Massachusetts Declaration of Rights to articulate standards for accessing confidential mental health records. The case involved Edward Bishop, who was convicted of sexually molesting two brothers. The Massachusetts appellate court upheld Bishop's conviction and rejected his contention that the trial judge, after reviewing the record, should have made the contents known to the defense (*Commonwealth v. Bishop*, 1993).

The Supreme Judicial Court of Massachusetts stated that it needed to describe a standard that defined the line between a less inclusive standard (that is, disclosure is not ordered when it should be ordered) and an overly inclusive standard (that is, disclosure is ordered when it should not be ordered). If there is doubt regarding whether information should be disclosed, then disclosure is appropriate. Hence, the Supreme Judicial Court of Massachusetts held that a defendant must make a threshold showing (that is, the minimum requirement) that records privileged by statute are likely to contain relevant evidence. The defendant need not show that the records actually contain information that carries the potential for establishing the unreliability of either the criminal charge or a witness on whose testimony the charge depends. Instead, the defendant must advance in good faith at least some factual basis that indicates how the privileged records are likely to be relevant to an issue in the case and show that he or she is not going on a "fishing expedition" hoping to find something helpful. If the judge finds, based on the defendant's **proffer** (that is, an argument to a judge explaining the relevance of evidence or testimony a party wants to introduce in his or her case), that the records are likely to be relevant to an issue in the case, the judge shall review the records *in camera* to determine whether the records contain communications that are relevant to the defense (*Commonwealth v. Bishop*, 1993).

The Supreme Judicial Court of Massachusetts illustrated the applicability of its test in another criminal case. This case involved a man who was accused of sexually molesting his two stepdaughters. His attorney sought access to the treatment records held by the Department of Social Services and the Family Care Center. The judge viewed these records in chambers and did not find anything beneficial to the defense. One of the girls had attempted suicide several months after the abuse was disclosed and was treated by a psychiatrist, but the defense attorney did not request access to these psychiatric records. The defendant was convicted and discharged his attorney. He appealed, in part, based on ineffective assistance of counsel because this attorney had failed to seek access to his stepdaughter's psychiatric records.

Applying the standards established in *Commonwealth v. Bishop* (1993), the new defense attorney's proffer was that the girl's suicide attempt occurred approximately nine months after she had revealed the sexual abuse to her mother, which was during a tumultuous time in the family home. The revelation had a major effect on family dynamics, but the mother did not call the police to report the abuse. Thus, the psychiatric records were likely to be relevant regarding the girl's credibility. Because the father was part of the family then, the records were likely to have information relevant to the charge. In the court's opinion, the defendant met the threshold standard, requiring the judge to review the records *in camera*. However, because the original defense attorney did not make the proffer, the defense attorney potentially violated the defendant's right to effective assistance of counsel, which is guaranteed by the Sixth Amendment. (The U.S. Constitution guarantees a defendant the right to **effective assistance of counsel.**

This does not mean that the counsel has to win the case or provide the best defense possible. But he or she has to perform professionally. For instance, an attorney who does not interview the defendant or who fails to interview a defense witness is not providing competent assistance. Essentially, it is malpractice by a defense attorney.) The trial judge was instructed to review the psychiatric records and if the records contained no beneficial evidence, the conviction would stand. However, if the psychiatric records had beneficial evidence, then the defendant was entitled to a new trial (*Commonwealth v. Oliveira*, 2000).

In a similar vein, California used *Pennsylvania v. Ritchie* (1987) and its state law to fashion a process for a criminal defendant to access mental health records. The appellate court in California established that a defendant must present good cause for accessing mental health records. Then, the trial court should (a) obtain the privileged records and review them *in camera;* (b) weigh the constitutional right to cross-examine against California statutory privilege; (c) determine which if any of the privileged materials are essential; and (d) create an adequate record for review (*People v. Reber,* 1986). Using this standard, the Court of Appeals of California affirmed the conviction of a defendant. In this case, Pack, the defendant, had convinced the court to review the accuser's records from Ventura County Mental Health Services. The records were subpoenaed and brought to the court sealed. After an *in camera* review, the judge returned the records, stating that there was no material in them beneficial to the defendant. However, the defendant wanted to use the fact that the accuser had mental health treatment and wanted information to use to attack the accuser's credibility. But the appellate court rejected such use, noting that the showing was too minimal to secure such a review (*People v. Pack,* 1988).

Although criminal defendants have achieved limited access to victims' mental health records, much to the disappointment of mental health professionals, victims have similarly gained access to the records of perpetrators. For instance, Jacqueline Pearson, following the sexual assault of her daughter, sued civilly the perpetrator, a foster child named George Miller, and the agencies involved in his placement, Luzerne County Children and Youth Services and KidsPeace.

After being placed in a foster home, George Miller abducted and sexually assaulted Ms. Pearson's daughter. Miller was subsequently convicted in criminal court. The basis of Ms. Pearson's civil suit was that Miller should not have been placed in a foster home, been allowed to attend school, or ride the bus unsupervised. Moreover, the suit claimed that both agencies knew that Miller had strong propensities to sexually assault young girls. Thus Pearson, armed with a release of information from Miller, moved during the discovery phase for access to Miller's records. The agencies claimed that despite Miller's granting Pearson permission to access his records, unfettered access would harm third parties identified in the records. Thus the agencies resisted granting access to Miller's records despite Miller's signed release. The case was being decided in the federal judiciary, but some of the privilege claims were being based on Pennsylvania state statutes. The lower district court fashioned a ruling favorable to Pearson, and the two agencies appealed.

The Third Circuit Court of Appeals rejected the recognition of privileges based on Pennsylvania statutes and ruled that the issue must be decided based on the federal rules regarding evidence. The Court of Appeals stated that privileges are decided on a case-by-case basis based on the Federal Rules of Evidence and that the judge could fashion a ruling based on federal rules. The upshot of the ruling was that Pearson would be given access to some information to build her case but that the confidentiality of third parties named in Miller's records would be respected (*Pearson v. Miller et al.*, 2000).

In another case, the U.S. Supreme Court seemed to endorse protecting the privilege between a client and a clinical social worker. The case involved a police officer, Mary Lu Redmond, who shot and killed a man. To address the trauma resulting from having killed someone, Redmond saw a clinical social worker over a period of time. When the victim's family filed a lawsuit against Redmond and the village that employed her, they learned of Redmond's involvement in counseling and sought the social worker's clinical records and notes. The social worker refused, and the trial judge instructed the jury to infer this refusal as indicating that the records contained information adverse to Redmond. As a result, the jury returned a verdict against Redmond (*Jaffee v. Redmond et al.*, 1996).

The Seventh Circuit Court of Appeals reversed, holding that the federal rules of evidence recognized a psychotherapist/client privilege. However, it held that a judge must employ a balancing test, weighing the need for disclosure against the individual's privacy rights. Employing such a test, the Court of Appeals held that the need for disclosure did not outweigh Redmond's privacy rights. But the U.S. Supreme Court rejected this balancing test and concluded that Federal Rules of Evidence recognize a social worker/client privilege in the federal legal system without a balancing test. Notwithstanding, the Court stressed that this was the first case in which it recognized a social worker/client privilege but conceded that this privilege may have to give way in some circumstances. However, the Court stated that it could not delineate the full contours that would govern all situations. The Court did indicate that the privilege would give way when a client has threatened harm to another person (*Jaffee v. Redmond et al.,* 1996).

Although social workers were pleased with the ruling in *Jaffee, Jaffee* involved a civil process. If the privilege recognized in *Jaffee* would give way in some circumstances in a civil process, the privilege likely would give way in a criminal process. Recall that the U.S. Supreme Court stated that when just money is involved, the legal system uses the lowest legal standard of proof, but when a person's life or liberty is threatened, due process requires significantly more. Accordingly, if the *Jaffee* ruling must yield in some circumstance in a civil process, it certainly must yield in a federal criminal trial.

IMPLICATIONS FOR SOCIAL WELFARE POLICY AND PRACTICE

Using the U.S. Constitution, the U.S. Supreme Court established the criteria for civil commitment for individuals with mental illness in this country. Although the Texas courts differed in the legal standard that should be used, the U.S. Supreme Court, in deciding which standard to use, established national policy for all states and the federal government. As in other areas, the Court grounded its decision in the liberty guaranteed by the Fourteenth Amendment and ruled that liberty required a higher standard than a preponderance of the evidence.

Although many state statutes now provide their citizens with severe mental illness with the right to mental health treatment, undoubtedly the law, and especially the U.S. Constitution, has provided the greatest influence on social welfare policy with respect to mental health. The U.S. Supreme Court was reluctant to rule explicitly that individuals have a constitutional right to treatment. But it certainly implied and inferred that there is a constitutional right to mental health treatment for people institutionalized for mental illness. In upholding the jury's award of damages in *O'Connor,* the Court stressed that Donaldson was not mentally ill and was not receiving treatment. If Donaldson had indeed been mentally ill and dangerous, he still would have won his case because of the lack of treatment. The hospital contended that Donaldson received milieu therapy, but the Court rejected it as insufficient and stated that individualized treatment was needed.

One can easily see how social welfare policy has affected social work practice in the mental health field. In *O'Connor,* Donaldson contended that he was not getting treatment. State officials contended that he received milieu therapy, which the courts rejected. They noted that an institutionalized person must have individualized treatment. This means that a social worker who is primarily involved in treatment has to make an individualized assessment, formulate a treatment plan, initiate specific activities designed to cure or alleviate the person's problems, and review this treatment plan periodically for modification. Although these practices are taught in schools of social work, institutional dynamics (for example, overcrowdedness, bureaucracy, psychologists and psychiatrists in charge) might affect services. Also, sometimes, when attention to a problem wanes, individuals in charge of institutions regress to previous behaviors.

The law has affected the policy of piercing the veil of confidentiality of mental health records. Much to the disappointment of mental health professionals, the law has given limited access to criminal defendants to accusers' mental health records when justified. Although such access to mental health records has emerged in sexual assault cases, the issue could also emerge in other cases where a victim is making an accusation against an accused. For instance, it could emerge in a homicide case if a defendant can make a proffer or offer of proof.

In the O. J. Simpson case, the defense attorney was able to make a proffer that Nicole Simpson might have discussed information in a counseling session. The judge ordered the file brought to court, and he reviewed it in chambers. Finding nothing to benefit the defense, the records were returned and the defense attorneys were denied access. This law could work for women who have been charged with killing a spouse. Conceivably, a man who had been in the military and who had been married previously might have in his military records mandated counseling for battering. This information would be useful to a second wife on trial for murder if she were arguing that she killed her husband in self-defense. The record of mandated counseling would help her to establish that her spouse was a violent person.

Another clear indication of the connection between policy and practice is in the area of accessing mental health records. Many individuals believe that records are private and confidential, which they are to some extent. But as was stated in the beginning of this book, few rights are absolute. Undoubtedly, as a limited right emerged to access mental health records, social workers and mental health professionals changed their practices regarding what they documented in clients' files.

Reportedly, some mental health counselors have been reluctant to document, fearing access to their clients' records. However, the problem with not documenting some events is that a lack of documentation might adversely affect a client's long-term treatment when a mental health counselor is forced to rely on memory. Attempting to remember what issues were fully addressed two years hence when a mental health counselor has numerous clients could be problematic for treatment. Another problem is that if the client sues the mental health counselor for malpractice, the lack of written records weakens the mental health counselor's defense.

CONCLUSION

This chapter discussed a basic principle regarding mental health policy: individuals have the right to act differently from others in society, and just because someone is idiosyncratic in his or her behavior does not mean society can put that person away. Another principle is that civil commitment requires that a person be both mentally ill and dangerous to self or others before this person can be institutionalized involuntarily. Just being mentally ill is not enough, nor is just being dangerous. When an individual is threatened with civil commitment for being both mentally ill and dangerous, the legal standard that must be used by a judge is clear and convincing evidence. There must be clear and convincing evidence of mental illness and current dangerousness. Then this chapter discussed the right to treatment in a mental institution and the right to mental health treatment in the least restrictive environment. Because the correction environment legally differs from a mental institution, this chapter discussed the right to mental health treatment in a correctional institution. In both environments, the right to refuse mental health treatment was discussed.

Finally, this chapter discussed the legal basis for accessing mental health records in a criminal case and explained that a court can order the production of mental health records for the judge to see. If information is found that is favorable to a defendant, this information must be given to the defense counsel. Equally, there is a legal basis for a victim who is suing in a civil process to access an alleged perpetrator's records.

Key Terms and Concepts

Habilitation

Confrontation
    Clause

Compulsory
    Process

In Camera

Proffer

Effective Assistance
    of Counsel

LEGAL LIABILITY
AND MALPRACTICE
AFFECTING SOCIAL
WORKERS

CHAPTER **7**

In all the areas previously discussed—child protection, adoption, and mental health—social workers may be liable for civil damages (Reamer, 1995; Sharwell, 1982), especially when children have been injured (Bullis, 1990; Jones & Alcabes, 1989). Social workers may incur this liability in removing children from their home (Besharov, 1984a) and for children who are injured in foster care placement (Besharov, 1984b). In such situations, both the child and the parents have a right to sue and collect damages if social workers have been negligent. Moreover, social workers may be sued for negligent supervision (Bloom, 1994). They may also be sued over parental termination of rights and adoption decisions.

In the mental health field, social workers may be sued for failing to provide mental health treatment. In addition, social workers may be sued for malpractice involving their mental health treatment (Dendinger, Hille, & Butkus, 1982; Gerhart & Brooks, 1985; Reamer, 1997; Watkins & Watkins, 1989; Whittington, 1988) and misdiagnosis of clients' problems (*Karasek v. LaJoie et al.*, 1997; *Karasek v. LaJoie et al.*, 1998). This chapter discusses how the law has affected malpractice in child protection, adoption, mental health counseling, and social work practice. Readers should keep in mind that every case discussed may not involve a professional social worker; a mental health counselor, caseworker, or adoption worker may have degrees in other academic fields, such as criminal justice, human ecology, or psychology. Nonetheless, all the cases discussed have direct application to social work.

MALPRACTICE IN CHILD PROTECTION

An African American couple had their child in day care. When one of the workers at the day care center was washing the child, the worker noticed what appeared to be a bruise, and she called child protective services. Sally Mauer, a social worker, responded to the report of possible child abuse and also examined the child. She called the police, who examined the child. The police advised that a physician should see the child, and Mauer took the child to the hospital. A physician, Dr. Lambrecht, examined the child and asked if the child had a history of Mongolian spots. To find out, the caseworker attempted to contact the child's pediatrician, but the pediatrician was unavailable. Dr. Lambrecht instructed Mauer to have the child's pediatrician examine the child or to have an expert at a children's hospital see the child, but Mauer did not do so. The child was put in protective custody, and the parents were separated from their child for several days. Later, a physician concluded that the child had not been physically abused and that the mark that had caused the initial concern was a Mongolian spot, which many African Americans have. In other words, the supposed bruise was a birthmark (*Lesley v. Department of Social and Health Services*, 1996).

The parents filed a lawsuit against Mauer, her supervisor, the Department of Social and Health Services, and Dr. Lambrecht. They charged that their constitutional rights to a familial relationship, care and proper treatment, and due process were violated. In the lower court, the parties involved were said to have qualified immunity, and the lawsuit was dismissed. However, the Court of Appeals of Washington, while upholding the granting of qualified immunity to Dr. Lambrecht, reversed the granting of immunity to the caseworker. The court noted that the issues raised by the parents, the Lesleys, required a trial (*Lesley v. Department of Social and Health Services*, 1996).

The Lesleys offered a declaration by Jon Conte, a professor of social work, that Mauer's investigation was unreasonable and biased. Further, a pediatrician at Harborview Medical Center, where Dr. Lambrecht urged Mauer to take the child, characterized Mauer's behavior as outrageous. The appellate court stated that Mauer was not entitled to qualified immunity. Among the errors that she had made were that she took the child from the day care center without informing the parents, that she failed to tell Dr. Lambrecht that the parents stated that their daughter had Mongolian spots, that the foster mother informed Mauer after several days that the mark had not changed, which would have indicated that the mark was not a bruise, and that Mauer failed to take the child to an expert after Dr. Lambrecht acknowledged that he was not qualified to determine whether the child had been abused.

The court ruled that Mauer violated established policy and practice in her conduct, a ruling that meant that she could not claim qualified immunity. To establish a civil rights complaint, the Lesleys had to show that Mauer's conduct constituted gross recklessness or deliberate indifference. The appellate court stated that whether Mauer's conduct was negligent was a question for a jury (*Lesley v. Department of Social and Health Services*, 1996).

MALPRACTICE IN THE ADOPTION PROCESS

Though the legal literature uses the term *wrongful adoption*, courts use a different term because the courts assert that the term *wrongful adoption* is really a claim of common law tort of fraud and misrepresentation. Though some agencies contend that public policy is harmed when adoption agencies are exposed to legal risk for not guaranteeing a healthy child five years after an adoption, a California court disagreed.

The California court stressed that condoning concealment of important information or intentional misrepresentation of information, both of which mislead prospective adoptive parents, cannot further public policy. (Courts sometimes consider the effect of their decisions as furthering or restricting public policy. A public policy may be to protect vulnerable children or elderly adults. Another public policy is that criminals not profit from their crimes. Thus, a criminal who commits a crime in which there is a reward cannot turn himself or herself in and then collect the reward. Or a criminal who robs a bank, hides the money, gets caught, and serves his or her time cannot retrieve the money and keep it. All are against public policy.) According to the court, the adoption of a child is an act of compassion, love, and humanitarian concern wherein the adoptive parent voluntarily assumes enormous legal, moral, social, and financial obligations. As a result, a trustworthy process benefits society, as well as the child and parent. As keepers of the conscience of the community, courts cannot accept conduct that would allow people who desire entrance into the emotional realm of parenting to be unprotected from schemes or tactics designed to discharge societal burdens onto the unsuspecting or unwary adoptive parents (*Michael J. et al. v. Los Angeles County Department of Adoptions*, 1988).

Michael J. et al. shows that courts understand the policy implications of deciding against adoption workers in malpractice allegations, but they also recognize that society cannot permit parents to be misled by adoption workers. Deliberately misleading prospective parents constitutes fraud, and several states have compared the definitions of *fraud* to the practices of adoption workers. Among these states are Ohio, West Virginia, and New York. In addition, a federal law has been used in questionable adoption practices.

Ohio, in a case involving an adoption by Russell and Betty Burr, was the first state to recognize wrongful adoption. The Burrs contacted the adoption unit of the Stark County Welfare Department in 1964. They requested a male child up to six months old. The caseworker in the adoption unit told them that finding a child that met their preferences would take from a year to a year and a half. Nonetheless, a few days later the Burrs were contacted and told that a 17-month-old male child was available (*Burr et al. v. Board of County Commissioners of Stark County et al.*, 1986).

The information the caseworker gave to the Burrs was that the child was born to an 18-year-old unwed mother in the Massillon City Hospital and that he was big and healthy. The alleged mother was living with her parents and trying to work and rear her child. Purportedly, the grandparents were mean to the child, and the mother decided to move to Texas for better employment and a better life. Unable to take care of the child, the mother left the child with the Stark County Welfare Department. Based on this reported history, the Burrs adopted the boy (*Burr et al. v. Board of County Commissioners of Stark County et al.*, 1986).

As the boy grew, the Burrs began to see a number of physical and mental problems. The child had physical twitching, speech problems, poor motor skills, and learning problems. When the primary school tested him, he was diagnosed as developmentally disabled but educable. When the boy was in high school, he began to hallucinate and was later diagnosed with

Huntington's disease. The Burrs obtained a court order to examine their son's sealed medical records, which they did not see prior to adoption (*Burr et al. v. Board of County Commissioners of Stark County et al.*, 1986).

What the Burrs learned was somewhat shocking. Their son had been born to a 31-year-old patient at the Massillon State Mental Hospital. His father was presumed to be a patient also. The biological mother had problems similar to those that the Burrs' adopted son had, including low intelligence and a speech impediment. Except for the boy's age, everything that the caseworker had told the Burrs was fabricated. There was no birth mother in Texas, no mean grandparents, no birth in the hospital, and no healthy boy. In fact, the boy had been placed in two foster homes prior to the adoption by the Burrs. He was born with a fever, and tests conducted before he was put up for adoption revealed that he had some problems and was developing slower than other infants his age. The adoption unit knew all this information before it placed the child with the Burrs (*Burr et al. v. Board of County Commissioners of Stark County et al.*, 1986).

Feeling deceived, the Burrs sued the Stark County Welfare Department, the director of the Stark County Welfare Department, the caseworker, and the Board of County Commissioners of Stark County. Following a jury trial, the Burrs were awarded $125,000. The Supreme Court of Ohio upheld the verdict under the theory that wrongful adoption is akin to the tort of fraud. For an adopting parent to succeed legally, the parent must prove each element of the fraud. Step by step, these elements are:

1. a representation or, where there is a duty to disclose, concealment of a fact;
2. which is material to the transaction at hand;
3. made falsely, with knowledge of its falsity, or with such utter disregard and recklessness as to whether it is true or false that knowledge may be inferred;
4. with the intent of misleading another into relying upon it;
5. justifiable reliance upon the representation or concealment;
6. a resulting injury proximately caused by the reliance (*Burr et al. v. Board of County Commissioners of Stark County et al.*, 1986, p. 1105).

Less flagrant in terms of truthfulness by the adoption worker but also constituting fraud, another wrongful adoption case was decided in West Virginia, where a couple sought to adopt a child from the Children's Home Society of West Virginia. Contradictory evidence existed regarding what the parents said they were told or not told and what the caseworkers indicated that they had conveyed to the parents. The key issue was whether the parents were told that the birth mother consumed alcohol during pregnancy and that the child had been treated for fetal alcohol syndrome. The caseworkers said that they told the parents these facts, but the parents said that they did not. The defendants moved for summary judgment in their favor, but the judge refused. For summary judgment to be granted, the moving party must establish that there are no genuine issues of material fact and that it is entitled to a judgment as a matter of law. The judge does not weigh the evidence but interprets the evidence favorable to the plaintiff. Moreover, the plaintiff must present some evidence that he or she is correct and could prevail if the lawsuit went to trial. In West Virginia, the essential elements of proving fraud are (a) that the act claimed to be fraudulent was the act of the defendant or induced by him or her; (b) that it was material and false; (c) that the plaintiff relied upon it and was justified under the circumstances in relying upon it; and (d) that the plaintiff was damaged because he or she relied upon it.

Using these criteria, the judge wrote that:

> viewed in the light most favorable to the plaintiffs, the evidence is sufficient to state a claim for fraudulent misrepresentation. The plaintiffs have support for their claim that CHS, through its employees, intentionally misrepresented facts regarding alcohol abuse by Jordan's [the adopted child's] birth mother. The plaintiffs have made a showing that CHS's alleged statements were false. The plaintiffs have offered evidence suggesting that CHS's alleged statements that Jordan's birth mother did not consume alcohol during pregnancy were material to their decision to adopt Jordan. The plaintiffs further testified that, in deciding to adopt Jordan, they reasonably relied upon the assurances of CHS employees that Jordan had no medical history of substance abuse. The plaintiffs claim that their reliance upon CHS's alleged misrepresentations caused them to incur unnecessary medical expenses in their attempt to treat Jordan's medical problems without an accurate medical history, and will cause them to incur extraordinary medical expenses well into the future. Finally, CHS was in a position to know about the birth mother's alcohol abuse, particularly since Sharon Powell [that is, the social worker] was present for Jordan's evaluation at Shawnee Hills, and the CHS had a duty to know under West Virginia Code § 48-4-6. Therefore the plaintiffs may establish CHS's liability for fraud without having to prove that CHS actually knew its representations were false (*Wolford v. The Children's Home Society of West Virginia*, 1998, pp. 584–585).

Both the Ohio case and the West Virginia case just discussed involved sustained violations of state laws. Another wrongful adoption case was based on a violation of a federal racketeering law—a much more serious law than fraud. The Cesniks, a Minnesota couple, sought to adopt a child from the New Beginnings Adoption and Counseling Agency, which was operated by the Edgewood Baptist Church in Georgia. Phoebe Dawson, the executive director of the New Beginnings Adoption and Counseling Agency, told the Cesniks that a child was available. According to the Cesniks, Dawson related that she had reviewed the medical records of a boy born in Columbus, Georgia, and that the boy was completely healthy. Further, the Cesniks were told that the birth mother had not used drugs and had prenatal care since the sixth week of pregnancy. Dawson delivered the baby to the Cesniks at a Minnesota airport and requested that the Cesniks sign a form indicating that they had received a copy of the boy's medical records, even though they had not. The reported reason for this request was to prevent Dawson from having to make another trip to Minnesota (*Cesnik v. Edgewood Baptist Church*, 1996).

Soon after getting the child, the Cesniks realized that the boy had significant health problems. They requested his medical records and discovered that the birth mother had not received any prenatal care, that the birth mother had tested positive for opiates and barbiturates, that the delivery had been complicated, and that the boy was born prematurely. By then, the boy's pediatrician had diagnosed the boy with cerebral palsy, asthma, developmental disorder, and severe behavioral problems. Most of these problems were attributed to the mother's drug use and lack of prenatal care. The Cesniks asked Dawson about the discrepancy between what the records showed and what she told them regarding the boy's health and mother. Dawson stated that she had not actually reviewed the boy's medical records because the records were switched at the agency by mistake with another mother's records with the same name. Also, Dawson reported that the boy's birth mother had lied about her health and drug use. The Cesniks accepted Dawson's explanations (*Cesnik v. Edgewood Baptist Church*, 1996).

Later, the Cesniks requested another child. This time they wanted a biracial or minority child. Dawson again flew to Minnesota, delivered an African American child to the Cesniks, and related the same story about the good health of this boy. She stated that the birth mother had prenatal care and did not use drugs. This child too developed serious health problems and again once the medical records were received, there were serious discrepancies. Dawson related the same story as she had with the first child, which was that she had not reviewed the records and that the records had been switched. This time, however, the Cesniks were not as believing as before. Moreover, this adoption had not been finalized. The Cesniks began inquiring about getting adoption assistance subsidies from the State of Georgia for both boys. Dawson flew to Minnesota, and while holding the boy, reportedly told the Cesniks that she would withhold consent for them to adopt the boy if they continued inquiring about his health and did not keep quiet. A few months later, the adoption was finalized, and the Cesniks had no contact with Dawson (*Cesnik v. Edgewood Baptist Church*, 1996).

However, the Cesniks filed a lawsuit in federal court against the church, the adoption agency, a social worker, and Dawson, contending in part that their dealings with the adoption agency and Dawson involved violations of the RICO statute. **RICO,** (Racketeering Influence and Corrupt Organization Act) is a federal statute that was designed to combat organized crime, but it can be used against any group of individuals involved in a continuing criminal enterprise or conspiracy. Committing fraud through use of the mail or through faxes is a federal offense. The Cesniks contended that they were victims of lies and a conspiracy that was carried out through the mail.

A U.S. District Court judge granted summary judgment in favor of the defendants, but the Eleventh Circuit Court of Appeals reversed the lower court ruling in some areas. The court indirectly criticized the attorneys for the Cesniks for filing a "shotgun" lawsuit, a lawsuit alleging a wide pattern of claims. They instructed the Cesniks' attorney to reframe some of their complaints and put them in acceptable form (*Cesnik v. Edgewood Baptist Church*, 1996). Though the Eleventh Circuit Court of Appeals could easily have agreed with the district court, it hinted in its ruling that the Cesniks may have basis for a winnable lawsuit, provided the lawsuit was properly drawn up and argued. Edgewood Baptist Church appealed to the U.S. Supreme Court, but it refused to hear the case (*Edgewood Baptist Church, DBA New Beginnings Adoption and Counseling Agency et al. v. Blane Cesnik et ux*, 1997).

The adoption cases discussed so far reflect adoption workers who gave erroneous information to parents. But adoption workers also have been cited for withholding information about a child's background that puts others at risk, which also constitutes fraud. In New York, two parents sought to adopt a girl from the Cardinal McCloskey School and Home for Children. The parents had previously adopted several children from this home. The administrator of the home, Cardinal McCloskey, contracted with a clinical social worker to aid in the adoption process. This social worker told the parents that the girl's mother had been a drug user and had abandoned the girl. The parents asked if there was any additional information that they should know about, and they were not given any additional information. The girl was taken home, where she later sexually molested two siblings. The parents then learned that the girl had a history of sexual abuse, which they believed was critical information that was unjustly withheld from them. The parents sued Cardinal McCloskey and the social worker. But the defendants moved for dismissal, and a dismissal was granted. An appellate court upheld the dismissal against the social worker because there was no evidence that the social worker had knowledge of the girl's sexual abuse. However, it reversed the dismissal against Cardinal McCloskey, noting that he was aware of the sexual abuse (*Jeffrey B. B. et al. v. Cardinal McCloskey School and Home for Children et al.*, 1999).

Essentially, the legal action against Cardinal McCloskey alleged fraud. To prove fraud, a plaintiff must establish (a) the defendant's misrepresentation or concealment of a material fact; (b) that such representation was false and known to be false; (c) the defendant's intention to deceive and induce the plaintiff to act upon such representation; (d) the plaintiff's reliance upon the representation; and (e) damages. Because there was clear evidence that the girl had been sexually abused, the parents were entitled to present their arguments to a jury (*Jeffrey B. B. et al. v. Cardinal McCloskey School and Home for Children et al.*, 1999).

But in another case, the court held that parents had sufficient warnings and were not misled. The Ferencs, a New Jersey couple, sought to adopt a Russian child. They consulted World Child Incorporation, which was assisted by The Frank Foundation Child Assistance International. They were told that two children were available for adoption, a boy and a girl. The Ferencs entered into a contract with the agencies to assist them in securing the children. They were given some information regarding the children, and they traveled to a Russian orphanage to see them. There they were told that the boy had some problems, but that his medical problems were minor or correctable with good medical treatment. In sum, the Ferencs were told that the boy was in generally good health. After consulting a Russian doctor and further inquiring about the boy's health, the Ferencs brought the boy, as well as the girl, back to the United States.

Although the girl appeared healthy, the boy was diagnosed as microcephalic and as having an attention deficit/hyperactivity disorder. He also exhibited symptoms of fetal alcohol syndrome. Initially informed that the boy had strabismus (that is, an eye muscle disorder) that was correctable, the Ferencs subsequently were told that the boy's strabismus was inoperable. Consequently, the Ferencs brought a lawsuit against both organizations and several defendants for wrongful adoption. The lawsuit claimed that the defendants either knew of the boy's deficits and intentionally concealed them from the Ferencs or knew little or nothing about them and negligently concealed their ignorance (*Ferenc et al. v. World Child Inc. et al.*, 1997).

All defendants moved for summary judgment in their favor. The judge noted that to make out a prima facie case of intentional misrepresentation, the Ferencs had to prove that the defendants (a) made false representation; (b) regarding a material fact; (c) with knowledge that the representation was false; (d) with intent to deceive; (e) which induced action in reliance on the representation. In addition, they claimed intentional infliction of emotional distress, a charge which required that the Ferencs prove that the defendants engaged in (a) extreme and outrageous conduct; (b) that intentionally or recklessly caused them to experience; (c) severe emotional distress.

Examining the contract the Ferencs signed, the judge observed that the contract was full of cautionary language. It referred to the risk of adopting a child internationally and stated that both organizations would supply medical and social information when it was available, but they could neither guarantee the completeness of the information nor its accuracy. The contract also noted that there were differences between Russians' and Americans' views of health and medicine. Finally, the contract urged adoptive parents to see the child; it stated that they were not required to adopt a child whom they did not believe to be healthy. In sum, the parents were forewarned and could not sustain a claim of fraud. Accordingly, their lawsuit was dismissed (*Ferenc et al. v. World Child Inc. et al.*, 1997).

DUTIES OF MENTAL HEALTH CLINICIANS

In conducting counseling or therapy, clinicians have a responsibility or duty to prevent physical injuries to individuals. A *duty* is a legal obligation to perform a task. Normally, whatever a client says to his or her therapist is confidential. However, in many jurisdictions confidcntiality dissipates when a client has threatened to harm a specific individual. Based on a lawsuit, California in 1974 established a **duty to warn** an individual when a client has made a specific threat of bodily harm against that individual. This duty to warn spread nationally, and now almost all states impose a duty upon therapists to prevent harm to individuals (McClarren, 1987; Waller, 1997). In a similar nature, another duty is emerging that requires therapists not to harm third parties socially or mentally. The first duty seeks to protect third parties from physical harm, and the second duty seeks to protect a person's reputation or prevent a person from being jailed. The following sections explain in more detail both duties.

Duty to Warn of Clients' Threats of Physical Harm

Prosenjit Roddar, undergoing counseling at Cowell Memorial Hospital at the University of California at Berkeley, told his psychologist that he was going to kill Tatiana Tarasoff when she returned from Brazil. The psychologist was assisted and supervised by three psychiatrists. The psychologist, joined by two psychiatrists, wanted to commit Roddar for treatment and fully inform the police of Roddar's threat, but the supervising psychiatrist overruled them. Roddar was detained briefly by law enforcement, but he was released after he appeared rational. Perhaps feeling that he was betrayed by his treatment professional, Roddar ceased psychiatric treatment. Several weeks later when Tarasoff returned from Brazil, Roddar killed her. Thereupon, her parents brought a lawsuit, contending that the treating mental health professional, his supervisor, and law enforcement violated their daughter's rights. The parents contended that the mental health professionals had a duty to warn them or their daughter of the threats. If the mental health professionals had warned the parents, the parents could have warned their daughter. The Supreme Court of California agreed with the Tarasoffs (*Tarasoff v. The Regents of the University of California et al.,* 1974).

Drawing upon a number of cases in other areas, the court extended a duty to warn to mental health professionals. The court, tracing the development of the common law, noted that initially no person owed a duty to control the conduct of another person. However, in California and other states, legal authorities began to recognize that some individuals indeed owed a duty to another. For example, a person responsible for a bulldozer was held to be liable when the key was left in it. A thief stole the bulldozer and jumped off while the bulldozer was running, caus-ing damage to property. Also, a driver who left a truck running in a high-crime area owed a duty when a thief stole the truck and damaged other vehicles. A doctor whose patient had a contagious disease owed a duty to family members to warn them.

Accepting these duties, the California court imposed the same duty on therapists. Thus, the court held that "when a doc-tor or a psychotherapist, in the exercise of his [or her] profes-sional skill and knowledge, determines, or should determine, that a warning is essential to avert danger arising from the med-ical or psychological condition of his patient, he [or she] incurs a legal obligation to give that warning" (p. 555). In addition, the California court concluded that the psychologist's conduct was ineffectual in having Roddar arrested and thus increased the danger to Tarasoff. Accordingly, the Supreme Court of California stated that "a duty to warn may also arise from a voluntary act or undertaking by a defendant. Once the defendant has com-menced to render service, he must employ reasonable care; if reasonable care requires the giving of warnings, he [or she] must do so. Numerous cases have held that if a defendant's prior con-duct has created or contributed to a danger, even if that conduct itself is non-negligent or protected by governmental immunity, the defendant bears a duty to warn affected persons of such impending danger" (p. 559).

An Ohio case shows how *Tarasoff* spread to another state. A young man, Matt Morgan, began experiencing mental health prob-lems when he was a senior in high school in Lancaster, Ohio. He progressively got worse and became violent in his parents' home. On one occasion, the police were called to get Matt out of the house. Matt was homeless for a while and migrated to Penn-sylvania. At a hospital in Pennsylvania, Matt was diagnosed as having a schizophreniform disorder, which meant that he had symptoms of schizophrenia but the symptoms had lasted less than six months. After six months of the same symptoms, Matt would qualify as having a diagnosis of schizophrenia. Matt was transferred to another mental health facility in Pennsylvania, where he was put on psychotropic medications. His symptoms, consisting of delusions that his parents and the government were out to get him, abated. Matt acknowledged to the mental health professionals in Pennsylvania that he was ill and that his medica-tions were helping him, and he indicated a willingness to continue taking his medications. Matt's parents were called in Ohio, and they came to pick him up. Matt was being followed by the Fairfield

Family Counseling Center (FFCC) in Ohio (*Estates of Morgan et al. v. Fairfield Family Counseling Center et al.*, 1997).

FFCC had a psychiatrist, Dr. Brown, on contract and he saw Matt. Dr. Brown, believing that Matt was malingering in order to get Social Security benefits, began to decrease Matt's medications. Matt's medication records from Pennsylvania were sent to Dr. Brown, but Dr. Brown did not read them. Besides brief visits from Dr. Brown, Matt was seeing two social workers and a licensed professional counselor. Matt began to deteriorate, and the family informed FFCC of Matt's condition. The parents also told FFCC that Matt had made a down payment on a gun. Matt was then seen by a social worker, who reported that FFCC had an unwritten policy that it would not initiate involuntary commitment but would assist the family if the family chose to initiate commitment. One night as the family was watching television, Matt excused himself, went upstairs, returned with a gun, killed his mother and father, and seriously injured his sister. The parents' estate and Matt's sister sued FFCC and all the professionals involved in Matt's treatment (*Estates of Morgan et al. v. Fairfield Family Counseling Center et al.*, 1997).

The trial court and the Ohio Court of Appeals granted summary judgment for all the defendants. However, the Supreme Court of Ohio reversed portions of the summary judgment, indicating that Dr. Brown, FFCC, and the social workers should have been proceeded against at trial and linking its decision to *Tarasoff*. The plaintiffs during discovery had expert mental health witnesses who testified that Dr. Brown, FFCC, and the social workers had deviated substantially from accepted standards of care. Apparently, the social worker and vocational counselor had made assessments regarding whether Matt was subject to involuntary hospitalization. The plaintiffs indicated that both the social worker and the vocational counselor were not qualified to make the decisions that they had made. Moreover, the plaintiffs testified that FFCC was competent to help individuals with problems in living but it was not qualified to work with individuals with severe mental illness. Because of this testimony, the Supreme Court of Ohio ruled that summary judgment was inappropriate and that a jury needed to decide the lawsuit (*Estates of Morgan et al. v. Fairfield Family Counseling Center et al.*, 1997).

Although a number of states have adopted the legal rationale of a duty to warn as established by *Tarasoff*, the Supreme Court of Texas explicitly chose to leave this issue to the Texas legislature (*Thapar v. Zezulka*, 1999). However, the Texas court has an interesting position on the duty to warn, a position it explains in *Thapar v. Zezulka* (1999). Dr. Thapar began treating Freddy Ray Lilly in 1985 for mental health problems, seeing him mostly as an outpatient. Lilly was hospitalized on some occasions, and during one hospitalization, he stated that he felt like killing Henry Zezulka, his stepfather. Dr. Thapar did not warn Henry Zezulka nor did she inform law enforcement. In addition, Dr. Thapar did not inform Lilly's family of his discharge from the hospital. Within weeks of getting out of the hospital, Lilly shot and killed Henry Zezulka, prompting Zezulka's wife to sue Dr. Thapar.

A lower Texas court had adopted the principles of *Tarasoff*, but the Supreme Court of Texas reversed the lower Texas court. The Supreme Court of Texas noted that three years after the *Tarasoff* case, the Texas legislature had an opportunity to adopt the *Tarasoff* principle of a duty to warn. Instead, it chose not to adopt it, deciding to create a strong law on mental health profession-al/client confidentiality.

However, the Texas statute on confidentiality has an exception. Other than in court proceedings, a mental health professional is permitted, but not required, to disclose confidential information to medical personnel or law enforcement when a mental health professional determines that there is a probability of imminent physical injury to the patient/client or to others (*Thapar v. Zezulka*, 1999). In other words, a mental health professional has discretion and may or may not warn law enforcement or others of a patient's threat to kill a specific person.

Duty to Not Harm Third Parties Socially and Mentally

A duty to protect third parties socially and mentally is not as widespread as the duty to warn others of physical harm. However, some state courts are ambivalent or have other legal options open to third parties. Reflecting ambivalence, the Pennsylvania Superior Court has ruled that there is a duty to parents regarding a mental health professional misdiagnosis of the parents' daughter, which harmed the parents. Although this case directly involved a psychiatrist (*Althaus v. Cohen*, 1998), it indirectly involved a social worker and thus applies to social workers as well. This case involved a 15-year-old girl who confided to her teacher that her father had touched her inappropriately. The teacher reported the allegation to Allegheny County Children and Youth Services, which took the child out of her home and placed her in foster care. Reportedly, the girl was encouraged to remember her abuse by the teacher and a social worker (Weidlich, 1995). As a result of the child's firm belief, the father was arrested.

The girl was referred for treatment at the Child and Adolescent Sex Abuse Clinic of the University of Pittsburgh Western Psychiatric Institute and was treated by a Dr. Cohen. As the child proceeded through therapy, her allegations became more bizarre. She claimed that both of her parents were involved in ritualistic torture and the killing of several babies. In addition, she claimed to have had a baby by cesarean section. The child's allegations of abuse widened to include all members of her family, her father's co-workers, and strangers. During this time, the father was arrested three times and the mother was arrested twice.

Both Dr. Cohen and a physician who examined the child concluded that much of the child's story was not true. For instance, the child did not have a scar from a cesarean section. However, Dr. Cohen refused to confront the child, fearing it would damage their therapeutic relationship. Dr. Cohen also refused to talk to other people and professionals in the child's life to ascertain whether abuse had occurred. In a meeting with the police, Dr. Cohen refused to discuss the child's veracity, contending that it was the job of the police to determine whether abuse had occurred. At the parents' preliminary hearing, Dr. Cohen testified under oath that she believed that the child had been abused. At trial, over Dr. Cohen's objection, the judge ordered an evaluation of the child.

Dr. Schecter was retained, and he hired two other psychologists to assist him. Dr. Schecter interviewed the parents, Dr. Cohen, the child, the child's grandparents, a previous therapist who had worked with the child, and the child's brother. In addition, Dr. Schecter reviewed the child's scholastic records and writings and administered psychological tests. Following his review of all the data, he concluded that the child suffered from a borderline personality disorder. Dr. Schecter also opined that this child could not determine fact from fantasy and that he doubted that any sexual abuse had occurred. The judge stated that one of the conditions for testifying under oath was that an individual had to have the capacity to distinguish between fact and fantasy. Thereupon, Dr. Cohen advised the child not to testify. The charges against the parents were dismissed.

After the dismissal, the parents and the child sued Dr. Cohen for negligence based on the theory that Dr. Cohen negligently diagnosed and treated the child, further exacerbating her undiagnosed borderline personality disorder. The parents also claimed that Dr.

Cohen owed them a duty of care because she knew that many of the child's allegations were not true and that the parents unfairly faced the criminal justice process. A jury found Dr. Cohen and the clinic liable for negligence in not recognizing that the sexual abuse claim was false. It awarded the girl and her parents $272,000 (Weidlich, 1995).

On appeal, the Pennsylvania Superior Court upheld the jury's verdict and recognized a duty of care to a third party. In Pennsylvania, a successful claim of negligence requires (a) a duty, or obligation, recognized by law requiring the actor to conform to a certain standard of conduct, for the protection of others against unreasonable risk; (b) a failure on the actor's part to conform to the standard required; (c) a reasonably close causal connection between the conduct and the resulting injury; and (d) actual loss or damage resulting to the interests of another.

Applying these criteria to Dr. Cohen, the court found that because Dr. Cohen treated the child for parental abuse, the parents were directly affected by Dr. Cohen's failure to diagnose properly and treat the child. Specifically, Dr. Cohen was aware of the criminal proceeding against the parents and actively participated in this process, and it was reasonably foreseeable that the parents would be harmed by Dr. Cohen's negligent diagnosis.

On further appeal, a majority of justices of the Supreme Court of Pennsylvania overruled the Superior Court of Pennsylvania's decision to impose a duty for Dr. Cohen's misdiagnosis of the Althauses' daughter (*Althaus v. Cohen*, 2000). In short, the Supreme Court of Pennsylvania stated that such a duty would have adverse consequences for individuals needing therapy and was not supported by precedent in that state. The malpractice verdict in the daughter's favor was not part of the appeal and was unaffected by the Supreme Court of Pennsylvania's ruling (*Althaus v. Cohen*, 2000). Although the Supreme Court of Pennsylvania's ruling reversed the imposition of a duty to third parties in Pennsylvania, the Supreme Court of Pennsylvania stated that its ruling would have been different if the idea of sexual abuse originated from Dr. Cohen. If that were the case, Dr. Cohen would have owed a duty to the Althauses (*Althaus v. Cohen*, 2000).

Like Pennsylvania, Illinois refused to recognize explicitly a duty to third parties but has an exception. The case involved a father, John Doe, whose adult daughter, Jane Doe, was in treatment with Dr. Bobbie McKay. During treatment, Jane Doe, with the aid of Dr. McKay, recovered repressed memories of being sexually abused at age 11 by her father. John Doe was invited to come to a therapeutic session in which Jane Doe would confront her father. Planned by Dr. McKay, the intent of the session was to shock the father into confessing. However, the father did not confess; instead, he denied having sexually abused his daughter. The father was then seen by an associate of Dr. McKay in order to deal with his alleged problem of repressing the abuse of his daughter. At some point, John Doe ceased treatment and sued Dr. McKay for damaging the father/daughter relationship, in addition to other claims. A lower Illinois court recognized John Doe's claim as valid, but the Supreme Court of Illinois rejected it, holding that the recognition of a third party's claim of injury would damage the mental health professional/client relationship (*John Doe v. Bobbie McKay*, 1998).

Although the Supreme Court of Illinois refused in *John Doe* to recognize a third party duty by mental health professionals, Illinois had, since 1977, a recognized concept called **transferred negligence,** which resembles a duty to third parties. The case that recognized transferred negligence was *Renslow v. Mennonite Hospital* (1977). In *Renslow*, a woman unknowingly was given the wrong blood during a transfusion at a hospital. As a result, her blood became sensitized (that is, her blood became hypersensitive to antigen, which causes the body to produce antibodies). Years later, the woman became pregnant, and her blood adversely affected her fetus. After being born, the child sued, arguing that the hospital was liable because of earlier negligence involving the mother. Although the court was quick to state that its *Renslow* decision did not recognize a duty to third parties in general, the court recognized an exception based on the close physical relationship between a fetus and its mother.

Duty to Not Sexually Exploit Clients

The law recognizes a duty not to sexually exploit clients, and some clients have prevailed in suing their abusers. Some cases are difficult for victims to prevail because of the law and public policy considerations. Some clients try unsuccessfully to sue agencies that employ social workers who have engaged in sexual malpractice. Then, some clients cannot recover significant damages because the insurance policy limits coverage in the area of sexual abuse. The courts have consistently upheld the practice of limiting insurance coverage.

In an unsuccessful case to attribute blame to an agency, *Ray v. County of Delaware* (1997) involves a case in which a nurse,

Jennifer Ray, sued the Delaware County Mental Health Clinic in New York for negligence. The claim presented was that she, while a client, had a sexual relationship with a social worker, Brian Hart, who was employed by the Delaware County Mental Health Clinic. She stated that the agency was negligent in hiring Hart and in supervising him. She also charged that the agency was negligent for not adopting a policy against client/employee sexual involvement and not enforcing the policy. The agency defended itself by noting that it had conducted a one-and-a-half-hour interview with Hart. His references did not indicate any abusive relationships, and he was qualified for the position. Thus, it was not negligent in hiring Hart. To refute Ray's contention that the agency should have made known to Hart that romantic relationships were inappropriate, it pointed to Hart's deposition in which he stated that he took a course in social work ethics.

Moreover, the agency contended that as a nurse, Ray knew that sexual relationships with clients were inappropriate and that she took steps to hide the relationship rather than report Hart. In effect, she contributed to any injuries that she may have incurred. Another witness, the director of mental health in Wayne County, testified that the Delaware County Mental Health Clinic was in conformity with the standards of the social work profession and had been granted an operating license by the State Office of Mental Health. Because Ray could not show that the agency was negligent in hiring, in making him aware of the code of conduct, and in supervision, the court granted summary judgment in favor of the defendant. Simply, the plaintiff could not show that the clinic had violated the standard of care (*Ray v. County of Delaware*, 1997).

In the other case that has national policy implications, the American Home Assurance Company went to court to seek a declaratory judgment involving Richard Levy, a social worker who had a malpractice insurance policy with the company. Levy was accused of having an improper sexual relationship with a client, Pamela Damian. Damian joined the legal action in opposing American Home Assurance Company's legal move to announce that fees it spent on Levy's defense reached the limits of Levy's policy. Damian argued that such a move was in violation of public policy. However, the Supreme Court of New York granted American Home Assurance Company's motion for declaratory judgment (*American Home Assurance Company v. Levy et al.*, 1999). The following discussion presents the facts and policy issues.

Levy was seeing Damian in a counseling relationship in 1988, 1989, and 1990. During this time no sexual relationship occurred, but Damian later complained that Levy was hugging her closely during those sessions. In addition, Damian stated that Levy was discussing her feelings and their relationship, which was later characterized as instances of transference and countertransference that often occur in counseling. On February 8, 1990, Damian ended her counseling relationship with Levy and began to see another therapist. On March 24, 1990, she began to have sex with Levy at her home and his office. She tried to end the relationship in May 1990 and could not, but it did end in September 1990. About a year later, in September 1991, Damian filed a complaint with the National Association of Social Workers (NASW) (*American Home Assurance Company v. Levy et al.*, 1999).

In addition, Damian filed a lawsuit against Levy. American Home Assurance Company was obligated to assist in Levy's defense because Levy had a malpractice insurance policy with the company that was issued through NASW. When American Home Assurance Company had spent $25,000 in Levy's defense, it went to court to let all parties know that it had spent the limit of Levy's policy and that if Damian won her lawsuit against Levy, American Home Assurance Company would not have further liability. The New York Supreme Court concurred with American Home Assurance Company in its ruling (*American Home Assurance Company v. Levy et al.*, 1999).

Levy's malpractice insurance policy had a maximum liability of $1,000,000, but it specifically stated that if the alleged malpractice involved an improper sexual relationship with a client, its liability would be limited to $25,000. An executive with American Home Assurance Company testified that the policy was written and approved by NASW. Specifically, NASW did not want a policy that would fully cover for malpractice involving sexual relationships because it believed that such a policy would encourage social workers to engage in sexual relationships with clients. Thus, the malpractice policy would have, in theory, a deterrent effect. Social workers were free to get additional insurance on their own, but NASW would not facilitate such coverage or broker such a policy with other insurance companies. Another reason that malpractice for sexual relationships was limited was to keep the cost of the insurance reasonable for the social workers. To cover fully malpractice involving sexual relationships would entail astronomical premiums (*American Home Assurance Company v. Levy et al.*, 1999).

Apparently, when notified that Levy's insurance company was seeking a judgment to announce its policy limits, Damian interceded, arguing that the American Home Assurance Company's position was against public policy. The New York Supreme Court ruled that such a position was not against public policy for the following five reasons:

First, a social worker's professional liability policy that limits coverage in cases involving claims of sexual misconduct is not void against public policy. A provision in an insurance policy is only against public policy when it violates a statutory mandate or prohibition or regulation of the Superintendent of Insurance. In New York, the Superintendent of Insurance approved the policy, and social workers in New York are not required to obtain malpractice or probability liability insurance.

Second, a social worker's professional liability policy that limits coverage in cases involving claims of sexual misconduct is not void as against public policy on the grounds that it has a discouraging effect on reporting sexual misconduct. Such claim suggests that clients are aware of social workers' insurance policies before suing and base the amount of damages on the amount of coverage. Also, clients do not refrain from complaining about sexual misconduct. Further, clients would not be able to conceal the cause of injury and litigate a malpractice lawsuit without alleging sexual misconduct. Moreover, the provision discourages sexual misconduct by social workers who would be exposed to personal liability without the protection of insurance.

Third, a social worker's professional liability policy that limits coverage for sexual misconduct is not against public policy on the grounds that it creates inequality in coverage. Because New York does not require social workers and therapists to carry malpractice insurance, it cannot be argued that various amounts of coverage based on the claims are contrary to public policy. Further, the insurance carrier only sets the amount of coverage. It does not limit the amount of recovery a client receives from a judge or jury.

Fourth, a social worker's professional liability policy that limits coverage for sexual malpractice is not void as being against public policy because it discriminates against women. New York insurance law prohibits any insurers from refusing to issue, renewing, or canceling a policy because of

sex or marital status. The focus of New York's law is prohibiting discrimination based on the sex of the policyholder.
Thus, women, even if they are clients, are not the victims of
discrimination.

Fifth, a social worker's professional liability policy that limits
coverage for claims of sexual misconduct is not void against
public policy on the grounds that there may be concurrent
proximate causes of injury. The concurrent proximate cause
theory has no role because the provision does not purport to
reduce liability solely for damages caused by the insured's
sexual misconduct.

IMPLICATIONS FOR SOCIAL WELFARE POLICY AND PRACTICE

Lesley v. Department of Social and Health Services (1996), the case
involving the child with Mongolian spots taken from day care,
reinforces the need for child protection workers to practice professionally. The caseworker should have contacted the parents
when she was called to the day care center, and she should have
allowed the parents to explain the spot on the child. Surely the
parents would have revealed that the spot was a birthmark, and
that information could have been verified. If the caseworker had
investigated further, she could have prevented the removal of the
child from her parents.

Lesley has implications for social welfare policy in two ways.
First, it shows that social workers cannot claim qualified immunity in this type of case. Recall that in two cases, the social worker
engaged in a number of activities that were not professional social
work practice. Recall further in Chapter 2 that the criteria for
qualified immunity is that a state agent did not violate laws that
reasonable people should know or that the law was not fully developed in an area. Here, the social worker did not fully investigate
the birthmark and took the child from day care without informing
the parents.

A second implication of *Lesley* is that social work professors
gave affidavits opining that specific practices by the social worker
were unprofessional. Social work professors are willing to get
involved in legal cases as expert witnesses and to give opinions
adverse to social work professionals who are defendants in lawsuits. Thus, if some social workers are practicing in a grossly
unprofessional manner, other social work professionals may be

likely to testify in court against such caseworkers. A social work professor who gives an affidavit or testifies for a plaintiff is powerful evidence of possible malpractice.

In the area of adoption, to avoid fraud and negligence in the adoption process, a social worker must be truthful. This would mean availing himself or herself of all relevant information and truthfully informing the adoptive parents of all the facts. To protect oneself fully and to avoid being accused later of fraud or negligence, a caseworker should give adoptive parents access to all the medical and social information available about a child. If confidentiality of other parties identified in these histories is an issue, then the names of such parties could be blacked out. If a social history indicates that John Brown was accused but not charged of abusing a child, then the name John Brown can be deleted or blacked out and the records would show that an unidentified person was accused but not charged with abusing the child. This might be similar to what the FBI does when information is requested under the Freedom of Information Act—it releases records with some information blacked out.

The law has had a major influence on social welfare policy and social work practice in the area of malpractice. Certainly, social work education emphasizes ethical behavior in social work practice. Equally certain, some social workers are faced with pressure to move children into adoptive homes, and giving misleading information or withholding information increases the likelihood of placing children in adoptive homes. Some adoption caseworkers have lied or misled adoptive parents regarding the health of children who would be difficult to place otherwise. Nevertheless, courts have indicated that lying or misleading adoptive parents is fraud. Furthermore, a caseworker cannot fail to access critical records for fear that they might reveal information injurious to the adoption process. The courts have ruled that such behavior is negligent. Hence, neither fraud nor negligence can occur in the adoption process. Social welfare policy cannot be advanced in this manner.

Although this book does not give legal advice, some cases indirectly tell social workers what to do and what not to do. In one case, a judge upheld the practices of adoption workers who repeatedly warn prospective parents of the lack of information or differences between good health in America and in the Soviet Union. Looking at this case and the other cases in which adoption workers lied, one can assume that professional practice would require an adoption worker to get signed acknowledgments of critical information. For example, an adoption worker should avail himself or herself of all information and specifically have parents sign forms specifically indicating their receipt of critical information. The adopting parents of the child who was sexually abused but the information was hidden from them could have been presented with a form indicating that they were told the child had been sexually abused and perhaps her treatment progress. In such an instance, there would have been no fraud, and no legal case against the adoption worker.

The law has had a significant effect on social welfare policy as it relates to the duties to third parties. One duty is a duty to warn of physical harm, and the other is a duty to protect third parties from social and emotional harm resulting from a mental health professional's malpractice. In *Tarasoff*, a duty was imposed on mental health professionals to warn a person or a person's family when a client has made specific threats to harm. Because this case was decided in the California courts, at first it was binding only in California. However, a significant number of other states have adopted the *Tarasoff* principle of a duty to warn, and thus this case has had a national effect on mental health policy. This case shows how one state may become a leader for the country in influencing social welfare policy.

Of course, some states have chosen not to adopt *Tarasoff*, but even in those states that have not adopted *Tarasoff*, there are limited duties for therapists not to harm others. Texas is one such state. In *Thapar v. Zezulka* (1999), a lower Texas court attempted to adopt *Tarasoff* but was rebuffed by the Supreme Court of Texas. The Supreme Court of Texas stated that the Texas legislature had chosen to ignore *Tarasoff* and instead adopted a strong confidentiality law regarding mental health professionals and their clients. According to the Supreme Court of Texas, if Texas were to adopt *Tarasoff*, this decision would be for the Texas legislature to make, not the Texas courts.

In adopting this decision in *Thapar v. Zezulka* (1999), the Supreme Court of Texas referenced Texas' statute on confidentiality pertaining to mental health professionals. The court stated that the statute indicated that mental health professionals could disclose information to law enforcement and others but were not mandated to do so. In effect, the Texas confidentiality statute gives mental health professionals the discretion to disclose or not to disclose. Furthermore, this statute has implications for social welfare policy in this state and in other states that have not adopted *Tarasoff* but have laws similar to those in Texas.

For example, a mental health policy in which a professional has the discretion to disclose or not to disclose a client's threat to kill someone is fraught with considerable problems for a state and mental health professionals. Such a policy has the potential for creating uneven policy in a state in which some people might feel that they were being treated unjustly. For example, a family of a victim who has been killed by a mental health professional's client is likely to be upset when they realize that such a tragedy might have been prevented. These feelings may be very troubling when an affected family learns or is told that another mental health professional chose to disclose a client's threat and this family's loved-one was saved. Regardless of the Texas law and its discretionary aspect, a victimized family who was not told of a client's threat will be quite upset and is likely to blame the mental health professional, personally if not legally.

Another problematic aspect of a discretionary law in the area of a duty to warn is that it might adversely affect the professional's mental health. Unquestionably, individuals enter the helping professions to assist others. These individuals are also members of their community and want a fair, just, and safe society. Thus, a mental health professional cannot feel good about himself or herself when learning that a client killed someone, such as Dr. Thapar learned in Texas. Although she won her case in the Supreme Court of Texas, she certainly has thought about what she could have done to prevent this tragedy and what she might do differently the next time. In states that follow *Tarasoff*, a mental health professional can say that he or she followed the law and warned a threatened person, although a tragedy still occurred. But in Texas, a mental health professional can say only that he or she exercised discretion, and then another professional second-guessed that discretion. Undoubtedly, a number of helping professionals leave their professions because of tragedies that they blame themselves, in part or wholly, for causing. *Thapar v. Zezulka* (1999) has such a potential, negative effect on the people who practice in the mental health field in Texas and similar states.

Two salient factors project from the Supreme Court of Pennsylvania's ruling in *Althaus v. Cohen* (2000), which reversed a lower Pennsylvania court regarding a duty to third parties in Pennsylvania. First, the Supreme Court of Pennsylvania's ruling, which was about a third of the size of the Superior Court of Pennsylvania's ruling, discussed Dr. Cohen's action differently from the Superior Court of Pennsylvania and more favorable toward Dr. Cohen. For example, the Supreme Court of

Pennsylvania stressed that Dr. Cohen did not testify in any criminal proceedings against the Althaus parents as evidence that Dr. Cohen's behavior was laudable. However, the justices of the Superior Court of Pennsylvania stated in their decision that Dr. Cohen testified under oath at the Althauses' preliminary hearing that she believed that the parents' daughter had been sexually abused. The Supreme Court of Pennsylvania did not state that the justices of the Superior Court of Pennsylvania had erroneous information and no attempt was made to clarify this apparent discrepancy regarding what Dr. Cohen did or did not do.

Then, the Supreme Court of Pennsylvania attributed the dismissal of the criminal charges against the parents to Dr. Cohen's forthright testimony at a competency hearing that the Althauses' daughter could not distinguish between fact and fantasy. However, the sequence of events in the Superior Court of Pennsylvania's ruling is different. As the criminal trial was nearing, the defense requested an independent evaluation of the daughter, which Dr. Cohen opposed. A team of evaluators, after conducting a full investigation of a number of individuals including testing of the daughter, concluded that the Althauses' daughter had not been sexually abused and was suffering from a borderline personality disorder. One member of the team, Dr. Schecter, testified first at the competency hearing about his findings and that the Althauses' daughter could not distinguish fact from fantasy. Then, Dr. Cohen testified and stated that she was best qualified to determine the daughter's competence to testify. On cross-examination by the defense attorney, Dr. Cohen admitted that much of the daughter's story was untrue and at times the daughter could not distinguish between fact and fantasy. Thereupon, the judge informed Dr. Cohen that one of the conditions to testifying in a court is that a witness must be able to distinguish between fact and fantasy. Then, Dr. Cohen advised the Althauses' daughter not to testify, which caused, then, the criminal charges against the Althaus parents to be dropped (*Althaus v. Cohen*, 1998). Again, no attempt was made by the Supreme Court of Pennsylvania to explain this discrepancy. If the Superior Court of Pennsylvania's version is correct, then Dr. Cohen cannot be given credit for the criminal charges being dropped against the parents.

A second salient factor in the Supreme Court of Pennsylvania's ruling is that although the justices were not prepared to impose a duty to third parties in Pennsylvania, they stated that mental health professionals could be sued under other conditions and theories. For instance, they indicate that in cases of a therapist implanting "false memories," which leads to criminal charges against a parent, a cause of action would be recognized in Pennsylvania. They observed that Dr. Cohen had not implanted any ideas of sexual abuse in the Althauses' daughter. In addition, a therapist who goes beyond the scope of medical diagnosis and treatment and thus harms others may be sued for defamation or intentional infliction of emotional distress (*Althaus v. Cohen*, 2000).

Like Pennsylvania, Illinois is another state that has chosen not to adopt *Tarasoff*. However, it leaves other possible options for third parties that might have been injured by a therapist. Illinois' transferred negligence has some features of a duty to third parties. The attorney in *John Doe v. Bobbie McKay* argued that *Renslow*, a precedent in Illinois involving a mother who was given the wrong blood by a hospital that later created problems for her baby, applied to Dr. McKay, but the Supreme Court of Illinois rejected the argument. One difficulty with John Doe's case was that his daughter was not suing Dr. McKay for malpractice. Given the holding in *Renslow*, another case might lead the Supreme Court of Illinois to extend transferred negligence to mental health professionals.

As a hypothetical example, consider a mental health counselor who was seeing a small child in therapy and helped the child to recover memories of sexual abuse by the child's father. What if a court of law severed the father's rights to his daughter after the mental health professional testified that the child's best interest required that the child be taken from the father's custody? Years later, the child, then a young woman, insists that she was never sexually abused or it was learned that the mental health counselor had personal issues that led her to see childhood sexual abuse in all her cases. Would the father have a case of malpractice against the mental health professional based on transferred negligence? The father might contend that losing his daughter led to a host of problems, such as drug use, a label as a child molester, loss of his marriage based on the memory recovery incidence, or inability to get married because he lost custody of his daughter. In short, the father could establish some type of serious injury to himself, as did the child who was injured when her mother received the wrong blood. No one knows how the Supreme Court of Illinois would rule in such a case, but it does suggest that it might extend transferred negligence to mental health professionals. Transferred negligence would be close to the duty to third parties that Pennsylvania has, at least, in false memory cases.

In the area of sexual malpractice, NASW has sought to influence practitioners into behaving professionally by not brokering insurance policies that pay considerable amounts of money in cases of sexual exploitation of clients. The courts have upheld such a practice. By limiting a policy in this area, a social worker is exposed to ruinous damages, which might act as deterrence. A social worker is free to pay for additional coverage for sexual misconduct, but the cost is likely to be exorbitant and thus may have a deterrent effect as well. On the other hand, having such a policy of attempting to deter social workers from misconduct prevents victims from receiving a just settlement of their claims.

CONCLUSION

This chapter discussed malpractice in a number of areas, beginning with child protection and the adoption process. Situations have occurred where social workers have deliberately misled parents in order to facilitate the adoption of children with serious medical problems. Then the chapter explained the duties of mental health professionals. One duty is to break confidentiality by informing third parties when a client has threatened to harm a specific person. Also, there is an emerging trend to impose another duty upon mental health professionals, which is not to harm third parties by their actions. The chapter discussed other forms of professional malpractice, such as by social workers who negligently remove children from their homes and who fail to follow proper procedures. The misdiagnosis of a client's problem is another form of malpractice discussed in this chapter. Finally, this chapter discussed malpractice involving sexual involvement with clients.

Key Terms and Concepts

RICO	Transferred
Duty to Warn	Negligence

LEGAL CONTENTIONS OF SOCIAL WORKERS

The previous chapters discuss the law's influence on those areas of social welfare policy and social work practice that are most recognizable to social workers: child protection, adoption, public assistance, and mental health. Although not stressed here because this book is about the judicial influence on social welfare policy and practice, social workers do also advocate for their clients' rights, such as helping qualified clients receive public assistance or helping clients adopted as children access their birth records.

Besides advocating for clients' rights, services, and social justice, social workers have advocated for their own rights and for social justice for themselves when they have perceived that they have been treated illegally and unfairly (*Tichon v. Harder et al.*, 1971). Social workers have contended that they have been discriminated against (Pardeck, 1999) and have argued violations of their liberty and property interests, which are protected by the Fourteenth Amendment (*Cunico v. Pueblo School District No. 60 et al.*, 1990). Also, social workers have argued in court that their rights under the Americans with Disabilities Act were violated, just as laypeople have argued.

This chapter discusses several legal cases involving professional social workers. Some social workers who are employed in public and private agencies have contended that they have been treated discriminatorily in promotion decisions (Gibelman, 1998). In addition, the issue of sexual harassment has emerged (Dhooper, Huff, & Schultz, 1989; Judd, Block, & Calkin, 1985; Maypole, 1986; Risley & Hudson, 1998; Singer, 1989; van Roosmalen & McDaniel, 1998).

The discussion of professional social workers does not suggest that the legal standards presented here pertain only to social workers. Rather than just list and briefly define the various laws to address social welfare concerns, such as the Americans with Disabilities Act, Age Discrimination in Employment Act, and sexual harassment or racial discrimination laws, this chapter shows their applications to real cases. One aim of this chapter is to illustrate further to students the use and application of legal concepts in social welfare policy and practice. A second aim is to show how the concepts of liberty and property manifest themselves intimately within social work environments.

After reading this chapter, students will be more knowledgeable not only about the law involving social workers but also about legal principles affecting future clients. For instance, this chapter discusses a legal case involving a social work supervisor who was fired reportedly for taking leave under the Family Medical Leave Act (FMLA). Other books likely describe this act and its passage by Congress and signing by the president. This book discusses how a court analyzes an alleged violation and identifies the legal framework for deciding such a case. This knowledge will be of benefit to students after they begin practicing professionally and working with clients. While not giving legal advice, a social worker with a client with an issue arising from FMLA would be able to explain the process and procedure, just as social workers do in explaining to crime victims what to expect in court. The same would be true for other areas, such as racial discrimination, sex discrimination involving a promotion, and equal pay.

SOCIAL WORK PROFESSIONALS AND EMPLOYMENT ISSUES

Most of the litigation involving social workers pertains to employment issues. The U.S. Supreme Court ruled on a case involving racial discrimination and established the criteria for deciding discrimination cases. This test has implications for other types of discrimination. Because some of the employment cases involving social work professionals that will be discussed involve discrimination claims, the test to establish an employment discrimination claim is explained here.

Standard for Deciding Discrimination in Employment

In 1973, the U.S. Supreme Court established the test to be used by lower courts and itself in deciding whether an African American could establish racial discrimination in employment (*McDonnell Douglas Corp. v. Green,* 1973). This case has far-reaching implications, applying both to initial employment and to promotions. In this case, Green, an African American, contended that his employer, McDonnell Douglas, engaged in discrimination in employment. Green, a mechanic, was laid off, and Green thought the decision to lay him off was tainted by racism. He protested and allegedly organized a "stall-in" in which several cars blocked the entrance to the plant during the morning shift change. Green was subsequently arrested. Later, when McDonnell Douglas began rehiring laid-off workers, Green applied but was rejected. Thereupon, Green sued, alleging racial discrimination. McDonnell Douglas' defense was that it did not rehire Green because of his illegal activity against the plant.

The U.S. Supreme Court unanimously decided how the courts were to decide racial discrimination cases filed under Title VII of the Civil Rights Act. It ruled that the complainant must carry the initial burden in establishing a prima facie case of racial discrimination. Such an establishment can be made by showing that (a) he or she belongs to a racial minority; (b) he or she applied for a job for which the employer was seeking applications; (c) he or she was rejected despite being qualified for the position; and (d) after the complainant's rejection, the employer continued to seek applications. Once the complainant establishes these facts, the burden shifts to the employer to show some legitimate, nondiscriminatory reason for the employer's adverse decision to the complainant. Then the complainant must be given an opportunity to show that the employer's purported reason is a pretext for a racially discriminatory decision (*McDonnell Douglas Corp. v. Green,* 1973). This type of process is called a **shifting burden analysis** because the burden begins with the plaintiff, shifts to the defendant, and then shifts back to the plaintiff. Thus, African Americans and others complaining of racial discrimination must establish all these criteria to prevail. Also, the shifting burden approach is used in sex discrimination and other areas of discrimination.

To establish a prima facie case of discrimination, a plaintiff must provide evidence of discrimination. This can be done by one of three methods or types of evidence. First, the plaintiff may use direct evidence of discrimination or discriminatory intent. Another term for direct evidence is *smoking gun*. Second, the plaintiff may use circumstantial evidence, using the *McDonnell Douglas* case as a paradigm. Third, the plaintiff may utilize statistical evidence demonstrating a pattern of discrimination (*Williamson v. Mississippi Department of Human Services,* 1997).

Having established both the criteria for determining whether a worker has been discriminated against by an employer and the types of evidence needed to support such a claim, the Court provided a basis for deciding discrimination cases involving employees or potential employees. Social workers would, of course, use these criteria and types of evidence in race, sex, and probably sexual orientation discrimination lawsuits. However, some social workers have grounded their lawsuits in claims of wrongful discharge in which the shifting burden of analysis was used.

Wrongful Discharge

Employing the shifting burden analysis, a case involving a social worker who was fired from a position at the Astor Home for Children shows the employer unable to satisfy its burden. The social worker alleged age discrimination and retaliation by her employer. Joan Hawkins, a 59-year-old social work student at New York University, was placed at Astor Home for Children for her field placement. Among its divisions were the Intensive Parenting Program and the Day Treatment Program. After graduating, she was offered and accepted a position at Astor in the Day Treatment Program. To assist another employee in transferring back to the Day Treatment Program from the Intensive Parenting Program, Hawkins was queried whether she was interested in moving to the Intensive Parenting Program. Hawkins agreed and was transferred in September 1995.

In February 1996, Hawkins had her first performance review by her two new supervisors. According to the agency's rules, a transferred employee would be on probation for three months, but Hawkins' new supervisors extended her supervision for six more months. They also told Hawkins that her work was unsatisfactory.

On May 1, Hawkins was told to resign by June 30. Hawkins requested written reasons from Dr. Ronna Weber, one of the supervisors and the one requesting the letter of resignation. Dr. Weber refused to provide the reasons in writing and fired Hawkins on May 17. On the day Hawkins was fired, Strum, the other supervisor, promised a letter of reference. When a younger woman replaced Hawkins, Hawkins filed a complaint with the Equal Employment Opportunity Commission (EEOC) for age discrimination. After being informed of Hawkins' action, Strum reneged on the letter of reference and would not return Hawkins' telephone calls (*Hawkins v. Astor Home for Children et al.*, 1998).

The EEOC issued a letter recognizing Hawkins' right to sue, and Hawkins did sue. Hawkins contended that her rights under the Age Discrimination in Employment Act (ADEA) and New York law were violated. In addition, she charged that the refusal of Strum to write the reference letter was retaliation for filing a complaint with EEOC. The defendants requested summary judgment in their favor. A U.S. District Court judge granted summary judgment for most of the claims, ruling that Hawkins could not provide proof of age discrimination.

Using the same standard for the retaliation claim that would be used for a claim of racial discrimination, the judge ruled that Hawkins had made a prima facie case and that Astor's explanation was unconvincing. Particularly, Astor stated that it had a policy of not writing reference letters for any former employee, a statement which was not supported by the evidence. Two people in the Day Treatment Program, in fact, wrote strong reference letters. Also, Astor claimed that Strum was willing to write a reference saying that Hawkins would perform well in nonclinical social work, but Strum was unwilling to write a reference involving Hawkins' ability to do clinical social work. Hence, the judge ruled that Hawkins could proceed to trial on the retaliation claim and ask for punitive damages for violating a protected activity in filing the age discrimination claim with EEOC (*Hawkins v. Astor Home for Children et al.*, 1998).

In another shifting burden analysis case, a social work supervisor, Bertha Williamson, took a leave under the Family Medical Leave Act (FMLA) from her position with the Mississippi Department of Human Services. She had been an employee of the department for 14 years and a supervisor for 7. When Williamson returned from her leave, she was summoned to a meeting with her supervisors, who expressed displeasure at the circumstances surrounding her leave. Shortly thereafter, Williamson, through two memoranda, requested social work coverage of a county under her jurisdiction. Her supervisor took offense at the tone of the memoranda, considering them to be unprofessional and insubordinate. Recommendations were made that Williamson be fired, and she subsequently was fired (*Williamson v. Mississippi Department of Human Services,* 1997).

Williamson filed a lawsuit contending that she was fired for taking leave under the FMLA. To make a prima facie case, Williamson had to prove that (a) the protections afforded by the FMLA extended to her; (b) that she suffered an adverse employment decision; and (c) that her employer treated her less favorably than a similarly situated employee who did not request FMLA leave or that her employer made the adverse employment decision because of her request for leave. An analysis of these factors suggested that Williamson established a prima facie case. Then, the burden shifted to the Mississippi Department of Human Services to rebut Williamson's prima facie case. Officials contended that Williamson did not follow its policy by specifying that she was requesting family leave. Because the department's policy contradicted aspects of the FMLA, the judge refused to grant summary judgment to the Mississippi Department of Human Services (*Williamson v. Mississippi Department of Human Services,* 1997).

Although not using a shifting burden analysis, a charge of wrongful discharge occurred at a Veterans Administration (VA) facility in Salisbury, North Carolina, where a licensed social worker sued several officials of the VA following her taking, as she contended, forced disability retirement. The social worker, Shelton-Riek, was hired at the Salisbury Veterans Medical Center in 1991. Four years later, she accepted a position of coordinator of the Specialized Inpatient Post Traumatic Stress Disorder Unit at the medical center. As perceived by administrators at the Medical Center, this unit in which Shelton-Riek worked had long suffered from administrative problems. For this reason, the VA solicited an outside consultant to evaluate the unit. Among the recommendations were that the medical center seek funding for a temporary coordinator of the unit and conduct a national search for a new coordinator. Dr. Katzin, the acting chief of staff, requested that Shelton-Riek resign. Before Shelton-Riek officially responded, Dr. Katzin announced her resignation. Thereupon, Shelton-Riek refused to resign (*Shelton-Riek v. Story et al.,* 1999).

The most interesting aspect of this case followed next. According to three nurses and a clinical psychologist, residents on the unit told them that Shelton-Riek had informed residents that the unit was about to be closed. Further, Shelton-Riek was alleged to have named to the residents specific staff members who were trying to close the unit and terminate her employment. The staff members contended that Shelton-Riek urged residents to keep the unit open and prevent her removal from the unit. The staff members felt that Shelton-Riek's conduct had put them in physical danger and was unethical. Some on the staff believed that Shelton-Riek had abused residents by soliciting their help for her own interests. Shelton-Riek denied that she had inappropriate discussions with residents regarding the problems surrounding the unit. Nonetheless, Shelton-Riek was reassigned to a different part of the medical center (*Shelton-Riek v. Story et al.*, 1999).

The clinical psychologist filed a complaint with the North Carolina Social Work Board. Shelton-Riek responded that this complaint to the social work board violated her rights under VA policy, which required that complaints should be handled internally rather than be reported to a licensing board. The North Carolina Social Work Board requested from the director of the VA, Dr. Story, its formal report regarding Shelton-Riek, but this information was not sent based on the advice of Story's counsel. Accordingly, the board dropped its investigation of Shelton-Riek. However, because a complaint to the North Carolina Social Work Board required Shelton-Riek to report to potential clients that she was under investigation, Shelton-Riek alleged that she lost money as a consultant and in her private practice. Shelton-Riek's physician diagnosed her with severe depression because of the issues on the unit and recommended that Shelton-Riek take a medical leave (*Shelton-Riek v. Story et al.*, 1999).

Shelton-Riek sued several officials at the VA. First, she contended that her right to due process was violated by officials who did not follow VA policy when passing over an internal resolution and filing the complaint with the North Carolina Social Work Board. She claimed further that the defendants' action forced her to take disability retirement, which deprived her without due process of her property interests in her employment. Finally, she claimed that her liberty interests, and specifically her reputation, were violated when the clinical psychologist filed a false complaint with the North Carolina Social Work Board. This complaint required her to disclose to potential clients that she was under investigation, and this disclosure caused her to lose money from her private practice (*Shelton-Riek v. Story et al.*, 1999).

The U.S. District Court rejected all of Shelton-Riek's claims and granted summary judgment for the defendants. According to the Civil Service Reform Act, a federal employee has an administrative remedy available to correct unfair employment treatment. If the defendants violated the policies of the VA, Shelton-Riek had open to her an avenue that could have led to her reinstatement with back pay. The court did not weigh the evidence regarding Shelton-Riek's removal to determine whether the removal violated the property interests of the Fourteenth Amendment. Instead, the court ruled that if Shelton-Riek's allegations were true, then an administrative remedy was available. This administrative remedy needed to be pursued first before going to federal court for relief (*Shelton-Riek v. Story et al.*, 1999).

In addition, Shelton-Riek's liberty interests allegation was rejected. In order to establish a liberty interests violation by the reporting of her to the North Carolina Social Work Board, Shelton-Riek, or any similarly situated social worker, needed to show (a) that the charges made by defendants were false; (b) that the charges were made public; (c) that the charges were made in the course of discharge or serious demotion; and (d) that the charge against the social worker might seriously damage the social worker's standing and associations in the community or otherwise impose on the social worker a stigma or other disability that foreclosed the social worker's freedom to take advantage of other employment opportunities. Although Shelton-Riek could factually satisfy three of the criteria, she could not satisfy the fourth one. Shelton-Riek stated that her private practice suffered somewhat and that she had fewer clients and income. Even if true, this loss did not constitute a serious damage, according to the court. As a result, Shelton-Riek could not satisfy all four criteria for establishing a deprivation of liberty (*Shelton-Riek v. Story et al.*, 1999).

Another case of alleged wrongful discharge affecting a social worker occurred when Rodney Scott, an African American male who was employed as a social worker with Parkview Memorial Hospital was told that his job was being eliminated. The hospital decided to downsize and reduce the number of social workers from nine to six. All the social workers were told that in effect all nine social work jobs were being eliminated, and that essentially they all would have to compete for the six jobs based on several interviews. A panel of interviewers, consisting of six women and one man, decided that a score of 39 or higher on the interview was passing. Scott received a 32 and was eliminated. He countered by filing a lawsuit alleging age and sex discrimination.

Scott's contention that he was subjected to age discrimination was met with considerable skepticism. Scott was 46, the social workers who survived the first round of interviews ranged in age from 32 to 46, and those who did not pass ranged in age from 42 to 48. The judges were quite skeptical that individuals in their 40s were viewed as old compared with people who were only a few years younger. They did note, however, that although in their circuit they have defined age discrimination as mostly involving older people, a difference in age of at least 10 years among employees could constitute possible age discrimination. This means that a person who is 55 and is removed from a position would have a difficult time convincing judges that he or she suffered from age discrimination if the person replacing the plaintiff was 51 or 50. However, if the replacement is 45 or less, this might give rise to a complaint of age discrimination.

In a case attempting to demonstrate sex discrimination, Scott contended that the questions posed at the interview for the six hospital social work jobs were geared to favor women, such as "Describe a situation where you went beyond your normal responsibilities in order to meet a patient's needs." Also, he pointed out that on one female social worker's evaluation sheet, the notation that the social worker "smiles warm" was made. The courts—the district court and the appellate court—concluded that Scott had no evidence of age or sex discrimination (*Scott v. Parkview Memorial Hospital,* 1999).

Though it was unnecessary to expand its explanation in ruling against Scott, the court discussed stereotypes. It said that:

> Let us suppose that women are more likely than men to display caring or generally warm-and-fuzzy attitudes—though this may be a stereotype about stereotypes, rather than an accurate description of traits in the population. How would this imply sex discrimination? Scott does not deny that caring about others' welfare, and eagerness to assist strangers, are appropriate traits for social workers. They are appropriate even when, as at Parkview Hospital, social work is evolving to include emphasis on negotiations with third-party payors. Questions about engagement with clients' needs are no less appropriate for social workers than questions about aggressiveness toward adversaries would be when hiring trial lawyers. Subjective interviews could be smokescreens for bias, but in professions such as social work (or law, medicine, architecture, and many others) they are also necessary. . . . Suppose supervisory social workers routinely disfavor aggressiveness and prefer warm smiles and going the extra mile. That might lead to unequal representation in the profession, if traits such as empathy are distributed unequally by sex. But it would not cause further disparate effects when selecting

from among social workers. Suppose more men than women have aggressive, competitive personas. That might explain why more men than women choose to be professional athletes, but it would not imply that male professional athletes are more competitive than female professional athletes, or that an evaluation of competitiveness would disfavor women seeking advancement (or longer careers) in sports. Just so with social work. [*sic*] People enter the field because they want to help others. A selection process limited to social workers therefore can ask about warmth or helpfulness without predictably screening out men, just as law firms can screen their existing trial lawyers for dogged combativeness without discriminating against women (*Scott v. Parkview Memorial Hospital*, 1999, pp. 525–526).

Another case of alleged discrimination in social work employment concerns promotion. A social worker with a master's degree, Belen Torres, sued her employer, Oakland County, Michigan Community Mental Health, after she was rejected for a promotion. She contended that she was discriminated against because of her national origin. She claimed that she was referred to as an "ass" or "asshole" by a supervisor. The case went to a jury, which ruled against her. Torres appealed the decision because an administrator who testified was asked whether Torres had been discriminated against by the person who made the actual promotion decision. Torres' attorney objected to this question as improper because it was a legal conclusion for the jury to make. The Sixth Circuit Court of Appeals agreed that the form of the question was improper, but it was a harmless error. Torres, during the deposition that she gave prior to trial, stated that she felt that she had not been discriminated against during the interview process. While testifying, she was impeached with her deposition. Accordingly, she was not seriously hurt by the improper question (*Torres v. County of Oakland et al.*, 1985).

Torres provided some additional information regarding discrimination allegations. For instance, the court stated that a one-time instance of a derogatory comment, such as calling someone an "ass" or "asshole," is not discrimination. Such a comment is not grounded in racial, ethnic, or gender negativity. In race and gender discrimination cases, a slur must be continuously used so as to alter the conditions of employment and create an abusive working environment (*Torres v. County of Oakland et al.*, 1985).

A case involving alleged discrimination in social work employment because of disability concerns was initiated by Virginia K. Parr, a registered nurse with a master's degree in social work from San Jose State University. In 1995, Parr began working as a part-time caseworker for a Virginia agency that provided counseling to people with developmental and mental disabilities. In 1997 after some restructuring, Parr became full time, and her supervisor was Juanita Johnson. Johnson noticed that Parr was not completing charting on time. Johnson began to work with Parr to improve her ability to complete charts on time. About three months later, Parr had not shown improvement. When Johnson spoke with Parr again about the charting, Parr stated that she had a learning disability. Administrators at the agency began to discuss this issue and whether they could legally terminate Parr, who was on probationary status. Administrators requested documentation of Parr's disability, and Parr supplied them with documentation that while at San Jose State University, Parr required more time to take examinations because of her learning disability. Some of the administrators indicated that Parr should be terminated as soon as possible and that Parr should not proceed past her probationary period. When a complaint was made against Parr regarding the manner in which a telephone call was handled, Parr was terminated from her position (*Parr v. District 19 Community Services Board*, 1999).

Parr filed a lawsuit contending that she was fired because of her disability. To prevail in a lawsuit alleging violation of the Americans with Disabilities Act (ADA), a plaintiff, such as Parr, has to establish that she has a disability; that she is a qualified person; and that her termination was the result of discrimination because of the disability. The ADA defines a *disabled person* as a person with a physical or mental impairment that substantially limits one or more of the major life activities; the person must have a record of such impairment or must be regarded as having an impairment. The courts concluded that Parr failed to present sufficient evidence showing that she was disabled according to the ADA. Moreover, Parr presented no evidence that the agency administrators really believed she was disabled as opposed to being ineffective in timely maintaining the charts. For these reasons, Parr's lawsuit was dismissed (*Parr v. District 19 Community Services Board*, 1999).

Employment Discrimination from Sexual Harassment

The cases just discussed involved employment discrimination. Another type of employment discrimination is sexual harassment. The legal standard for establishing sexual harassment is the same regardless of whether the alleged harassment occurred in a business or a social work agency. Although the number of lawsuits involving social work agencies is small compared to other settings, a few social workers have alleged sexual harassment by other social workers. A discussion of one case in the literature reveals the application of the sexual harassment definition.

The case in the literature reveals that one claim of sexual harassment by a social worker against a social work agency and its employees was determined by the courts to be groundless. This case involved a social work supervisor named Melvina Lake, who sued pro se (that is, acting as her own attorney) Concord Family Services in New York City. From October 1991 to August 1992, Lake worked as a social work supervisor. During this period, Lake herself received supervision from three people: Luz Liburd, who was for a while the director of Concord's Social Work Department; Mario Drummonds, the program director; and Lelar Floyd, the executive director.

During her employment at Concord, Lake began to accuse various employees at Concord of sexual harassment and harassment in general. She accused a co-worker of harassment by making derogatory remarks and being antagonistic. The agency investigated the complaints but found them unsupported. Then she accused the program director, Drummonds, of looking into her home window and making hostile comments about female employees. Lake made this complaint to the Child Welfare Agency, which investigated. Its report indicated that although Lake truly believed her allegations, they were unfounded. Lake was then informed by Concord that complaints of sexual harassment would be taken seriously, but groundless allegations could lead to Lake's dismissal.

A month later, Lake accused a temporary social worker of making sexually derogatory comments to her in the agency's waiting area. She alleged that two clients heard the remarks, and she informed the director of the Social Work Department. When the executive director investigated, the purported witnesses denied the claim. Lake also accused one administrator of sending people to her home to harass her. The executive director asked Lake to resign. Refusing to resign, Lake was terminated from the agency. Lake brought suit, and her case was summarily dismissed (*Lake v. Concord Family Services*, 2000).

Lake accused the agency of quid pro quo sexual harassment and of allowing a hostile working environment. A hostile working environment violates Title VII of the Civil Rights Act. Drawing on existing case law, the judge noted that Title VII prohibits discrimination with respect to the terms, conditions, or privileges of employment because of the sex of the employee. An employer violates this provision by requiring people to work in a discriminatorily hostile and abusive environment. For a plaintiff to prevail, he or she must show that the conduct was so severe and pervasive that it created a hostile or abusive environment that altered the terms and conditions of employment (*Lake v. Concord Family Services*, 2000).

Quid pro quo harassment involves an employer's use of submission to or rejection of unwelcome sexual conduct by an individual as the basis for employment decisions. For a plaintiff to prevail, he or she must present evidence that (a) he or she was subject to unwelcome sexual conduct and (b) his or her reaction to that conduct was then used as the basis for decisions affecting the compensation, terms, conditions, or privileges of employment. Because Lake presented no evidence of quid pro quo sexual harassment or a hostile working environment, her claim was rejected (*Lake v. Concord Family Services*, 2000).

Religious Objections to Some Clients

A case emerging from the Division of Family Services within the Department of Social Services in Missouri reflects a legal concept explained in Chapter 2—immunity and religious freedom within a social work agency. This case involved a social worker, Phillips, who worked for the Division of Family Services of the State of Missouri Department of Social Services, and who was supervised by Collings. Phillips, who assessed primarily applicants for foster parents, had received a favorable first evaluation, and his supervisor wrote him a recommendation for a graduate program in social work.

During one conversation between Phillips and Collings, Phillips stated that he, because of his religious views, could not approve, as foster parents, unmarried couples, people involved in extramarital relationships, and openly gay couples. A meeting occurred the next day with Collings' supervisor, Wilson, Collings, and Phillips to discuss what Phillips had stated. Wilson stated that she had been told that Phillips' religious beliefs interfered with his ability to do his job. Phillips' response was that his religion taught him that homosexuality was wrong, unmarried couples living together was wrong, and a spouse who cheated on the other spouse was wrong. As a result, he could not approve or sanction any of these couples as foster parents. Phillips asked that he not be assigned any cases that conflicted with his religious views (*Phillips v. Collings*, 2001).

According to Phillips, his relationship with Collings deteriorated immediately after his revelation. Collings ignored him in meetings and was abrupt with him when he tried to discuss matters with her. Shortly thereafter, Collings wrote an evaluation of Phillips and suggested that Phillips be fired for not adopting a nondiscrimination role, which was caused by his religious, moral, and value beliefs. The evaluation went up the supervisory chain with comments and revisions by Collings' superiors. Collings' original recommendation that Phillips be fired was changed to "needs improvements." Collings' original evaluation consisted of four pages. The revised evaluation evolved into a 53-page document that criticized all aspects of Phillips' work performance. This was the longest evaluation in the department's history. The revised evaluation consisted of numerous "Corrective Action Plans."

Because of the continuing problems with Collings, Phillips sought and received a transfer into another division of the department in a different city. When Phillips was working for the child abuse and neglect division with a different supervisor and a different job description, Collings sent the 53-page document to Phillips although he was no longer in her department and she was not supervising him. Phillips sued the department for religious discrimination, and a jury found for him. The jury awarded him $1,500 in compensatory damages and $25,000 in punitive damages (*Phillips v. Collings*, 2001).

Collings appealed to the Eighth Circuit Court of Appeals and based this appeal on three grounds for reversal. She claimed that the trial judge erred in instructing the jury. Also, she argued that Phillips suffered no adverse employment action and that she was entitled to qualified immunity. Normally, **adverse employment action** is defined as being fired, being demoted, or losing pay. But on some occasions, the lack of these types of actions still may constitute adverse employment action (*Bassett v. Minneapolis*, 2000).

In *Kim v. Nash Finch Co.* (1997), the Eighth Circuit Court of Appeals ruled that a reduction in duties, disciplinary action, negative personnel reports, "papering" a personnel file, and employer-required remedial training constitute adverse employment action. The Eighth Circuit Court of Appeals concluded that Collings' behaviors constituted adverse employment action, although Phillips was not fired or demoted. (Phillips was subsequently fired, but it had nothing to do with the issues in the appeal.) Collings created the unprecedented-in-length 53-page evaluation that criticized everything about Phillips. No other employee had received a lengthy evaluation of this nature, and, in a very short time, it contradicted the first positive evaluation and her letter of recommendation to a graduate school of social work. Then, Collings' next evaluation recommended that Phillips be fired for his religious beliefs, which she was persuaded to change to "needs improvements." Last, Collings had delivered to Phillips the 53-page document though he was no longer being supervised by her. These actions, taken as a whole, constituted adverse employment action (*Phillips v. Collings*, 2001).

Collings' second ground for appeal stated that she was entitled to qualified immunity. But the Eighth Circuit Court of Appeals rejected this claim. A state employee is entitled to qualified immunity when a law has not been clearly established. The Eighth Circuit Court of Appeals stated that the law requiring employers to accommodate employees' sincerely held religious beliefs is clearly established. The court of appeals noted that only a small number of homosexual couples sought to be approved as foster parents. Moreover, Phillips had requested that he not be assigned those cases because of his religious beliefs. Thus, the department could have easily accommodated Phillips, but chose instead to castigate him for his belief and drive him away from the department. The jury instruction, last, was said to be adequate; therefore, the Eighth Circuit upheld the verdict against Collings (*Phillips v. Collings*, 2001).

IMPLICATIONS FOR SOCIAL WELFARE POLICY AND PRACTICE

Shelton-Riek provides insight into how liberty and property interests are viewed in relation to employment. As stated earlier, a job is viewed as property. *Shelton-Riek* confirms that a job is property. This case also reveals that a social worker's reputation is understood as falling under liberty. To establish a liberty interest violation based on a contention of injury to a social worker's reputation, a social worker has to establish four criteria, consisting of (a) false charges; (b) charges made public; (c) charges made in the course of discharge or serious demotion; and (d) injury. A social worker who is fired based on false information may have both liberty and property interest violations under the Fourteenth

Amendment to the U.S. Constitution. *Shelton-Riek* tells social work administrators how far they may go without violating a social worker's liberty in a reassignment as discipline. A lateral transfer with no loss in pay does not constitute a serious demotion. Thus, a social work professional who is moved for disciplinary reasons from one unit to another unit with no loss in pay cannot claim a violation of his or her liberty interests.

The entire discussion about discrimination and how it is established reveals how racial and other discrimination can occur without being addressed by the legal system. Both social welfare policy and social work practice are implicated in these cases. As one judge noted, an interview in which subjective factors are reportedly assessed can mask discrimination. This observation is discernible from *McDonnell Douglas Corp. v. Green* (1973) and how systemic discrimination may occur that is difficult to root out.

McDonnell Douglas Corp. v. Green (1973) provides insight in how discrimination occurs that is difficult to refute. For instance, if white employees have an advantage in tenure, then the decision to lay off can be made by tenure for reduced positions. However, an advantage can be given to white employees by having them compete for reduced positions in job interviews. Interviewers can conclude that whites interviewed better, which cannot be disproved because it is a subjective factor. In either event, the African American or other minorities may come up short. Moreover, legally there would be nothing that the African American could do to overturn these decisions. The courts have ruled that both are fair, while acknowledging that an interview can mask discriminatory intent.

The same would be true for women or people of different sexual orientation. For example, suppose a woman applied for a position that went to a white male that she thought she should have gotten and decided to file a sex discrimination lawsuit. The woman would be required to go through the shifting burden analysis. All the employer would need to do after the woman established her prima facie case would be to argue that the white male interviewed better and expressed a stronger vision for the position than the other candidate or candidates. The woman would not be able to prove, probably, that the employer's response is a pretext for sex discrimination. Judges are not going to assess which candidate presented the stronger or strongest vision. In order for an employer to lose such a case, the employer would have to be incredibly stupid, putting sex-biased information in writing or publicly stating sex-biased views.

Phillips v. Collings (2001) has implications for social work agencies. The social work code of ethics forbids discrimination of any sort, which includes discrimination based on sexual orientation. Also, the social work profession has sought to eliminate homophobia among social workers and the public. Likely, the supervisor in *Phillips* was attempting to uphold the ethics of the profession. However, the law supersedes social work ethics here. If a social worker, for religious reasons, has a problem with providing services to gays and lesbians, the agency must accommodate this social worker, if accommodations can be reasonably done. In this case, Phillips asked that he not be assigned any cases, and because there were few gay couples seeking approval as foster parents, these cases could have been reassigned to other workers. This case likely has implications for social workers who conduct marital or relationship counseling and who object for religious reason to counseling gay couples or unmarried cohabitating couples.

CONCLUSION

This chapter indicated that social workers advocate at times for clients, but social workers also need to advocate at times for themselves in the employment community. Most of the cases discussed involved social work professionals in public and private agencies. This chapter presented the standard for deciding racial discrimination in employment, which also is applied in other areas. The standards for establishing sexual harassment were discussed. Last, this chapter discussed how a social worker's religious belief must be accommodated, if possible, although it may conflict with social work's values.

Key Terms and Concepts

Shifting Burden
  Analysis

Adverse
  Employment
  Action

CONCLUSION

This book endeavors to inform students primarily about constitutional law's impact on social welfare policy and social work practice. In all areas of this book, social work students and professionals may see and experience the law's effect. Depending upon students' practice area upon graduation, students will see, and hopefully better understand, how constitutional law has an effect on policy in child protection, adoption, public assistance, mental health, professional practice in which malpractice is alleged, and social workers' employment. Hopefully, no student will experience discrimination in his or her employment fields. However, it is plausible and especially in employment where several people are competing for the same positions. Specific portions of the U.S. Constitution touch all of these areas.

Often, the law is viewed as too complicated for laypeople to grasp, but the approach, which students have learned, is similar to the generic model for social work practice. A problem exists in which judges must decide the outcome. To aid them in their decision-making process, they consider the problem and choose the appropriate legal test or standard, apply it to the problem, and arrive at a decision. Social workers perform tasks that are similar in the social work arena. They are presented with a problem, such as a person seeking social services, they apply a test, and they arrive at a decision.

Some decisions, as these chapters have shown, immensely shape and influence social welfare policy and social work practice. This book focuses on pertinent amendments to the U.S. Constitution, emphasizing the First, Fourth, Eighth, and Fourteenth Amendments. Of these amendments, probably the Fourteenth, and particularly the liberty component, has the most effect on social welfare policy. Liberty is implicated when states have tried to restrict the movement of people receiving public assistance. Liberty is involved when a person has been civilly committed and is not receiving treatment. Liberty is implicated when colleges seek to dismiss students for academic misconduct or for disciplinary reasons. Liberty is potentially affected when a social worker complains that he or she has been unfairly reported to a social work licensing board, which results in damage to his or her reputation and income.

In a similar vein, students know what property interests—protected by the Fourteenth Amendment—include. A social worker's job is property, a social work degree is property, and a social worker's license is property. Equally, depending upon the wordings of a state or federal statute, rehabilitation may be property, mental health treatment may be property, public assistance may be property, professional training may be property, and a program for facilitating social workers' returning to school for a graduate degree may be property.

Some decisions are likely to be in law for a relatively long time, such as the right to mental health treatment for civilly committed people, but some decisions, or victories, are temporary. For instance, in *Ferguson et al. v. City of Charleston et al.* (2001), the U.S. Supreme Court ruled that the involvement of law enforcement at the beginning stages of a policy to force drug addicted women who had delivered babies to undergo testing was unconstitutional. On the surface, this may be perceived as a victory for poor women and minority women who were mostly affected by this policy. Although this decision was rendered by a 6-to-3 vote, at least one justice suggested that he would rule differently if law enforcement had no role in the initial policy. There might be other justices that follow this line of reasoning. Even the attorneys for the women suggested that the decision gave indications that a revised policy would be viewed differently by some of the justices, who clearly differentiated this case from previous cases involving mandatory drug testing, which the Court had sanctioned.

The South Carolina Department of Social Services was initially involved in the development of this policy and could easily help formulate a policy similar to what is done in child abuse cases that come to the hospital. Hence, the issue of coercing drug addicted new mothers into treatment is not over.

This book also provides many of the legal standards used to decide discrimination cases. Because the book is intended solely for social work students, cases involving social workers were selected involving professional social workers. The purpose in choosing these types of cases was that social work students would, hopefully, be more excited and interested in reading about cases in their profession. A social work student might not have much enthusiasm for reading about a lawyer who was disciplined by the bar association and sued but would be interested in a social worker who was disciplined by a social work board and sued, such as in the *Shelton-Riek* case. Although a few social work students may go next to law schools, most are going to practice social work and be licensed by a social work board. Thus, they might be more interested in legal action in the social work arena.

In a similar fashion, social work students know more about the legal standard used to decide discrimination cases. Hopefully, no social worker is going to experience discrimination in the workplace, but in reality these situations sometimes occur. Social work students now have an idea of what is needed to prevail in a lawsuit involving discrimination based on race or gender. This knowledge concerns both hiring and promotion.

Another significant case concerns the extent to which a social work agency, or any agency, must reasonably accommodate a social worker's sincerely held religious belief. Although the Council on Social Work Education mandates nondiscrimination, some exemptions have been made for social work schools within religious institutions. In addition, some social work schools have Christian social work organizations. The *Phillips* case reminds us that social workers who have sincere religious beliefs and ask not to work with certain groups must be accommodated if it can be reasonably done.

If students want to do additional reading on the cases discussed here or other cases, finding cases is quite easy. Some public and college libraries have sections where legal casebooks are shelved. In addition, law libraries have these same casebooks and others. As shown in the diagram in Chapter 1, the federal judiciary consists of the U.S. Supreme Court, Courts of Appeals, and U.S. District Courts. Retrieving a case from one of these levels is similar to retrieving an article from a social work journal. For example, one source for the U.S. Supreme Court decisions is the *United States Reports.* The citation for famous abortion decision is *Roe v. Wade,* 410 U.S. 113 (1973). This means that this decision is in volume 410 of the *United States Reports,* beginning on page 113. The year of the decision is 1973. For a decision in the Court of Appeals, one would look at the *Federal Reporter.* Take the case *Anderson v. University of Northern Iowa et al.,* 779 F.2d 441 (8th Cir. 1985). This case would be found in volume 779 of the *Federal Reporter,* 2nd series, beginning on page 441. Also, this decision was rendered by the Eighth Circuit Court of Appeals in 1985. For a case decided in the U.S. District Court, one would look in the *Federal Supplement. Shelton-Riek v. Story et al.,* 75 F. Supp. 2d 480 (MD NC 1999) means that this case would be found in volume 75 of the *Federal Supplement* beginning on page 480 of the 2nd series. Also, this decision was rendered in the Middle District in North Carolina in 1999. These cases may also be retrieved electronically by searching Westlaw or LexisNexis. One can search by name or some unique phrase in the decision. For instance, in one famous case involving affirmative action in colleges, a judge used the phrase "jump up and slap us in the face." One could type in that exact phrase and retrieve this case.

GLOSSARY OF TERMS

Absolute Immunity—absolute protection for governmental agents

Adverse Employment Action—being fired, being demoted, or losing pay

Appellee—the party responding to an appeal

Appellate Court—court that hears appeals

Best Interest of the Child—the principle that the decisions involving children should serve what is best for that child

Beyond a Reasonable Doubt—used in criminal cases, it is the degree of certainty necessary to convict a defendant of a crime. It does not mean beyond all possible doubt but beyond any doubt based upon reason and common sense.

Certiorari—a written order by the U.S. Supreme Court to a lower court to send certified records of a proceeding in the court below. The Court will either grant certiorari, which means it will hear the case, or deny certiorari, which means it will not hear a case.

Claimant—the person who makes a claim

Clear and Convincing Evidence—an intermediate standard that requires a fact finder be persuaded that the fact to be proved is highly probable

Common Law—rules created by judges in the 11th century to decide cases

Compelling State Interest—a very strong reason put forth by the government

Compulsory Process—the court's authority to issue a subpoena

Confrontation Clause—the clause in the Sixth Amendment that gives defendants the right to confront their accuser

Danger Creation Theory—a theory that if a state's affirmative conduct places a person in jeopardy, then the state may be liable for the harm inflicted on that person by a third party

Defendant—the person or entity that defends itself in a civil lawsuit

Disability—an inability to engage in any substantially gainful activity because of a physical or mental impairment that could be expected to result in death or to last continuously for at least 12 months

Disability Test—five requirements a person must meet to receive disability benefits from Social Security

Domicile—the place at which a person is physically present and that the person regards as home; a person's true, fixed, principal, and permanent home to which that person intends to return and remain even though currently residing elsewhere

Duty to Warn—a legal requirement to warn a third-party individual of possible harm

Effective Assistance of Counsel—adequate representation by a defense attorney generally in a criminal case

Eminent Domain—the power of government to take individual property for the public's good

Fundamental Rights—rights that the courts consider to be critical to free people enjoying liberty, as opposed to nonfundamental rights

Guardian Ad Litem—a special guardian appointed by the court in which a particular litigation is pending to represent an infant, ward or unborn person in particular litigation. The status of guardian ad litem exists only in that specific litigation in which the appointment occurs.

Habilitation—the teaching of basic skills

Harmless Error—the doctrine that minor or harmless errors during a trial do not require reversal of the judgment by an appellate court

Immunity—freedom or exemption from penalty, burden, or duty

In Camera—in the judge's chambers

Intermediate Scrutiny Test—a test utilized for content-neutral restrictions. It involves a court determining whether governmental action is substantially related to an important governmental objective.

Nonfundamental Rights—rights that the courts consider to be not fundamental, such as receipt of welfare benefits or a promotion

Parens Patriae—in its early form, it was the principle that the king was the ultimate guardian of dependent groups. Presently, this responsibility lies with the state and the federal government.

Penumbra—a surrounding area or periphery of uncertain extent. For example, the Fourth Amendment provides for freedom from unreasonable searches and seizures. This implies a right to privacy that surrounds the right to be free from unreasonable searches and seizures.

Plaintiff—the person or entity that is bringing a civil lawsuit. For instance, a person or a corporation, such as Firestone or Ford Motor Corporation, may be the plaintiff. In contrast, the person or entity that defends itself in a civil lawsuit is the defendant.

Police Power—the power of government to protect the health, safety, welfare, and morals of its citizens

Preponderance of the Evidence—the lowest standard of proof and the degree of persuasion necessary to find for the plaintiff in most civil cases. It requires just enough evidence to persuade a jury or judge that a fact is more likely to be true than not true.

Prima Facie Case—the establishment of essential facts just on appearance but subject to further evidence or information

Privileges—particular and peculiar benefits or advantages enjoyed by a person, company, or class, beyond the common advantages of other citizens

Procedural Due Process—the way in which government may act

Procedural Law—the methods used in investigating, presenting, managing, and deciding legal cases, and specifically the body of law that determines which of these methods will be allowed and the body of law that governs how they will be used

Proffer—an initial showing of evidence made by an attorney to a court for immediate acceptance

Qualified Immunity—limited protection for governmental agents

Qualified Individual with a Disability—a disabled person who is capable of doing the essential functions of a job when that job provides reasonable accommodations

Quasi-Suspect Classification—the law's classification of certain people based on gender and illegitimacy

Rational Basis Test—in a free society, a test based on the determination whether a challenged law bears a reasonable relationship to the accomplishment of some legitimate governmental objective

Reasonableness Test—a test that is similar to the rational basis test but is used only in a prison environment

RICO—(Racketeering Influence and Corrupt Organization Act) a federal statute that was designed to combat organized crime

Right to Privacy—the right of individuals to retain certain information about themselves and prevent others from learning of it

Shifting Burden Analysis—the changing of burden between a plaintiff and a defendant

Special Needs—in criminal cases, a balancing test used by the U.S. Supreme Court to determine whether certain searches (such as administrative, civil-based, or public-safety searches) impose unreasonably on individual rights

Special Relationship Theory—the theory that a state has assumed control over an individual sufficient to trigger an affirmative duty to protect that individual; then the state may be liable for the harm inflicted on the individual by a third party

Strict Scrutiny Test—a test based on the extent to which the governmental body passing the legislation shows that the legislation in question promotes a compelling interest and is the least intrusive and extreme

Substantial Evidence—such relevant evidence that a reasonable mind might accept as adequate to support a conclusion

Substantial Gainful Activity—work activity involving significant physical or mental abilities for pay or profit

Substantive Due Process—restricts the government and requires the government to be reasonable in the rules and norms it seeks to establish

Substantive Law—the entire body of law that establishes and defines those rights and duties that the legal system exists to protect and enforce

Suspect Classification—the law's classification of certain individuals, consisting of groupings by race, ethnicity, national origin, and alienage

Transferred Negligence—the position that negligence toward one person transfers to a second person when the two parties are linked, such as negligence involving the mother, which affected the child

Trier of Fact—a judge or jury who decides the facts of a case

REFERENCES

A. J. et al. v. L. O., 697 A.2d 1189 (DC App. 1997).

Abramovitz, M., & Blau, J. (1984). Social benefits as a right: A re-examination for the 1980s. *Social Development Issues, 8,* 50–61.

Addington v. Texas, 441 U.S. 418 (1979).

Alexander, R., Jr. (1988). Mental health treatment refusal in correctional institutions: A sociological and legal analysis. *Journal of Sociology and Social Welfare, 15,* 83–99.

Alexander, R., Jr. (1989). The right to treatment in mental and correctional institutions. *Social Work, 34,* 109–112.

Alexander, R., Jr. (1991). The United States Supreme Court and an inmate's right to refuse mental health treatment. *Criminal Justice Policy Review, 5,* 225–240.

Alexander, R., Jr. (1995). Social workers and immunity from civil lawsuits. *Social Work, 40,* 648–654.

Alexander, R., Jr., & Brown, K. A. (2000). Field placements in correctional institutions: Issue, problems, and benefits. *Arete, 24,* 40–47.

Althaus v. Cohen, 710 A.2d 1147 (PA 1998).

Althaus v. Cohen, 756 A.2d 1166 (PA 2000).

Alvarez et al. v. Shalala et al., 189 F.3d 598 (7th Cir. 1999).

American Home Assurance Company v. Levy et al., 686 N.Y.S.2d 639 (1999).

Anderson v. University of Northern Iowa et al., 779 F.2d 441 (8th Cir. 1985).

Atherton, C. R. (1990). A pragmatic defense of the welfare state against the ideological challenge from the right. *Social Work, 35,* 41–45.

Banay, R. S., & Davidoff, L. (1942). Apparent recovery of a sex psychopath after lobotomy. *Journal of Criminal Psychopathology, 4,* 59–66.

Barahal, H. S. (1958). 1,000 prefrontal lobotomies: A five to ten year follow-up study. *Psychiatric Quarterly, 32,* 653–690.

Barron, J. A., Dienes, C. T., McCormack, W., & Redish, M. H. (1992). *Constitutional law: Principles and policy* (4th ed.). Charlottesville, VA: Michie Company.

Barth, R. P. (1996). Effects of age and race on the odds of adoption versus remaining in long-term out-of-home care. *Child Welfare, 76,* 285–308.

Bassett v. Minneapolis, 211 F.3d 1097 (8th Cir. 2000).

Bates, K. L. (1999, January 31). Lessons of history: Eugenics left a haunting legacy: Early 20th century movement had a goal of race betterment. *Detroit News,* p. A15.

Bentley, K. J. (1994). The right of psychiatric patients to refuse medication: Where should social workers stand? *Social Work, 38,* 101–106.

Berstein, D. E. (1999). Sex discrimination laws versus civil liberties. *University of Chicago Legal Forum, 1999,* 133–197.

Besharov, D. J. (1984a). Liability in child welfare. *Public Welfare, 42,* 28–33.

Besharov, D. J. (1984b). Malpractice in child placement: Civil liability for inadequate foster care services. *Child Welfare, 63,* 195–204.

Black's Law Dictionary (1990). St. Paul, MN: West.

Blackburn, C. E. (1990). The therapeutic orgy and the right to rot collide: The right to refuse antipsychotic drugs under state law. *Houston Law Review, 27,* 447–513.

Blau, J. (1989). Theories of the welfare state. *Social Service Review, 63,* 26–38.

Blome, W. B. (1996). Reasonable efforts, unreasonable effects: A retrospective analysis of the "reasonable effort" clause in the Adoption Assistance and Child Welfare Act of 1980. *Journal of Sociology and Social Welfare, 23,* 133–150.

Bloom, R. B. (1994). Institutional child sexual abuse: Prevention and risk management. *Residential Treatment for Children and Youth, 12,* 3–18.

Board of Regents of State Colleges v. Roth, 408 U.S. 564 (1972).

Bowring v. Godwin, 551 F.2d 44 (4th Cir. 1977).

Boyer, B. (1999, March 19). No black and white rules in transracial adoption. *Chicago Tribune,* p. 25.

Bragdon v. Abbott et al., 524 U.S. 624 (1998).

Braslow, J. (1999). Therapeutic effectiveness and social context:

The case of lobotomy in a California state hospital, 1947–1954. *Western Journal of Medicine, 170*, 293–296.

Breggin, P. (1972). Lobotomy—It's coming back. *Liberation, 17*, 30–35.

Brooks, W. M. (1990). Reevaluating substantive due process as a source of protection for psychiatric patients to refuse drugs. *Indiana Law Review, 31*, 937–1017.

Brown, P. (1984). The right to refuse treatment and the movement for mental health reform. *Journal of Health Politics, Policy and Law, 9*, 291–313.

Bullis, R. K. (1990). Cold comfort from the Supreme Court: Limited liability protection for social workers. *Social Work, 35*, 364–366.

Burke, R. K. (1985). Privileges and immunities in American law. *South Dakota Law Review, 31*, 1–39.

Burr et al. v. Board of County Commissioners of Stark County et al., 491 N.E.2d 1101 (Ohio 1986).

Butchers' Union Slaughter-House and Live Stock Landing Company v. Crescent City Live-Stock Landing and Slaughter-House Company, 111 U.S. 746 (1884).

California Family Code § 7851.

California Health & Safety Code § 120140.

California Insurance Code § 799.10.

California Welfare & Institution Code § 366.26.

California Welfare & Institution Code § 5325.2.

California Welfare & Institution Code § 5332.

Carey, C. A. (1998). Crafting a challenge to the practice of drug testing welfare recipients: Federal welfare reform and state response as the most recent chapter in the war on drugs. *Buffalo Law Review, 46*, 281–345.

Cesnik v. Edgewood Bapist Church, 88 F.3d 902 (11th Cir. 1996).

Cichon, D. E. (1992). The right to just say no: A history and analysis of the right to refuse antipsychotic drugs. *Louisiana Law Review, 53*, 283–426.

City of Boerne v. Flores, 521 U.S. 507 (1997).

Clapp, J. E. (2000). *Dictionary of the law*. New York: Random House.

Clark, J. J. (1999). Clinical risk and brief therapy: A forensic mental health perspective. *Psychiatric Social Work, 6*, 219–235.

Clark, L. D. (1995). A critique of Professor A. Bell's thesis of the permanence of racism and his strategy of confrontation. *Denver University Law Review, 73*, 23–50.

Clayton, E. W. (1987). From Rogers to Rivers: The rights of the mentally ill to refuse medication. *American Journal of Law and Medicine, 13*, 7–52.

Cleveland v. Policy Management Systems Corporation et al., 526 U.S. 795 (1999).

Code of Alabama § 22-11A-38.

Commonwealth v. Bishop, 617 N.E.2d 990 (Mass. 1993).

Commonwealth v. Oliveira, 2000 Mass. LEXIS 255 (Mass. 2000).

Council on Social Work Education (2000). *Handbook of accreditation standards and procedures* (4th ed.). Alexandria, VA: Author.

Court finds 1,500 ways to say no. (1997, October 7). *The Atlanta Constitution,* p. A1.

Courtney, M. E. (1998). The costs of child protection in the context of welfare reform. *The Future of Children, 8,* 88–103.

Coy v. Iowa, 487 U.S. 1012 (1988).

Crawford, J. M. (1999). Co-parent adoptions by same-sex couples: From loophole to law. *Families in Society, 80,* 271–278.

Cunico v. Pueblo School District No. 60 et al. 917 F.2d 431 (10th Cir. 1990).

Currier v. Doran, 23 F. Supp. 2d 1277 (Dist. NM 1998).

Curtis, C. M. (1996). The adoption of African American children by whites: A renewed conflict. *Families in Society, 77,* 156–165.

Curtis, C. M., & Alexander, R., Jr. (1996). The Multiethnic Placement Act: Implications for Social Work Practice. *Child & Adolescent Social Work Journal, 13,* 401–410.

Dendinger, D. C., Hille, R., & Butkus, I. T. (1982). Malpractice insurance for practicum students —an emerging need? *Journal of Education for Social Work, 18,* 74–79.

Department of Health and Human Services (2001). *Standards for privacy of individually identifiable health information.* 65 Fed. Reg. 82462. Washington, DC: Author.

Derzack v. County of Allegheny, Pennsylvania County of Allegheny Children and Youth Services et al., 1996 U.S. Dist. LEXIS (WD Pa. 1996).

DeShaney v. Winnebago County Department of Social Services, 489 U.S. 189 (1989).

Dhooper, S. S., Huff, M. B., & Schultz, C. M. (1989). Social work and sexual harassment. *Journal of Sociology and Social Welfare, 16,* 125–138.

DiNitto, D. M. (2000). *Social welfare: Politics and public policy* (5th ed.). Boston: Allyn and Bacon.

Doe et al. v. Sundquist et al., 1998 Tenn. App. LEXIS 597.

Doe v. Sundquist, 106 F.3d 702 (6th Cir. 1997).

Doe v. Sundquist, 943 F. Supp. 886 (M.D. Tenn. 1996).

Ducat, C. R., & Chase, H. W. (1988). *Constitutional interpretation.* St. Paul, MN: West.

Duchschere, K., & O'Connor, A. (1995, June 6). Jurgens to be freed from prison today. *Star Tribune,* www.startribune.com/ stOnline/cgi-b . . . ord=homicide& word=homicide&word=adopting.

Dvorak, P. (1998, June 12). Patient with TB found in N.O. She was labeled as health threat. *Times-Picayune,* p. B1.

Edgewood Baptist Church, DBA New Beginnings Adoption and Counseling Agency et al. v. Blane Cesnik et ux, 519 U.S. 1110 (1997).

Equality Foundation of Greater Cincinnati v. City of Cincinnati, 128 F.3d 289 (6th Cir. 1997).

Equality Foundation of Greater Cincinnati et al. v. The City of Cincinnati, 860 F. Supp. 417 (SD OH 1994).

Estates of Morgan et al. v. Fairfield Family Counseling Center et al., 673 N.E.2d 1311 (OH 1997).

Estelle v. Gamble, 429 U.S. 97 (1976).

Faimon v. Winona State University et al., 540 N.W.2d 879 (Minn. 1995).

Ferenc et al. v. World Child Inc. et al., 977 F. Supp. 56 (DC 1997).

Ferguson et al. v. City of Charleston, 186 F.3d 469 (4th Cir. 1999).

Ferguson et al. v. City of Charleston et al., 121 S. Ct. 1281 (2001).

Fisher, L. (1999). *American constitutional law* (3rd ed). Durham, NC: Carolina Academic Press.

Foucha v. Louisiana, 504 U.S. 71 (1992).

Fred Phillips and Yolanda Lopez v. Texas Department of Protective and Regulatory Services, 25 S.W. 348 (Tex. 2000).

Freeman, W. (1957). Frontal lobotomy 1936–1956: A follow-up study of 3,000 patients from one to twenty years. *American Journal of Psychiatry, 113*, 877–886.

Garner, B. A. (1999). *Black's law dictionary*. St. Paul, MN: West.

Gentile, L. (1996). Giving effect to equal protection: Adarand Constructors, Inc. v. Pena. *Akron Law Review, 29*, 397–421.

Genty, P. M. (1998). Permanency planning in the context of parental incarceration: Legal issues and recommendations. *Child Welfare, 77*, 543–559.

Gerhart, U. C., & Brooks, A. D. (1985). Social workers and malpractice: Law, attitudes, and knowledge. *Social Casework, 66*, 411–416

Gibelman, M. (1998). Women's perceptions of the glass ceiling in human service organizations and what to do about it. *Affilia, 13*, 147–165.

Gibelman, M., & Schervish, P. H. (1993). *Who we are: The social work labor force as reflected in the NASW membership*. Washington, DC: NASW Press.

Gideon v. Wainwright, 372 U.S. 335 (1963).

Gifis, S. H. (1996). *Law dictionary* (4th ed.). Hauppauge, NY: Barron's Educational Series.

Goldberg v. Kelly et al., 397 U.S. 254 (1970).

Goodman, E. (2001, March 25). Privacy and pregnancy. *Boston Globe*, p. E7.

Griswold v. Connecticut, 381 U.S. 479 (1965).

Griswold v. The State of Wyoming, 994 P.2d 920 (WY 1999).

Guthrie, P. M. (1991). Drug testing and welfare: Taking the drug war to unconstitutional limits? *Indiana Law Journal, 66*, 579–607.

H. C. by Hewett v. Jarrard, 786 F.2d 1080 (11th Cir. 1986).

Hamid, A. (1992). Drugs and patterns of opportunity in the inner city: The case of middle-aged, middle-income cocaine smokers. In A. V. Harrell & G. E. Peterson (Eds.), *Drugs, crime, and social isolation: Barriers to urban opportunity* (pp. 209–239). Washington, DC: Urban Institute Press.

Hammond v. Apfel, 2000 U.S. App. LEXIS 6893 (6th Cir. 2000).

Hansen, J. O. (2000, January 16). From birth on, drugs play major role in children's deaths. *Atlanta Constitution*, p. A19.

Harper v. the State of Washington, 110 Wn. 873 (1988).

Hawkins v. Astor Home for Children et al., 1998 U.S. Dist. LEXIS 3699 (SD NY 1998).

Heller v. Doe, 509 U.S. 312 (1993).

Hentoff, N. (2000, January 8). Don't welfare recipients have rights? *Washington Post*, p. A19.

Higginbotham, J. S. (1998, November 5). Uncomfortable exchanges prompted solely by ethnic disparity. *Chicago Tribune*, p. 31.

Howard, D. E. (1999, December 7). Drug testing helps people quit welfare. *Detroit News*, p. A12.

Hunter, M. J. B. (1997). Special report: Minnesota Supreme Court foster care and adoption task force. *Hamline Journal of Public Law & Policy, 19*, 1–253.

Huppke, R. W. (2000, April 3). Gay man allowed to adopt boys but not their sister: Man who fought the adoption later molested her. *Columbus Dispatch*, p. A2.

Idelson, H. (1996, July 6). Conferees prepare for clash on welfare proposals. *Congressional Quarterly Weekly Report, 54*, 1922–1924.

In re Lora Faye Wirsing v. Michigan Protection and Advocacy Service, 456 Mich. 467, 573 N.W.2d 51 (Mich. 1998).

In re Lukas B. et al. v. Rungsun, 79 Cal. App. 4th 1145 (2000).

In re Rashad H. et al. v. Steven H., 78 Cal. App. 4th 376 (2000).

In re Winship, 397 U.S. 358 (1970).

In the Interest of D. B. et al., 2000 Ga. App. LEXIS 332 (2000).

In the Interest of L. S. D. et al., 2000 Ga. App. LEXIS 508 (2000).

In the Interest of M. C., 534 S.E.2d 442 (Ga. App. 2000).

In the Matter of Department of Social Services v. Bonnie Mitchell, 710 N.Y.S.2d 509 (2000).

In the Matter of the Welfare of P. R. I., 606 N.W.2d 72 (Minn. 2000).

Jackson v. Indiana, 406 U.S. 715 (1972).

Jaffee v. Redmond et al., 518 U.S. 1 (1996).

Jane Does v. The State of Oregon, 993 P.2d 822 (OR 1999).

Jansson, B. S. (1993). *The reluctant welfare state: A history of American social welfare policies* (2nd ed.). Pacific Grove, CA: Brooks/Cole.

Jansson, B. S. (1997). *The reluctant welfare state: American social welfare policies: Past, present, and future* (3rd ed.). Pacific Grove, CA: Brooks/Cole.

Jeffrey B. B. et al. v. Cardinal McCloskey School and Home for

Children et al., 689 N.Y.S.2d 721 (1999).

John Doe v. Bobbie McKay, 700 N.E.2d 1018 (Ill. 1998).

Johnson, L. C. (1995). *Social work practice: A generalist approach* (5th ed.). Needham Heights, MA. Allyn and Bacon.

Jones, J. A., & Alcabes, A. (1989). Clients don't sue: The invulnerable social worker. *Social Casework, 70,* 414–420.

Jordan ex rel. Jordan v. Jackson, 15 F.3d 333 (4th Cir. 1994).

Judd, P., Block, S. R., & Calkin, C. L. (1985). Sexual harassment among social workers in human service agencies. *Arete, 10,* 12–21.

Kansas Constitution Bill of Rights § 20.

Karasek v. LaJoie et al., 660 N.Y.S.2d 125 (NY 1997).

Karasek v. LaJoie et al., 699 N.E.2d 889 (NY 1998).

Karger, H. J., & Stoesz, D. (1998). *American social welfare policy: A pluralist approach* (3rd ed.). New York: Longman.

Kaufman, B. L. (2000, March 2). Countersuit over adoption filed: Social worker says accuser racist, greedy. *Cincinnati Enquirer,* http:// enquirer.com/editions/2000/03/ 02/loc_countersuit_over.html.

Kelsey v. Green, 69 Conn. 291, 37 A. 679 (1897).

Kennedy, R. (2000). Race relations law in canon of legal academia. *Fordham Law Review, 68,* 1985–2010.

Kim v. Nash Finch Co., 123 F.3d 1046 (8th Cir. 1997).

Kim, R. Y. (2001). Welfare reform and ineligibles: An issue of constitutionality and recent court rulings. *Social Work, 46,* 315–323.

Kitchen, B. (1979). The dilemma of the welfare state: The right to remain rich and the right to escape poverty. *Canadian Journal of Social Work Education, 5,* 25–42.

Knecht v. Gillman, 488 F.2d 1136 (8th Cir. 1973).

Kupenda, A. M., Thrash, A. L., Riley-Collins, J. A., Dukes, L. Y., Lewis, S. J., & Dixon, R. R. (1998). Law, life, and literature: Using literature and life to expose transracial adoption laws as adoption on a one way street. *Buffalo Public Interest Law Journal, 17,* 43–69.

Lake v. Concord Family Services, 2000 U.S. Dist. LEXIS 3126 (ED NY #2000).

Lesley v. Department of Social and Health Services, 83 Wn. App. 263, 921 P.2d 1066 (Wash. 1996).

Lewin, T. (1998, October 27). New families redraw racial boundaries. *New York Times,* p. A1.

Louisiana Revised Statute 40: 4 (2000).

M. L. B. v. S. L. J., 519 U.S. 102 (1996).

MacFarquhar, N. (1995, May 11). Ex-nursery workers to sue over ordeal of sex charges. *New York Times Current Event Edition,* p. B4.

MacGregor, B. J., Peltason, J. W., Cronin, T. E., & Magleby, D. B. (1998). *Government by the people: National, state, and local version*

(17th ed.). Upper Saddle River, NJ: Prentice Hall.

Mackey v. Procunier, 477 F.2d 877 (9th Cir. 1973).

Madden, R. G., & Parody, M. (1997). Between a legal rock and a practice hard place: Legal issues in "recovery memory" cases. *Clinical Social Work Journal, 25*, 223–247.

Maldonado et al. v. Houstoun et al., 157 F.3d 179 (3rd Cir. 1998).

Mapp v. Ohio, 367 U.S. 643 (1961).

Marbury v. Madison, 5 U.S. 137 (1803).

Marshall, S., & Wasson, H. (2000, February 28). Pictures of daughter in bath submerge mom in hot water: Ohio case of sexually oriented material could be settled today. *USA Today*, p. 5A.

Maryland v. Craig, 497 U.S. 836 (1990).

Mayer, C. (1989). Survey of case law establishing constitutional minima for the provision of mental health services to psychiatrically involved inmates. *New England Journal of Criminal and Civil Confinement, 15*, 243–275.

Mayhood, K. (2000, January 7). Girl, 14, to remain in foster home: The teen had been taken away from her parents because her weight had increased to 300 pounds. *Columbus Dispatch*, p. B1.

Maypole, D. E. (1986). Sexual harassment of social workers at work: Injustice within? *Social Work, 31*, 29–34.

McClarren, G. M. (1987). The psychiatric duty to warn: Walking a tightrope of uncertainty.

University of Cincinnati Law Review, 56, 269–293.

McDonnell Douglas Corp. v. Green, 411 U.S. 792 (1973).

McInnis-Dittrich, K. (1994). *Integrating social welfare policy & social work practice*. Pacific Grove, CA: Brooks/Cole.

McKay, D. (2000). *Essentials of American government*. New York: Westview.

Meyers v. Contra Costa County Department of Social Services, 812 F.2d 1154 (9th Cir. 1987).

Michael J. et al. v. Los Angeles County Department of Adoptions, 201 Cal. App. 3d 859, 247 Cal. Rptr. 504 (1988).

Michaud, A. (1999a, April 21). County delays transracial adoptions, suit says. *Cincinnati Enquirer.*

Michaud, A. (1999b, May 11). Family joins adoption lawsuit: Says county wanted black home for boy. *Cincinnati Enquirer.*

Michaud, A. (1999c, April 22). County denies adoption bias, *Cincinnati Enquirer.*

Miley, K. K., O'Melia, O., & Dubois, B. L. (1995). *Generalist social work practice: An empowering approach*. Boston: Allyn and Bacon.

Miranda v. Arizona, 384 U.S. 436 (1966).

Mississippi Band of Choctaw Indians v. Holyfield et al., 490 U.S. 30 (1989).

Mittlestedt v. Apfel, 204 F.3d 847 (8th Cir. 2000).

Morales v. Turman, 383 F. Supp. 53 (S.D. Tex. 1972).

Mother of four charged with endangerment (1997, April 24). *New York Times*, p. B6.

New York Constitution Article I § 1.

Newton v. Apfel, 2000 U.S. App. LEXIS 7607 (5th Cir. 2000).

Nirode, J. (2000a, May 4). Law professor pushes for greater access to adoption records. *Columbus Dispatch*, p. C7.

Nirode, J. (2000b, May 16). Fight for adoption aid goes on: The state is appealing a court ruling saying a woman's adopted daughter is entitled to a subsidy. *Columbus Dispatch*, pp. C1, C2.

O'Connor v. Donaldson, 422 U.S. 563 (1975).

O'Connor, K., & Sabato, L. J. (1993). *American government: Roots and reform.* New York: Macmillan.

Official Code of Georgia Annotated, § 31-22-9.1.

Olmstead et al. v. L. C. et al., 527 U.S. 581 (1999)

Pardeck, J. T. (1999). Disability discrimination in social work education: Current issues for social work programs and faculty. *Journal of Teaching in Social Work, 19*, 151–163.

Parham v. Hughes, 441 U.S. 347 (1979).

Parr v. District 19 Community Services Board, 1999 U.S. App. LEXIS 4220 (4th Cir. 1999).

Pearson v. Miller et al., 2000 U.S. App. LEXIS 8072 (3rd Cir. 2000).

Pennsylvania Department of Corrections et al. v. Yeskey, 524 U.S. 206 (1998).

Pennsylvania Statute 35 § 7607.

Pennsylvania v. Ritchie, 480 U.S. 39 (1987).

People v. Pack, 201 Cal. App. 3d 679 (1988).

People v. Reber, 177 Cal. App. 3d 523 (1986).

Perry v. Louisiana, 110 S. Ct. 1317 (1990).

Phillips v. Collings, 2001 U.S. App. LEXIS 16000 (8th Cir. 2001).

Planned Parenthood of Central Missouri et al. v. Danforth, 428 U.S. 52 (1976).

Planned Parenthood of Southeastern Pennsylvania v. Casey, 112 S. Ct. 2791 (1992).

Plotkin, R. (1978). Limiting the therapeutic orgy: Mental patients' right to refuse treatment. *Northwestern University Law Review, 72*, 461–525.

Poythress, N. G., & Miller, R. D. (1991). The treatment of forensic patients: Major issues. In S. Shah & B. Sales (Eds.), *Law and mental health: Major developments and research needs* (pp. 81–113). Bethesda, MD: National Institute of Mental Health.

Prigmore, C. S., & Atherton, C. R. (1979). *Social welfare policy: Analysis and formulation.* Lexington, MA: D. C. Heath.

Promise Doe et al. v. Sundquist et al., 1998 Tenn. App. 597 (Court of Appeals of Tenn. 1998).

Ray v. Apfel, 2000 U.S. App. LEXIS 6144 (10th Cir. 2000).

Ray v. County of Delaware, 239 A.D.2d 755 (NY 1997).

Reamer, F. G. (1995). Malpractice claims against social workers:

First facts. *Social Work, 40,* 595–601.

Reamer, F. G. (1997). Managing ethics under managed care. *Families in Society, 78,* 96–101.

Redlich, N., Schwartz, B., & Attanasio, J. (1995). *Understanding constitutional law.* New York: Matthew Bender.

Reitz, M. (1999). Groundswell change in adoption requires anchoring by research. *Child and Adolescent Social Work Journal, 16,* 327–354.

Rennie v. Klein, 458 U.S. 1119 (1982).

Rennie v. Klein, 462 F. Supp. 1131 (D. N.J. 1978).

Renslow v. Mennonite Hospital, 67 Ill.2d 348, 367 N.E.2d 1250 (1977).

Rhode Island Constitution 1, § 6.

Rhoden, N. K. (1980). The right to refuse psychotropic drugs. *Harvard Civil Rights-Civil Liberties Law Review, 15,* 363–413.

Riggins v. Nevada, 112 S. Ct. 1810 (1992).

Riggins v. Nevada, 860 P.2d 705 (NV 1993).

Risley, C. C., & Hudson, W. W. (1998). Sexual harassment of social work students. *Affilia, 13,* 190–210.

Ritter, J. (1999, June 14). Mother jailed when she refuses TB medication: Authorities deemed her a health threat to family. *USA Today,* p. A16.

Robinson v. California, 370 U.S. 660 (1962).

Roe v. Wade, 410 U.S. 113 (1973).

Rogers v. Okin, 478 F. Supp. 1342 (D. Mass. 1979).

Romer v. Evans et al., 517 U.S. 620 (1996).

Rosenson, M. K. (1994). Social work and the right of psychiatric patients to refuse medication: A family advocate's response. *Social Work, 38,* 107–112.

Ruiz v. Estelle, 553 F. Supp. 567 (S.D. Tex. 1982).

Saenz v. Roe and Doe et al., 526 U.S. 489 (1999).

Sanchez v. Apfel, 2000 U.S. App. LEXIS 6769 (10th Cir. 2000).

Santosky et al. v. Kramer et al., 455 U.S. 745 (1982).

Scott v. Parkview Memorial Hospital, 175 F.3d 523 (7th Cir. 1999).

Segal, E. A., & Brzuzy, S. (1998). *Social welfare policy, programs, and practice.* Itasca, IL: F. E. Peacock.

Shapiro v. Thompson, 394 U.S. 618 (1969).

Sharwell, G. R. (1982). Avoiding legal liability in the practice of school social work. *Social Work in Education, 5,* 17–25.

Shelton-Riek v. Story et al., 75 F. Supp. 2d 480 (MD NC 1999).

Shobat, S. (1985). Pathway through the psychotropic jungle: The right to refuse psychotropic drugs in Illinois. *The John Marshall Law Review, 18,* 407–443.

Siegal, L., & Senna, J. (2000). *Juvenile delinquency: Theory, practice, and law* (7th ed.). St. Paul, MN: West.

Simon & Schuster v. New York State Crime Victims Board, 502 U.S. 105 (1991).

Simon, S. (1999, December 18). Unlikely support for drug tests on welfare applicants. *Los Angeles Times*, p. 1.

Singer, T. L. (1989). Sexual harassment in graduate schools of social work: Provocative dilemmas. *Journal of Social Work Education, 25*, 68–76.

Skidmore, R. A., Thackeray, M. G., & Farley, O. W. (1997). *Introduction to social work* (7th ed.). Boston: Allyn and Bacon.

Smith v. Wayne Probate Judge, 231 Mich. 409, 204 N.W. 140 (1925).

South Carolina Code § 20-7-610.

Sparkman v. Sparkman, 217 Ala. 41, 114 So. 580 (1927).

Spencer Kellogg & Sons Inc. v. Lobban, 315 S.W.2d 514 (Tenn. 1958).

State v. Horne, 282 S.C. 444, 319 S.E.2d 703 (1984).

State v. Perry, 610 So.2d 746 (La. 1992).

Stein, T. J. (1998). *Child welfare and the law* (Rev. ed.). Washington, DC: CWLA Press.

Strausberg, C. (1999, March 15). Baby T saga spurs politicians to push for black adoption bill. *Chicago Defender*, p. 1.

Szasz, T. (2001, November 23). Commentary: Assisted suicide is bootleg suicide. *Los Angeles Times*, p. B17.

T. M. et al. v. Carson et al., 2000 U.S. Dist. LEXIS 5302 (Dist. WY 2000).

Tarasoff v. The Regents of the University of California et al., 529 P.2d 553 (1974).

Teare, R. J., & Sheafor, B. W. (1995). *Practice-sensitive social work education: An empirical analysis of social work practice and practitioners*. Alexandria, VA: Council on Social Work Education.

Teicher, S. A. (1999, April 14). Fight over mixed-race adoptions: A Rhode Island case shows how changes in attitude don't always follow. *Christian Science Monitor*, p. 1.

10 children taken out of Brooklyn apartment (1997, March 12). *New York Times*, p. B2.

Texas Administrative Code § 700.1502.

Texas Administrative Code § 700.1504.

Texas Administrative Code § 700.1505.

Texas Government Code § 501.054.

Texas Health & Safety Code § 597.049.

Thapar v. Zezulka, 994 S.W.2d 635 (Tex. 1999).

Tichon v. Harder et al., 438 F.2d 1396 (2nd Cir. 1971).

Title 20 C.F.R. § 404.1520.

Title 25 USCS § 1901.

Title 25 USCS § 1902.

Title 25 USCS § 1915.

Title 42 U.S.C. § 12132.

Title 42 USCS § 671.

Title 42 USCS § 1996b.

Torres v. County of Oakland et al., 758 F.2d 147 (1985).

Turner v. Glickman et al., 2000 U.S. App. LEXIS 4020 (7th Cir. 2000).

Turner v. Safley, 107 S. Ct. 2254 (1987).

Ulman, L. (1939). Law as a creative force in social welfare. In F. Lowry (Ed.), *Readings in social* case work 1920–1938: Selected reprints for the case work practitioner (pp. 736–746). New York: Columbia University Press.

Underwood v. Commissioner of Social Security, 200 U.S. App. LEXIS 436 (6th Cir. 2000).

United States of America v. Scott William Moses, 137 F.3d 894 (1998).

Van Roosmalen, E., & McDaniel, S. A. (1998). Sexual harassment in academia: A hazard to women's health. Women and Health, 28, 33–54.

Virginia offers regret for sterilizations (2001, February 15). USA Today, p. 3A.

Vitek v. Jones, 445 U.S. 480 (1979).

Waller, T. (1997). Estates of Morgan v. Fairfield Family Counseling Center: Application of traditional tort law post-Tarasoff. Akron Law Review, 31, 321–347.

Walton et al. v. Hammons, 192 F.3d 590 (6th Cir. 1999).

Washington v. Harper, 110 S. Ct. 1028 (1990).

Watkins, S. A., & Watkins, J. C. (1989). Negligent endangerment: Malpractice in the clinical context. Journal of Independent Social Work, 3, 35–50.

Watson, R. A. (1985). Promise and performance of American democracy (5th ed.). New York: John Wiley & Sons.

Weidlich, T. (1995, January 9). False memory, big award. The National Law Journal, p. A6.

White by White v. Chambliss, 112 F.3d 731 (4th Cir. 1997).

White v. Thompson et al., 569 So.2d 1181 (Miss. 1990).

Whitner v. State, 328 S.C. 1, 492 S.E.2d 777 (1997).

Whitner v. State, 523 U.S. 1145 (1998).

Whittington, R. (1988). Button your lips. Journal of Independent Social Work, 3, 93–100.

Williamson v. Mississippi Department of Human Services, 1997 U.S. Dist. 9968 (ND Miss. 1997).

Wolford v. The Children's Home Society of West Virginia, 17 F. Supp. 2d 577 (SD WV 1998).

Woods, J. (2000, May 22). Trying to make the right choices: South High School senior has overcome long odds. Columbus Dispatch, pp. 1A, 2A.

Wyman v. James, 400 U.S. 309 (1971).

Yamamoto, E. K., Serrano, S. K., Fenton, M. S., Gifford, J., Forman, D., Hoshijo, B., & Kim, J. (2001). Civil rights in the new decade: Dismantling civil rights: Multiracial resistance and reconstruction. Cumberland Law Review, 31, 523–567.

Yngvesson, B. (1997). Negotiating motherhood: Identity and difference in "open" adoption. Law and Society Review, 31, 31–80.

Youngberg v. Romeo, 457 U.S. 307 (1982).

Yvonne L. v. New Mexico Department of Human Services, 959 F.2d 883 (10th Cir. 1992).

INDEX

TO THE OWNER OF THIS BOOK:

We hope that you have found *Understanding Legal Concepts that Influence Social Welfare Policy and Practice* useful. So that this book can be improved in a future edition, would you take the time to complete this sheet and return it? Thank you.

School and address: _____

Department: _____

Instructor's name: _____

1. What I like most about this book is: _____

_____

_____

2. What I like least about this book is: _____

_____

_____

3. My general reaction to this book is: _____

_____

4. The name of the course in which I used this book is: _____

_____

5. Were all of the chapters of the book assigned for you to read? _____

   If not, which ones weren't? _____

6. In the space below, or on a separate sheet of paper, please write specific suggestions for improving this book and anything else you'd care to share about your experience in using the book.

_____

_____

_____

_____

_____

Optional:

Your name: _____ Date: _____

May Brooks/Cole quote you, either in promotion for *Understanding Legal Concepts that Influence Social Welfare Policy and Practice* or in future publishing ventures?

Yes: _____ No: _____

Sincerely,

Caroline Concilla

Attention Professors:
Brooks/Cole is dedicated to publishing quality publications for education in the social work, counseling, and human services fields. If you are interested in learning more about our publications, please fill in your name and address and request our latest catalogue, using this prepaid mailer. Please choose one of the following:

☐ social work   ☐ counseling   ☐ human services

Name: _____

Street Address: _____

City, State, and Zip: _____

FOLD HERE

- -

NO POSTAGE
NECESSARY
IF MAILED
IN THE
UNITED STATES

BUSINESS REPLY MAIL
FIRST CLASS   PERMIT NO. 358   PACIFIC GROVE, CA

POSTAGE WILL BE PAID BY ADDRESSEE

ATT: *Marketing* _____

**The Wadsworth Group
10 Davis Drive
Belmont, CA 94002**

FOLD HERE